EVERYDAY COOKING

FOR THE

JEWISH HOME

MORE THAN 350 DELECTABLE RECIPES

ETHEL G. HOFMAN

A John Boswell Associates/King Hill Productions Book

HarperCollins*Publishers*

To Walter, whose constant support and love of food make life an endless adventure.

HarperCollins books may be purchased for educational, business, or sales promotional use. For information please write: Special Markets Department, HarperCollins Publishers, Inc., 10 East 53rd Street, New York, NY 10022.

FIRST EDITION

Designed by Barbara Cohen Aronica
Index: Maro Riofrancos

Library of Congress Cataloging-in-Publication Data

Hofman, Ethel G., 1939—
    Everyday cooking for the Jewish home : more than 350 delectable recipes / Ethel Hofman.—1st ed.
        p.   cm.
    Includes index.
    ISBN 0-06-017295-9
    1. Cookery, Jewish.   I. Title.
TX724.H64   1997
641.5′676—dc21   97-30089
                                                            CIP

97 98 99 00 01 HC 10 9 8 7 6 5 4 3 2 1

Contents

Everyday Cooking
for the
Jewish Home

Cooking in the Jewish Home

I grew up in the only Jewish family living in the remote Shetland Isles, north of Scotland. While my playmates sat down to suppers of fried herring, I cut my teeth on pickled herring and gefilte fish, dishes my mother had learned from her mother, my Lithuanian grandmother. Along with steaming cups of tea, my mother served mandelbrot and strudel, instead of bannocks and scones, to appreciative friends and neighbors.

From my mother I learned to "cook Jewish." In an environment totally isolated from any Jewish community, she quickly assimilated local ingredients into the Ashkenazic dishes she had been brought up with in Glasgow, Scotland, where a large number of European Jews had settled in the early 1900s. We observed the Sabbath and the High Holy Days, and kosher, traditional Ashkenazic dishes were daily fare on our table. Each summer, my Russian-born father hauled a barrel of salt herring into our garage to be on hand for my mother so she could put up batches of pickled herring in five-pound glass "sweetie" jars or make chopped herring, which he loved. Items for Passover, such as matzohs and matzoh meal, unavailable in local shops, were shipped to us from Morrison's Deli in Glasgow, and, as my mother never fails to point out, "I was cooking with olive oil long before it became fashionable." Indeed, in my mother's kitchen, everything from fried fish and chips, the typical British supper, to gefilte fish patties was all cooked in oil rather than in the lard commonly used at that time.

History has had a profound effect on Jewish cuisine. At college and on my travels, I discovered that my mother's Ashkenazic cooking wasn't the whole picture. Through the centuries, Jewish life has been turbulent, rarely calm, so that Jews have wandered into every corner of the world. As with my mother's, their cooking was influenced by locale and the need to keep within the laws of kashruth. This has led to a unique blending of distinctive ingredients by the kosher cook.

Simply put, the Jewish community is divided into two main groups: Ashkenazic and Sephardic. Each has its own unique culinary flair. The chopped liver, blintzes, and briskets typical of Ashkenazic cuisine come from the Jews of Eastern and Central Europe. (*Ashkenaz* is the old Hebrew word for Germany.) Because of the cold climates and the ingredients available, their dishes tend to "stick to the ribs," with lots of dairy products and root vegetables, and simple flavorings, such as onions, garlic, dill, and sweet-sour combinations.

I always think of Sephardic dishes as exotic. Sephardic Jews (*Sepharadh* is Hebrew for "Spain"), many the descendants of Spanish Jews who were expelled from Spain during the Inquisition in 1492, are from Mediterranean and Middle Eastern countries. Sephardic cooking was influenced by popular Mediterranean foods, such as olives, pita bread, hot peppers, and a cornucopia of vegetable salads, which almost always begin a Sephardic meal. Pungent herbs and spices, such as cumin, ginger, and cilantro, are used lavishly; lamb is often the meat of choice; and grains, fruits, and vegetables are main menu items—right in step with today's nutritional recommendations. Little wonder this cuisine is gaining a firm foothold on American menus.

Happily, the explosion of exotic sauces, seasonings, meats, and farmed game has been accompanied by an incredible increase in kosher certified products, so that many ethnic dishes can be duplicated easily. Because my Jewish home cooking is for every day and not just for a few special holidays a year, I have used convenience foods wherever possible, so that many of these dishes require the least possible time and effort on the part of the cook, in the hope that they may become standard family favorites. In this collection, you'll also find recipes for old-fashioned cholents and spicy, fruity tagines from Morocco. All are quick, easy, and well within the expertise of any cook. As for the tricky subject of cholesterol (as in *schmaltz*), I use fat sparingly, but I do add some, for there's no substitute for that indescribable flavor; and what's a tablespoon divided by six servings? In accordance with the laws of kashruth, meat and milk are not mixed within a recipe, and, of course, no pork products or shellfish are used.

In the modern melting pot that is Israel, I have delighted in dishes from cooks hailing from Romania to Morocco, each recipe suggestive of its source—a living heritage and nostalgic reminder of its cook's roots. The more than 350 recipes that make up *Everyday Cooking for the Jewish Home* reflect centuries of a rich, varied cuisine made easy by computer-age appliances and an ever-growing range of high-quality kosher ingredients. The result is both healthy simplicity and lively good taste in a compendium I hope you'll refer to again and again. Eat well and enjoy, or as the Israelis say, *"B'tayavon."*

WHAT'S KOSHER?

Even to people who are not Jewish, products that bear the seal of kosher certification are perceived as meeting a sterling standard of quality and as being superior, cleaner products. Think of kosher chickens and frankfurters. Kosher certified foods make up one of the fastest growing segments of today's food business, and giant conglomerates have latched onto that segment as a winning way to present products that will be highly acceptable to the general public. In 1996, according to Integrated Marketing Communications in New York, 8,100 companies were producing certified kosher products. Over 36,000 products are certified, and the dollars spent buying all those products have zoomed to 35 *billion.*

Not surprisingly, the kosher certification business is also booming. Rabbis and religious organizations supervise the inspections of manufactured items and each has its own symbol. Over 275 different kosher certifications are applied to foods all over the world. Annual site inspections are usually unannounced. Other symbols are certified by local and international rabbis. The OU symbol Ⓤ, the most highly regarded, is attached to about 80 percent of kosher foods produced in the United States. Often a P for parve, an M for meat, or a D for dairy appears near the certification. The K symbol for kosher is not as rigorous, and is not accepted by many orthodox Jews.

What does it mean when a label or recipe is marked "parve,"

"meat," or "dairy"? *Kosher* is the Yiddish word for fit or proper. According to Jewish law, when applied to food it means "fit to eat." The dietary laws, or laws of kashruth, which dictate how to make food fit and proper for eating, are set out in the Book of Leviticus in the Bible. There are three categories of kosher food:

Meat: In order for an animal to be kosher, it must have split hooves *and* chew its cud. Kosher animals include the cow, goat, lamb, and deer. But these animals must also be slaughtered according to Jewish law to be kosher. Killing animals for sport is regarded as cruelty. In order not to inflict suffering, the jugular vein must be severed with one stroke of a razor sharp knife that has no nicks or flaws so that the animal dies immediately. As much blood as possible must be removed from the meat before cooking, which is why observant kosher cooks soak meat or poultry in salted water, then coat it with kosher salt and let it drain. The salt is rinsed off before cooking. The tenderest steaks come from the hindquarters of large animals but the process of removing the sciatic nerve and blood vessels is so costly that packing houses sell these parts on the general market, and they are not available kosher.

Nonkosher animals include pig, camel, horse, and rabbit. No part of these animals my be eaten in any form; bacon, for example, is not kosher. *Glatt kosher* relates specifically to animal foods. "Glatt" is Yiddish for smooth. If the lung of an animal is scarred or damaged, that animal is considered nonkosher and therefore the meat is not kosher.

Dairy: Milk and milk products from a kosher animal are dairy. They may not be eaten with meat or poultry or used in cooking meat dishes. If a recipe is quoted as dairy or a meal is dairy, this means that absolutely no meat or any ingredient containing or having come in contact with meat has been included.

Parve: This brings in a huge group of foods that contain neither meat nor dairy ingredients. They are in essence neutral and as such may be included in either a meat or dairy meal. All fruits, vegetables, and grains are parve. Kosher fish—those with fins and scales—are parve. Eggs are also parve, though chicken is considered meat.

When buying parve convenience foods, it's important to check the label to be sure the food doesn't have the less rigorous "K" certification. Some parve foods contain casein, which is derived from milk, and depending upon the amount and the level of your observance, you may or may not consider the ingredient truly parve.

At Passover, special dietary laws are observed. Besides being certified kosher, foods must be labeled "kosher for Passover," and specific foods are forbidden. These forbidden foods are those that contain anything that might ferment and rise: grain and cereal products, like corn and rice, and their derivatives, such as grain alcohol and vinegar, and legumes, such as peas and beans. (Many Sephardic Jews do allow rice.) Wheat flour is used to make matzohs, but for Passover, matzoh preparation and baking must be completed within eighteen minutes so that fermentation is impossible.

To ensure separation of dairy and meat, the kosher kitchen is stocked with at least two separate sets of dishes, pots, pans, silverware, and utensils, plus two additional sets for Passover. These are not interchangeable. Most Jews allow the same dishwasher to be used for both meat and dairy, since the water temperature used for each washing is high enough to thoroughly clean the machine as well as the dishes; but ultraorthodox Jews may have two dishwashers, two sinks, and two refrigerators, one for meat and one for dairy. Glass dishes are considered nonporous and so may be used at either meat or dairy meals.

CHAPTER ONE

Appetizers and Snacks

*I*n Yiddish, the word for appetizers is *forspeise*. For Jews all over the world, whether Ashkenazic or Sephardic, these tasty tidbits are expected to begin a meal. Unlike French hors d'oeuvres, which were originally designed for the rich, the humblest Jewish family in the Pale of Settlement (an overcrowded area stretching from the Black Sea to the Baltic and the only place in Eastern Europe where Jews were allowed to live) started their meals with some kind of appetite teaser, granted that it was usually made from ingredients that were cheap and plentiful.

A traditional Jewish appetizer might be a dish of schmaltz herring steeped in vinegar and bay leaves; chicken giblets and livers cooked with onions, then chopped and served with black bread; or even *rotach,* a large black radish grated and tossed with a little chicken fat to add flavor and richness. *Forspeise* served a double purpose: to use every bit of any edible ingredient on hand and to curb the appetite when there was little else to follow.

The recipes in this chapter reflect the cultural diversity of the *forspeise* table and the ease with which dishes tinged with nostalgia can be duplicated in simpler fashion today. Besides traditional foods, such as Chopped Pickled Herring and Arbis (peppered chickpeas), you'll find updated versions of familiar classics—Roasted Eggplant and Olive Hummus and Vegetarian Chopped "Liver"—adjusted for the availability of new ingredients and with an eye to modern nutritional standards. With timesaving appliances like the food processor and microwave and with the rapidly expanding number of kosher certified foods, all these recipes can fit neatly into the contemporary Jewish kitchen.

CHOPPED PICKLED HERRING

*M*y mother made her own pickled herring with fish fresh from the boats. She had to gut, scale, and fillet the fish before beginning, and then she started chopping. Now it's a snap with a food processor and store-bought pickled herring.

MAKES 1⅓ CUPS; 6 TO 8 SERVINGS

1 (8-ounce) jar pickled herring in wine sauce
1 heel from a loaf of rye bread (4×3×½-inch) or 1 stale
   slice
½ apple, peeled, cored, and cut up
1 hard-cooked egg, quartered

1. Drain herring, reserving liquid. Place herring and any onions from jar in a food processor.

2. Soak rye bread in reserved liquid. Add moistened bread and any remaining herring liquid to processor along with apple and three-quarters of egg.

3. Pulse until coarsely chopped. Transfer to a serving dish.

4. To garnish, press remaining egg through a coarse wire sieve held over chopped herring.

PICKLED HERRING AND APPLE

*I*n Eastern Europe, herring was fresh and cheap and it was common to salt the fish in barrels to last through the winter. Herring appeared in scores of different dishes. Using a jar of pickled herring, this appetizer is made in a jiffy.

MAKES 1⅓ CUPS; 4 TO 6 SERVINGS

1 (8-ounce) jar pickled herring tidbits, drained
2 tablespoons chopped onion
1 sweet apple, peeled, cored, and cut into ½-inch dice
2 teaspoons fresh lemon juice

1. Place herring and onion in a small bowl. Toss to mix.

2. Sprinkle apple with lemon juice and stir into herring.

3. Serve with cocktail picks or transfer to a lettuce-lined plate and serve as a salad.

DANISH HERRING

Serve this easy appetizer with soda crackers or matzohs.

8 SERVINGS

1 (16-ounce) jar pickled herring, drained
1 medium onion, chopped
1 tart apple, peeled, cored, and finely diced
2 kosher dill pickles, finely diced
1 cup ketchup

Place herring, onion, apple, and pickles in a small serving bowl. Pour ketchup over all and stir gently to mix. Cover and refrigerate until serving time.

SARDINE AND ONION SPREAD

When I was growing up in the Scottish isles, this was a favorite snack, which we spread on hot toast or matzohs. To keep parve, use margarine instead of butter on the toast.

2 SERVINGS

1 (3¾-ounce) can whole sardines, drained
1 tablespoon cider vinegar
1 teaspoon Dijon mustard
1 tablespoon minced onion

In small bowl, mash together sardines, vinegar, and mustard. Stir in onion.

FRESH SALMON SPREAD

*A*ny time you cook fresh salmon and have some leftovers, they can be transformed into this chunky breakfast spread to spoon onto toasted bagels. Just begin with step 2.

4 TO 6 SERVINGS

3 tablespoons distilled white vinegar
1 bay leaf
8 ounces salmon fillet
1 small red onion, minced
8 slices of cucumber, finely diced
3 tablespoons capers
3 tablespoons chopped fresh dill
2 tablespoons mayonnaise

1. In a medium skillet, bring 1 inch of water to a simmer. Stir in 3 tablespoons vinegar and add bay leaf. Add salmon, cover, and simmer over medium-low heat until salmon is just opaque throughout, about 10 minutes. Remove from heat and let cool in the liquid. Remove skin; flake salmon, discarding any small bones.

2. In a medium bowl, combine salmon, red onion, cucumber, capers, dill, and mayonnaise. Mix with a fork; do not mash.

3. Cover and refrigerate until chilled.

BABA GANOUSH

*O*ften called "poor man's caviar," this cool, smoky egg-plant spread is popular in Israeli homes and restaurants. For best flavor, make it one to two days ahead to give the flavors a chance to mellow. Serve at room temperature with fresh, Soft Matzohs (page 20), pita bread, or sliced oranges.

MAKES 1 CUP; 4 TO 6 SERVINGS

1 medium eggplant (about 1 pound)
3 tablespoons chopped parsley
2 tablespoons tahini (stir well before using)
2 tablespoons fresh lemon juice
1 tablespoon olive oil
2 garlic cloves, quartered and smashed
¼ teaspoon salt
Pinch of cayenne

1. Prick eggplant all over, wrap loosely in microwave-safe paper towels, and microwave on High for 8 to 10 minutes, or until eggplant is soft when pressed with fingers. Or bake in a 400°F. oven for 1 hour, or until soft. Set aside until cool enough to handle.

2. Cut eggplant in half lengthwise and place in a colander to drain off any excess liquid. Scoop out pulp and place in a food processor. Add 2 tablespoons parsley, tahini, lemon juice, oil, garlic, salt, cayenne, and 1 tablespoon water. Process until almost smooth.

3. Spoon baba ganoush into a serving dish and garnish with remaining 1 tablespoon chopped parsley. Serve at room temperature.

CLASSIC HUMMUS

Here's a quick dip, perfect for last-minute entertaining. Just dump everything into a food processor and blend. It will hold its flavor and texture for up to three days in the refrigerator. Serve with warm pita breads or with carrot and celery sticks.

MAKES 2 CUPS; 6 TO 8 SERVINGS

1 (15-ounce) can chickpeas, with their liquid
½ cup tahini (stir well before using)
2 teaspoons chopped garlic
3 tablespoons fresh lemon juice
1 teaspoon distilled white vinegar
Salt and white pepper

1. Place chickpeas with their liquid in a food processor. Add tahini, garlic, lemon juice, and vinegar. Process until smooth and creamy.

2. Pour into a serving bowl and season to taste with salt and white pepper. Serve at room temperature or cover and refrigerate for up to 3 days.

BLACK BEAN HUMMUS

MAKES 1½ CUPS; 6 TO 8 SERVINGS

1 (19-ounce) can black beans, drained but not rinsed
⅓ cup tahini (stir well before using)
Juice of 1 lemon
2 teaspoons minced garlic
¼ cup cilantro sprigs
1 teaspoon salt
¼ teaspoon pepper
2 teaspoons ground cumin

Place black beans, tahini, lemon juice, garlic, cilantro, salt, pepper, and cumin in a food processor. Puree until smooth.

HUMMUS WITH ZA'ATAR SEASONING

*C*hickpeas are an Israeli staple. I like to use canned to save time; dried chickpeas need soaking overnight and long cooking. Za'atar is a salty mixture of blended herbs, including thyme, marjoram, and sumac, which is available at Middle Eastern food shops and many supermarkets. I've included my version—minus the sumac—just in case you can't find za'atar.

MAKES 1 CUP; 4 TO 6 SERVINGS

2 garlic cloves, cut in half
1 (15-ounce) can chickpeas, drained and rinsed
¼ cup tahini (stir well before using)
¼ cup fresh lemon juice
3 tablespoons extra-virgin olive oil
1 teaspoon ground cumin
1 teaspoon ground coriander
½ teaspoon Za'atar Seasoning (recipe follows)
½ teaspoon crushed hot red pepper
½ teaspoon salt
Paprika and chopped fresh parsley, for garnish

1. With machine on, drop garlic through feed tube of a food processor and chop coarsely.

2. Add chickpeas, tahini, lemon juice, 2 tablespoons olive oil, cumin, coriander, Za'atar Seasoning, hot pepper, salt, and 3 tablespoons water. Process until smooth but still grainy.

3. Transfer to a serving dish. Drizzle the remaining 1 tablespoon olive oil on top. Garnish with paprika and parsley. Serve at room temperature, with warm pita triangles for dipping.

ZA'ATAR SEASONING

Za'atar is a Middle Eastern blend of seasonings used in hundreds of Israeli dishes. You'll find it on pizza and in pasta, dairy, and egg dishes. There are many variations, some including hyssop, a biblical herb. Try this mix if you can't find za'atar at the store.

MAKES ¾ CUP

- ¼ cup dried marjoram
- ¼ cup toasted sesame seeds
- 3 tablespoons kosher salt
- 1 tablespoon dried rosemary
- 1 tablespoon ground cumin
- 2 teaspoons dried thyme leaves

In a small jar, place marjoram, sesame seeds, salt, rosemary, cumin, and thyme. Cover tightly and shake to mix well. Store in a cool, dry place.

ROASTED EGGPLANT AND OLIVE HUMMUS

Roast the eggplant the day before and refrigerate. Then it's quick to just measure and mix. Serve with bagel thins or warm pita bread.

MAKES 2 CUPS; 6 TO 8 SERVINGS

1 medium eggplant (about 1 pound)
1 (15-ounce) can chickpeas, rinsed and drained
½ cup tahini (stir well before using)
½ cup fresh lemon juice
2 teaspoons minced garlic
3 tablespoons chopped pitted kalamata olives
Salt

1. Preheat the oven to 400°F. With a sharp knife, pierce eggplant all over 6 to 8 times. Bake for 30 minutes, until soft. Set aside until cool enough to peel.

2. In a food processor, combine roasted eggplant with chickpeas, tahini, lemon juice, and garlic. Process to a grainy consistency. Stir in 2½ tablespoons chopped olives. Season with salt to taste.

3. Transfer to a serving dish. Garnish with remaining ½ tablespoon chopped olives. Serve at room temperature or slightly chilled.

TAHINI DIP

*T*his silky, nutty-flavored dip is made from tahini, a Middle Eastern ground sesame seed paste, available at supermarkets. The oil from the sesame seeds tends to separate, so bring the tahini to room temperature and stir to mix well before using. Store in the refrigerator to prevent the paste from turning rancid. This classic dip is great with cut-up raw vegetables or pita bread triangles.

MAKES ¾ CUP; 4 TO 6 SERVINGS

½ cup tahini
¼ cup fresh lemon juice
¼ cup chopped fresh cilantro
1 teaspoon chopped garlic
¼ teaspoon salt
⅛ teaspoon white pepper

In a small bow, mix tahini, lemon juice, and ¼ cup cold water until smooth. Stir in cilantro, garlic, salt, and white pepper. Serve at room temperature.

ARBIS

*A*rbis, or peppered chickpeas, is traditionally served at *Shalom Zachar,* a ceremony to welcome a newborn baby boy, which is celebrated at home on the Friday night following the birth. To save time, I use well-drained canned chickpeas instead of dried. These are usually spooned onto a small plate and eaten with your fingers.

MAKES 2³/₄ CUPS

2 (15-ounce) cans chickpeas, drained
1 tablespoon olive oil, preferably extra-virgin
1 tablespoon coarse kosher salt
1 tablespoon coarsely ground black pepper

1. Spread chickpeas on 3 layers of paper towels to absorb moisture. Let drain 5 or 10 minutes.

2. Transfer to a bowl and toss with olive oil, salt, and pepper. Cover and refrigerate for up to 3 days. Serve chilled.

VEGETARIAN CHOPPED "LIVER"

PARVE

My friend Sima makes the best mock chopped "liver" I've ever tasted. It's a hit at every party. Sima's secret: plenty of browned onions. Spread on warm pita bread or thickly sliced cucumbers.

MAKES 4 CUPS; 6 TO 8 SERVINGS

3 tablespoons vegetable oil
2 large onions, sliced
¾ cup walnuts
1 (15-ounce) can peas, drained
3 hard-cooked eggs, quartered
1 tablespoon mayonnaise
2 tablespoons fresh lemon juice
1 teaspoon salt
¾ teaspoon pepper
Paprika

1. In a large skillet, heat oil over medium heat. Add onions and cook, stirring occasionally, for 10 minutes, or until golden brown.

2. In a food processor, chop walnuts coarsely. Add browned onions, peas, eggs, mayonnaise, lemon juice, salt, and pepper. Pulse until coarsely chopped; do not process to a paste.

3. Transfer to serving dish. Dust lightly with paprika. Serve at room temperature.

SOFT MATZOHS

*T*his bread is baked daily by Alberto Delbello at his Roman-Jewish restaurant, Tiramisu, in Philadelphia. Unlike the hard, dry matzohs we eat at Passover, these are soft and warm and should be served almost as soon as they are made. They are irresistible for nibbling.

MAKES 6

1½ cups all-purpose flour
½ teaspoon salt
½ cup cold water
¼ cup garlic-flavored olive oil
Coarse kosher salt and freshly ground pepper

1. In a medium bowl, combine flour and salt. Make a well in center and pour in water. Mix with your hands (not a food processor) until dough forms a ball. Add a little more water, 1 tablespoon at a time, if needed, to make a soft, pliable dough.

2. Turn out onto a lightly floured board and knead for 2 to 3 minutes. Let dough stand 10 minutes at room temperature.

3. Divide dough into 6 equal pieces. On a floured surface, roll out 1 piece into a round as thin as possible.

4. Heat a 7-inch nonstick skillet over medium heat. Sprinkle a little flour into skillet. Add 1 round of dough and cook, flipping every 30 seconds, until dry throughout and slightly browned, about 2 minutes. Brush with garlic oil and season lightly with salt and pepper. Cut into triangles. Keep warm wrapped in a kitchen towel while you cook remaining rounds of dough. Serve warm.

BROWN-BOILED EGGS

Several years ago, on Rosh Hashanah, when I visited Kibbutz Hagoshrim, just a few miles from the south Lebanese border, the Turkish cook in the kibbutz served these Sephardic-style brown eggs. He called them *charinadus*. Oil helps keep the water from evaporating during the long cooking process.

MAKES 12

12 eggs
1 cup cold strong coffee
2 tea bags
Brown skins of 2 large onions
½ cup vegetable oil

1. Place eggs in a large heavy saucepan with 3 to 4 inches of cold water to cover. Add coffee, tea bags, onion skins, and oil.

2. Bring to a simmer, cover, and reduce heat to lowest setting. Liquid should never be more than just barely simmering. Cook for 6 hours, adding more water as needed.

3. Remove from liquid. Refrigerate until ready to serve. Serve cold, in the shell.

KOSHER DILL PICKLES

*T*hese are easy and cheaper and more delicious than any store-bought pickles. Just make sure to scrub the cucumbers well before preparation to remove any wax or sediment. Sterilize the canning jars by running them through the dishwasher or submerge them in a pot of boiling water.

MAKES 2 QUARTS

8 to 10 small kirby cucumbers, rinsed and dried
8 sprigs of fresh dill with stems
8 garlic cloves, peeled and cut in half
1 tablespoon pickling spice
2 tablespoons cider vinegar
½ cup coarse kosher salt

1. Trim stem ends off cucumbers.

2. Divide dill, garlic, pickling spice, and cider vinegar between 2 sterilized 1-quart canning jars. Pack whole kirbys in jars, arranging them so they stand upright.

3. Dissolve salt in 1½ quarts boiling water. Pour enough boiling salted water over kirbys to cover, leaving ½ inch of space at top of jars.

4. Cover jars tightly with lids. Store in a cool, dark place for 1 to 2 weeks. After 1 week, the pickles will be half-sour. After 2 weeks or so, they will be full-fledged kosher dills. At that point, store in refrigerator for up to 1 month.

SPICED GREEN OLIVES

PARVE

*T*hese great cocktail pickups always appear at Israeli weddings. Serve with toothpicks or tiny forks for spearing.

4 TO 6 SERVINGS

1 (16-ounce) can large pitted green olives
1 plum tomato, finely diced
2 tablespoons olive oil
1 pickled lemon (recipe follows), sliced and cut into quarters, or 3 slices of fresh lemon, quartered and tossed with ⅛ teaspoon salt
1 teaspoon hot pepper flakes
2 tablespoons barbecue sauce (your favorite kosher brand)

1. In a small nonreactive saucepan, mix olives with tomato, oil, pickled lemon, and pepper flakes. Cook over low heat for 5 minutes.

2. Stir in barbecue sauce and simmer 3 minutes longer.

3. Serve cold or at room temperature. These keep well in refrigerator for up to 3 or 4 days.

PARVE

PICKLED LEMONS

Moroccan Jews are partial to these pickled lemons, which impart their unique taste to tagines, stews, and even salads. Sometimes they are thinly sliced and served as an hors d'oeuvre with black and green olives.

MAKES 1 QUART (8 LEMONS)

8 lemons
Coarse kosher salt
Olive oil

1. Bring a large saucepan of water to a boil. Add lemons and cook for 2 minutes. Drain and rinse under cold running water.

2. Almost quarter 7 lemons lengthwise, leaving the wedges attached at one end. Sprinkle 1 rounded teaspoonful salt into each lemon.

3. Sprinkle 1 tablespoon salt over bottom of a clean 1-quart canning jar. Pack lemons into jar, pressing each down to fit snugly.

4. Cut remaining lemon in half and squeeze juice into jar. Sprinkle 1 teaspoon salt into each squeezed lemon half and press on top, cut side down. Pour enough olive oil into jar to cover lemons.

5. Cover jar tightly with lid and let stand at room temperature 10 to 14 days, until lemon skins are translucent and have lost their bitterness. Store in refrigerator for up to 3 months.

BROWNED ONION AND EGG SPREAD

"*C*holesterol be damned," insists my eighty-seven-year-old mother who still feeds us this delicious spread slathered on crusty bread as a snack. Rye bread is the traditional base, but she uses whole wheat bread, since rye is usually unavailable in the Shetland Isles.

MAKES 2 CUPS

2 tablespoons plus 1½ teaspoons schmaltz
1 large onion, chopped
6 hard-cooked eggs, shelled
Salt and white pepper

1. Heat 2 tablespoons schmaltz in a medium skillet. Add onion and fry over medium-high heat until onion is nicely browned at edges but not burned, 4 to 6 minutes.

2. In a medium bowl, chop eggs coarsely. Add browned onions with any fat remaining in skillet and mix well. Stir in remaining 1½ teaspoons schmaltz.

3. Season with salt and white pepper to taste. Serve at room temperature.

Tip: To chop eggs neatly, use an egg slicer. First slice egg, then keeping slices together, turn whole egg to slice in opposite direction into small dice.

REDUCED-FAT FRIED ONION AND EGG SPREAD

*F*or this lower-fat, reduced-cholesterol version of the traditional spread, I substitute egg whites for some of the whole eggs and use just a tad of chicken fat for genuine taste. Serve with crackers or thickly sliced cucumber.

MAKES 1¼ CUPS; 6 TO 8 SERVINGS

6 hard-cooked eggs
1 tablespoon Asian sesame oil
½ teaspoon schmaltz
1 large onion, finely diced
1 tablespoon low-fat mayonnaise
2 teaspoons Dijon mustard
½ teaspoon salt
Parsley sprigs, for garnish

M E A T

1. Cut hard-cooked eggs in half. Remove 4 yolks and set aside for another use. Chop together 2 egg yolks and 6 egg whites.

2. In large nonstick skillet, heat sesame oil and schmaltz over medium heat. Add onion and cook until golden and crisp, about 10 minutes. Do not burn, or taste will be bitter. Transfer to a mixing bowl.

3. Stir in chopped eggs, mayonnaise, mustard, and salt. Mix well. Spoon into a serving dish. Garnish with parsley sprigs. Serve at room temperature or slightly chilled.

BAKED PARTY SALAMI

*E*veryone helps themselves to this easy appetizer. This idea is from my longtime friend Barbara Desky, who tells me, "At parties, this is always the first appetizer to disappear."

15 TO 18 SERVINGS

1 (1½-pound) kosher beef salami
¼ cup apricot preserves
½ cup Dijon mustard
Party rye bread

1. Preheat oven to 350°F. Remove casing from salami. With a small sharp knife, score crosswise, with lines ¼ inch apart. Line a small baking pan with foil and put the salami in pan.

2. In a small saucepan, warm apricot preserves over low heat just until melted, 2 to 3 minutes. Stir in mustard and blend well. Smear mixture all over salami.

3. Bake salami for 1 hour, turning after 30 minutes, until crisp and browned.

4. Transfer salami to a serving platter. Present with rounds of party rye and a knife for slicing.

MEAT

CHOPPED LIVER

*T*here is no substitute for schmaltz, or rendered chicken fat, in this recipe. Beef liver may be used in place of calf's liver, but the mixture will be darker. Serve on small rounds of party rye or with crackers.

MAKES ABOUT 2²/₃ CUPS; 6 TO 8 SERVINGS

1 pound calf's liver
¼ cup schmaltz
2 medium onions, sliced
2 hard-cooked eggs, quartered
½ teaspoon salt
¼ teaspoon pepper
2 tablespoons chicken broth or water

1. Rinse liver and pat dry. Cook under preheated broiler for 5 to 7 minutes, turning once, until no pink remains.

2. In a medium skillet, heat 1 tablespoon schmaltz. Add onions and cook over medium heat for about 5 minutes, or until soft.

3. Cut liver into 8 pieces. Place in a food processor with onions, remaining schmaltz, three-quarters of the eggs, salt, and pepper. Pulse until finely chopped; do not overprocess to a paste. Add chicken broth or water if mixture seems dry.

4. Press remaining egg through a sieve to garnish. Serve at room temperature.

MEAT

SWEET-AND-SOUR TURKEY COCKTAIL MEATBALLS

*F*eel free to double or triple this recipe, because you can never make enough of these tangy, mini-meatballs. They're great for a party or buffet and because they're made with matzoh meal, you can even offer them during Passover.

6 TO 8 SERVINGS

1½ pounds ground turkey
3 tablespoons chicken broth or water
¼ cup matzoh meal
¼ cup chopped parsley
2 teaspoons grated lemon zest
1 teaspoon salt
⅛ teaspoon pepper
1½ cups chili sauce
¼ cup red currant jelly
3 tablespoons fresh lemon juice
2 tablespoons dried currants or raisins

M E A T

1. In a mixing bowl, combine turkey, broth or water, matzoh meal, parsley, lemon zest, salt, and pepper. Blend well. Roll into balls about 1 inch in diameter. Set aside.

2. In a large nonreactive saucepan, heat chili sauce, currant jelly, lemon juice, and currants over medium heat. Place meatballs in sauce. Stir gently, spooning sauce over meatballs to coat.

3. Cover, reduce heat to medium-low, and simmer, partially covered, for 20 minutes, stirring often to avoid sticking. Serve hot, with toothpicks.

DILLED SALMON MOUSSE

Here's a never-fail appetizer, which for years graced every Bar Mitzvah appetizer table and is still a favorite. It is best made with fresh dill. Serve with party pumpernickel rounds or cucumber coins.

10 TO 12 SERVINGS

1 (¼-ounce) envelope unflavored gelatin
½ cup boiling water
2 tablespoons fresh lemon juice
½ cup tartar sauce
1 teaspoon paprika
4 to 5 stems of fresh dill, cut up, plus sprigs for garnish
1 (16-ounce) can salmon, drained
¾ cup heavy cream
¼ teaspoon hot pepper sauce
Salt and pepper

1. In a blender or food processor, combine gelatin, boiling water, and lemon juice. Let stand for 5 minutes to allow gelatin to soften.

2. Add tartar sauce, paprika, dill, and salmon. Whirl about 10 seconds to chop dill coarsely and blend. Add cream and hot sauce and process again to mince dill and blend well. Season with salt and pepper to taste.

3. Rinse a 2-quart mold with cold water. Without wiping dry, immediately pour salmon mousse into mold. Cover with plastic wrap and refrigerate at least 8 hours or overnight to set completely. Turn onto a platter. Garnish with fresh dill sprigs. Serve chilled.

DAIRY

WHITEFISH SPREAD

*C*hubs, small smoked whitefish, are too dry for this popular spread. Instead, buy a thick steak cut from a large smoked fish.

MAKES 2 CUPS; 6 TO 8 SERVINGS

1 pound smoked whitefish, skinned and boned
½ cup shredded carrot
¼ cup finely chopped celery
3 tablespoons minced scallions
1 tablespoon mayonnaise
1 tablespoon sour cream
Dash of cayenne

Flake fish with a fork. Add carrot, celery, scallions, mayonnaise, sour cream, and cayenne. Mix well. Refrigerate, covered, until serving time.

MARINATED FETA CHEESE

MAKES 1 POUND; 6 TO 8 SERVINGS

1 pound feta cheese, cut into ½-inch dice
2 tablespoons tiny (nonpareil) capers
1½ cups basil-flavored olive oil
1 tablespoon minced jalapeño pepper
1 teaspoon ground cumin

1. In a wide-mouthed jar or small deep bowl, layer half of feta. Sprinkle capers over cheese and cover with remaining feta.

2. In a 2-cup glass measure or bowl, mix olive oil with minced jalapeño pepper and cumin. Pour over feta cheese. Cover and refrigerate overnight. Let return to room temperature before serving.

DAIRY

ISRAELI EGGPLANT ROLLS

Eggplant is a staple vegetable in Middle Eastern cooking. Many contemporary as well as traditional dishes, such as this *mele-mah*, are created around it. I first tasted this at the Sonesta Hotel in Jerusalem, where I attended a wedding in which the bride insisted on a totally vegetarian menu.

MAKES 10; 4 TO 5 SERVINGS

1 medium eggplant
Olive oil
½ cup seasoned dry bread crumbs
½ cup shredded carrot
½ cup shredded zucchini
¼ cup ricotta cheese
1 teaspoon ground cumin
⅛ teaspoon salt
Lettuce leaves, for serving

1. Preheat broiler. Oil a large baking sheet.

2. Peel eggplant and cut lengthwise into ¼-inch-thick slices. Brush generously on both sides with olive oil and dip in bread crumbs to coat both sides. Place on baking sheet and broil 2 to 3 minutes on each side, or until eggplant is tender and crumbs are lightly browned. Let cool.

3. In a small bowl, mash together carrot, zucchini, ricotta, cumin, and salt. Spread a rounded tablespoon ricotta mixture on an eggplant slice. Roll up like a jelly roll. Repeat with remaining filling and eggplant.

4. Arrange on lettuce-lined platter. Serve at room temperature with a fork and knife as a first course.

DAIRY

NOVA ENCHILADAS

Jewish cooking is becoming more and more international. Here the craze for Mexican food gets mixed with the traditional lox— with corn tortillas standing in for bagels.

MAKES 8; 4 SERVINGS

8 corn tortillas
4 ounces cream cheese, softened
3 to 4 ounces nova smoked salmon
2 medium tomatoes, thinly sliced
1 sweet onion, thinly sliced
1 lime

1. Heat a large skillet, preferably cast-iron, over high heat. Warm tortillas, 1 or 2 at a time, until pliable, about 30 seconds on each side.

2. Spread cream cheese over warm tortillas. Layer one fourth of smoked salmon, tomato slices, and onion on top of each. Squeeze a little lime juice over each. Roll up and serve immediately.

DAIRY

CHAPTER TWO

Soups

✶

For Jewish cooks, soups, beginning with chicken soup and borscht, have always been an important part of the cuisine, not least because a liquid supper in a bowl provided a cheap way to feed a hungry family. For Jewish immigrants in the early part of this century, soup was often the main dish of the meal, served with hunks of bread chewed as a filler. Often the vegetables were wilted (bought for a few cents at the end of the market day), but pulses (lentils and beans) and cereals, or whole grains, gave substance while stretching meager supplies of meat and poultry. Whatever the ingredients, the final potion was satisfying, nutritious, and when Grandmother had anything to do with it, heavenly tasting.

Such is the case with chicken soup, the proverbial "Jewish penicillin," which has crossed all ethnic borders to become the cure-all for whatever ails you. There's no secret in its making. Besides an uncomplicated recipe for basic chicken soup, I've included a number of variations and a repertoire of other soups that range from hearty, rib-sticking Beef-Barley Soup with Mushrooms and Kale and Fresh Tomato Soup with Kasha to light, warm-weather fare, such as Chilled Cherry Wine Soup and Kibbutz Minted Peach Soup from Israel.

As a base, when I don't have homemade broth on hand, I use bouillon granules or bouillon cubes or canned broth, so that soup can be a regular item on my year-round menus no matter how busy I am; just don't tell Grandma. You'll find kosher versions of beef, chicken, and vegetable flavors of both canned broth and bouillon granules or cubes in almost all markets. Vegetable stocks are particularly useful for flavoring parve soups, which can be served with either a milk or a meat meal, and for soups that include dairy products.

Most of these recipes can be made ahead and refrigerated for two to three days. Almost all freeze well. When reheating any refrigerated or frozen soup, though, be sure to taste and check the seasonings. Often a little extra salt and pepper or a splash of lemon juice are needed the second time around.

VEGETARIAN BORSCHT FROM KIEV

My friend Rosa, who was born and raised in Kiev, Russia, makes borscht the old-fashioned way. "You must use fresh beets, big and juicy," she insists, "and as a side dish, boiled potatoes with fresh garlic and dill."

6 TO 8 SERVINGS

2 large beets, peeled
2 large carrots, peeled
1 large green bell pepper, diced
1 large sweet onion, chopped
6 tablespoons fresh lemon juice
¼ to ⅓ cup sugar
Salt and pepper

1. Shred beets and carrots coarsely in a food processor or on the large holes of a hand grater. Place in a large wide saucepan or flame-proof casserole.

2. Add bell pepper and onion and enough cold water to cover vegetables by 1 inch. Stir and cover pot. Bring to a boil, reduce heat to low, cover, and cook for 1 hour.

3. Stir in lemon juice and ¼ cup sugar. Season to taste with salt and pepper. Cook 15 minutes longer. Taste and add remaining sugar if you think it needs it. Serve hot, at room temperature, or chilled.

CREAM OF LEEK AND POTATO SOUP

*P*arsley root adds a distinctly Jewish taste to this French classic. By using nondairy creamer in place of cream, this parve soup can be served at a meat or dairy meal.

6 TO 8 SERVINGS

2 tablespoons margarine
3 leeks (white and tender green), trimmed, rinsed well, and cut into 1-inch pieces
3 large baking potatoes, peeled and thinly sliced
2-inch piece of parsley root, peeled and sliced
4 cups vegetable broth
2 teaspoons salt
¼ teaspoon white pepper
2 cups nondairy creamer
1 tablespoon lemon juice

1. Melt margarine in large soup pot. Add leeks, potatoes, and parsley root. Cover and cook over low heat for 20 minutes, or until leeks are soft.

2. Add broth, salt, and pepper. Cover and bring to a boil. Lower heat to medium and cook 20 minutes longer, until potatoes are soft. Remove from heat. Let cool slightly.

3. Puree soup in a blender or food processor (you'll need to do this in 2 batches). Return to pot.

4. Stir in nondairy creamer, then lemon juice. Reheat if necessary. Serve hot.

RED LENTIL SOUP

*T*he small reddish-orange lentils that give this soup its color are known as Egyptian lentils. The story goes that Esau sold his birthright for a dish of lentils. This is a better deal.

6 SERVINGS

2 tablespoons vegetable oil
2 medium onions, chopped
1 medium carrot, peeled and chopped
1 medium parsnip, peeled and thinly sliced
1 tablespoon chopped garlic
6 cups vegetable broth
¾ cup dried red lentils
¼ cup tomato paste
3 tablespoons chopped parsley
1 teaspoon dried oregano
1 bay leaf
Pinch of crushed hot pepper flakes
Salt and pepper

1. Heat oil in a large heavy pot over medium-high heat. Add onions, carrot, and parsnip and cook 5 minutes.

2. Add garlic, broth, lentils, tomato paste, 2 tablespoons parsley, oregano, bay leaf, and hot pepper flakes. Bring to a boil. Cover and simmer, stirring often, for 20 minutes, or until lentils are tender.

3. Season with salt and pepper to taste. Remove and discard bay leaf. Serve hot, garnished with remaining 1 tablespoon chopped parsley.

SCHAV

*S*chav, or sorrel, must be picked and used in the spring when the sour leaves are young and tender. Sorrel grows wild in Eastern Europe and makes a tart, cool soup. Spinach, which is less sharp, may be substituted for the tangy green, but more lemon juice will be needed.

4 SERVINGS

3 cups vegetable broth
6 cups sorrel leaves, shredded
1 scallion, sliced
3 tablespoons fresh lemon juice
2 teaspoons sugar
1 egg
Chopped fresh dill and finely diced cucumber

1. Bring broth to a boil. Add sorrel and scallion. Return to a boil and cook for 3 minutes. Remove from heat and stir in lemon juice and sugar.

2. Lightly beat egg in a small heatproof bowl. Gradually whisk 1 cup hot soup into egg. Slowly mix egg mixture into soup in pot, whisking constantly to avoid curdling.

3. Let cool slightly. In batches if necessary, puree soup in a food processor or blender until smooth. Transfer to a bowl, cover, and refrigerate until cold.

4. Serve chilled, with small bowls of chopped fresh dill and diced cucumber on the side.

FRESH TOMATO SOUP WITH KASHA

*T*hickened with kasha straight from the box, this is a great way to use up overripe tomatoes. For a complete dairy meal, serve with sharp cheese, crusty rolls spread with sweet butter, and a salad.

4 TO 6 SERVINGS

2 tablespoons olive oil
3 very ripe beefsteak tomatoes (about 1½ pounds), cut into ½-inch dice
1 yellow bell pepper, cut into thin strips about 1-inch long
4 cups vegetable juice, such as V-8
2 tablespoons kasha
¼ cup shredded fresh basil
2 garlic cloves, chopped
2 tablespoons fresh lemon juice
1 teaspoon sugar
Salt and pepper

1. Heat oil in a large pot over medium heat. Add tomatoes and cook, stirring, until soft and broken down, about 5 minutes.

2. Stir in pepper strips, vegetable juice, kasha, fresh basil, garlic, and 1 cup water. Simmer for 5 minutes, or until kasha is soft.

3. Stir in lemon juice and sugar. Season with salt and pepper to taste. Serve hot.

CHILLED CHERRY WINE SOUP

*T*he timesaving secret here? Baby food is used to thicken the soup instead of cornstarch, which tends to lump and needs cooking.

6 SERVINGS

2 (16-ounce) cans pitted sweet cherries
1 cup kosher sweet wine
½ cup water
2 teaspoons grated lemon zest
2 tablespoons fresh lemon juice
Pinch of nutmeg
2 (6-ounce) jars plum/tapioca baby food
1 to 2 tablespoons honey
Lemon peel, slivered (optional)

1. In a medium bowl, mix together cherries and their juice, wine, water, lemon zest, lemon juice, and nutmeg.

2. Stir in plum baby food. Sweeten to taste with honey, if desired.

3. Serve chilled or at room temperature. Garnish with slivers of lemon peel.

NOTE: This soup may be garnished with a teaspoon of sour cream, which would make the dish dairy.

KIBBUTZ MINTED PEACH SOUP

Served daily in summer in the communal dining room of Kibbutz Hagoshrim in northern Israel, this soup is sweetened mainly by the natural juices of the peaches and plums. Especially popular in Israel during Succoth, when grapes are plentiful and traditional, it is served as a refreshing first course.

6 SERVINGS

4 very ripe peaches
4 purple plums
¼ cup sugar
2 tablespoons chopped fresh mint
½ teaspoon ground cardamom
1 cup seedless red grapes, halved

1. Remove pits from peaches and plums and cut into thin slices.

2. Place fruit in a medium saucepan with sugar, mint, cardamom, and 5 cups water. Bring to a boil over high heat, stirring to dissolve the sugar. Cover, reduce heat to medium-low, and simmer for 10 minutes.

3. Remove from heat and stir in grapes. Serve soup at room temperature or chilled.

EINLAUF

*T*hese fluffy little egg-drop dumplings make a light garnish for clear broths, such as the Old-Fashioned Chicken Soup on page 46.

4 SERVINGS

1 egg
½ teaspoon finely chopped fresh dill or ¼ teaspoon dried
⅛ teaspoon salt
Pinch of white pepper
3 tablespoons flour

1. Beat egg and 2 teaspoons water with dill, salt, and white pepper. Add flour and beat with a fork until smooth.

2. Drop batter by teaspoonfuls into boiling water, broth, or soup. Reduce heat to low and cook for 5 minutes.

MANDLEN

Mandlen, little pastry nuts, are usually used as a soup garnish. These are more substantial and not as light as store-bought.

MAKES 30

1 egg
1 tablespoon vegetable oil
½ teaspoon salt
About ⅔ cup flour

1. Preheat oven to 400°F. Coat a large baking sheet with nonstick cooking spray.

2. In a small bowl, whisk egg, oil, and salt. Stir in ½ cup flour. Add enough of remaining flour to make a soft dough.

3. Divide dough in half. With floured hands, shape each piece into a rope ½ inch in diameter. Slice ropes into pieces of dough ½ inch thick and place them on prepared cookie sheet.

4. Bake in preheated oven for 5 minutes. Turn over with a wide spatula and bake until golden, about 5 minutes longer. Let cool, then store in airtight container and use as needed.

BEEF-BARLEY SOUP WITH MUSHROOMS AND KALE

*H*ere's a thick, rib-sticking soup that's a pleasure to come home to on a cold winter night. Since it tastes even better reheated, you can prepare it well in advance. If you don't have a butcher who can accommodate you with coarsely ground chuck, do it yourself: Buy cubed trimmed beef chuck; then cut it into smaller chunks and coarsely grind it by pulsing a few times in the food processor.

6 TO 8 SERVINGS

1 pound beef chuck, coarsely ground
¼ cup pearl barley
2 teaspoons salt
1 large onion, chopped
2 large carrots, peeled and sliced
1 small parsnip, finely diced
2 cups thinly sliced fresh mushrooms
2 cups packed shredded kale
½ teaspoon pepper
½ cup chopped fresh parsley

1. Place beef and barley in a large pot with 2½ quarts water. Add salt and bring to a boil. Skim off any froth.

2. Add onion, carrots, parsnip, and mushrooms. Reduce heat, cover, and simmer for 1 hour.

3. Stir in kale and pepper and cook for 10 minutes. Season with additional salt and pepper to taste. Stir in parsley just before serving.

MEAT

OLD-FASHIONED CHICKEN SOUP

*U*se this basic chicken soup to make Chicken Soup with Matzoh Balls (page 366) or as a flavorful base whenever chicken broth is called for. Chicken soup can be divided among covered containers and frozen for up to 6 months.

MAKES ABOUT 3½ QUARTS

1 (6- to 7-pound) whole chicken, preferably a stewing hen, neck and gizzard reserved
2 large onions, quartered
3 large carrots, cut into 1-inch pieces
2 celery ribs, cut into 2-inch lengths
2 medium parsnips, peeled and cut into 1-inch pieces
1 medium turnip, peeled and cut into 1-inch pieces
6 to 8 large sprigs and stems of parsley
1 teaspoon whole black peppercorns
2 whole cloves
2 bay leaves
Salt (optional)

1. Remove fat from chicken. Rinse chicken, neck, and gizzard under cold running water. Place in a large stockpot and add 4 to 5 quarts water. Bring to a boil over medium heat, skimming off foam as it rises to the top. Immediately reduce the heat so the liquid is just barely simmering.

2. Add onions, carrots, celery, parsnips, turnip, parsley, peppercorns, cloves, and bay leaves. Partially cover and simmer, skimming occasionally, for 4 to 5 hours. Add more water if soup reduces too much.

3. Strain soup. Return to rinsed-out pot and boil until reduced to 3 to 4 quarts. Skim off fat. If there's time, refrigerate first; the fat will lift right off. If using as soup, season with salt to taste. If saving for broth to use as a base for other soups, you may want to leave it unsalted.

CHICKEN AND ESCAROLE SOUP WITH MUSHROOMS AND CHICKEN KNAIDLACH

With the mushrooms, vegetables, and meaty *knaidlach*, this is a substantial soup that can serve as a main course. When you use it as one, be sure to pass a basket of good bread, preferably whole grain, on the side. Without the *knaidlach,* it makes a fine first course.

6 SERVINGS

2 tablespoons olive oil
½ pound mushrooms, sliced
2 shallots, thinly sliced
2 celery ribs, thinly sliced
1 carrot, shredded
2 cups packed shredded escarole
8 cups chicken broth
Chicken Knaidlach (recipe follows)

1. Heat oil in large pot. Add mushrooms, shallots, celery, and carrot. Cook over medium heat, stirring occasionally, for 5 minutes.

2. Add escarole and chicken broth. Bring to a boil, reduce heat to medium, and simmer for 10 minutes.

3. Ladle into bowls and serve hot with Chicken Knaidlach.

CHICKEN KNAIDLACH

*I*talian Jews make their Passover *knaidlach* with chicken, but chicken is also traditional for Jews from the Chechnyan city of Grozny, which is where my recipe comes from.

MAKES 20 TO 22

½ pound skinless, boneless chicken breast
1 egg
⅓ cup matzoh meal
2 tablespoons chopped chives
½ teaspoon salt
½ teaspoon pepper
Pinch of nutmeg

1. Cut chicken into 2-inch pieces. Chop finely by pulsing in a food processor, but be careful not to grind to a paste.

2. Transfer ground chicken to a small bowl. Add egg. matzoh meal, chives, salt, pepper, and nutmeg. Blend well. Mixture should be stiff. Add more matzoh meal if needed. With wet hands, form into small balls 1 inch in diameter.

3. Bring a large saucepan of salted water to a simmer. Gently add chicken *knaidlach,* cover, and cook over medium heat until balls are almost dry in center, 15 to 20 minutes. Drain and serve with hot chicken soup.

CHICKEN SOUP WITH LOKSHEN

4 TO 6 SERVINGS

1½ tablespoons vegetable oil
2 medium parsnips, diced
2 medium carrots, grated
1½ cups fine egg noodles, broken
1 garlic clove, chopped
6 cups chicken broth
1 cup frozen peas
2 tablespoons chopped fresh parsley
Salt and pepper

M E A T

1. Heat oil in a large soup pot. Add parsnips and carrots. Cook over low heat, stirring occasionally, until parsnips are softened, about 10 minutes. Stir in noodles and garlic.

2. Pour in chicken broth and peas. Bring to a boil, reduce heat to medium, and simmer, partially covered, for 15 minutes.

3. Just before ladling into bowls, stir in parsley and season with salt and pepper to taste.

CHICKEN SOUP WITH VEGETABLES

*T*he addition of soft baby lettuces adds color and a new dimension to this age-old favorite. If available, use a hen instead of a chicken for superior flavor.

10 TO 12 SERVINGS

1 (5-pound) whole chicken, neck and gizzard reserved
2 large onions, quartered
3 large carrots, cut into 1-inch pieces
2 celery ribs, cut into 2-inch lengths
1 medium parsnip, cut into 1-inch pieces
4 stems of fresh dill
1 tablespoon salt
4 peppercorns
2 bay leaves
Freshly ground pepper
3 cups shredded butter lettuce

M E A T

1. Remove fat from chicken. Rinse chicken, neck, and gizzard under cold running water. Place in a large soup pot and add water to cover. Bring to a simmer over medium heat, skimming off foam as it rises to the top.

2. Add onions, carrots, celery, parsnip, dill, salt, peppercorns, and bay leaves. Cover, reduce heat to low, and cook slowly, partially covered, for 4 to 5 hours, the longer the better.

3. Let soup cool. Skim off fat. Remove chicken for use in another dish. Strain soup and discard bay leaves and peppercorns. Dice vegetables and return to soup.

4. Before serving, bring soup to a boil. Season with additional salt and pepper to taste. Stir in shredded lettuce. Serve hot.

CHICKEN SOUP WITH WINTER VEGETABLES

*E*ven though for speed this soup is prepared with canned broth, the infusion of fresh vegetables and herbs makes this impossible to distinguish from the long, slow-cooked version.

6 TO 8 SERVINGS

1 tablespoon schmaltz or vegetable oil
1 large onion, thinly sliced
2 leeks, trimmed, washed and thinly sliced
1 cup thinly sliced fennel
1 medium rutabaga, peeled and diced
1 (10-ounce) package frozen mixed vegetables
2 teaspoons celery seed
1 cup coarsely chopped fresh parsley
1 (46-ounce) can chicken broth or 6 cups homemade chicken broth
Salt and pepper

MEAT

1. In a large soup pot, heat schmaltz. Add onion, leeks, fennel, and rutabaga. Cook over medium heat, stirring occasionally, for 10 minutes, or until vegetables are softened.

2. Add frozen mixed vegetables, celery seed, parsley, and broth.

3. Bring to a boil over high heat. Lower heat, cover, and simmer for 15 minutes.

4. Season with salt and pepper to taste. Serve hot.

SUMMER CHICKEN SOUP

*E*ven in Israel, hot soup is eaten year-round. Fresh tomatoes and basil add bright summer color and flavors to this basic broth. Serve with bread sticks.

4 SERVINGS

1 tablespoon olive oil
1 medium green zucchini, cut into thin julienne strips
1 medium yellow zucchini or summer squash, cut into thin julienne strips
1 cup corn kernels, fresh or frozen
1 pound ripe tomatoes (3 medium), cut into ½-inch dice
4 cups chicken broth
¼ cup shredded fresh basil
2 teaspoons lemon-pepper seasoning
Salt

MEAT

1. Heat oil in a large pot. Add green and yellow zucchini and corn. Cook over medium heat, stirring often, 3 to 5 minutes, or until zucchini is barely tender.

2. Add tomatoes, chicken broth, basil, and lemon-pepper seasoning. Bring to a boil. Reduce heat to low, cover, and simmer for 5 minutes. Season with salt to taste and serve at once.

EGG AND LEMON SOUP

*T*his light, comforting soup is popular with Greek Jews for breaking the fast on Yom Kippur. The slightly sharp taste is similar to schav, the Eastern European sorrel soup. I add a little chopped fresh cilantro for color and combine lemon and lime juice to enhance the citrus flavor.

4 SERVINGS

4 cups chicken broth
½ cup long-grain white rice
2 eggs
2 tablespoons fresh lemon juice
1 tablespoon fresh lime juice
1 tablespoon finely chopped fresh cilantro or parsley

1. In a 3-quart saucepan, bring chicken broth to boil. Add rice, lower heat to a simmer, cover, and cook for 20 minutes, or until rice is tender. Remove from heat.

2. In a small bowl, whisk together eggs, lemon juice, and lime juice until well blended. Slowly add about ½ cup hot broth, whisking constantly to avoid curdling.

3. Blend egg mixture back into saucepan, whisking constantly. Return to medium-low heat, add cilantro, and cook, whisking, for 2 to 3 minutes, until soup is hot and begins to thicken slightly. Do not let boil, or liquid will curdle. Serve at once.

KRUPNIK

Barley, potatoes, and onions were year-round affordable staples for Russian Jews. On special occasions, beef was added. I use ground beef instead of chunks to quickly release a rich, meaty flavor.

8 TO 12 SERVINGS

2 tablespoons vegetable oil
½ pound lean ground beef
2 large onions, thinly sliced
2 large potatoes, cut into ½-inch dice
2 medium carrots, shredded
¼ cup pearl barley
8 cups beef broth
2 garlic cloves, chopped
2 teaspoons caraway seeds
2 teaspoons salt
¼ cup chopped flat-leaf parsley

1. Heat oil in a large soup pot. Add ground beef and cook over medium-high heat, stirring to break up lumps, until no trace of pink remains, about 5 minutes. Drain off any fat.

2. Add onions, potatoes, carrots, barley, and beef broth. Bring to a simmer over medium heat. Skim off any foam as it forms.

3. Add garlic, caraway seeds, and salt. Cover, reduce heat to medium-low, and cook for 40 minutes, stirring occasionally. Stir in parsley just before serving.

MEAT

SPLIT PEA SOUP WITH FRANKFURTERS

*F*or kosher cooks, the smokiness of frankfurters takes the place of the meatiness of the ham bone used in nonkosher recipes.

4 TO 6 SERVINGS

3 frankfurters, thinly sliced
2 tablespoons vegetable oil
1 large onion, chopped
¾ cup dried split green peas
10 peeled baby carrots
1 cup coarsely chopped rutabaga
6 cups beef broth
Salt and pepper

M E A T

1. In a large pot, cook frankfurters in oil over medium-high heat, stirring, until lightly browned, about 5 minutes.

2. Add onion, split peas, carrots, rutabaga, and broth.

3. Bring to a boil, skimming off any froth. Cover and simmer for 45 minutes, or until vegetables and peas are tender.

4. Season with salt and pepper to taste. Ladle into bowls, making sure each serving gets a whole baby carrot.

"STONE" SOUP

*R*emember the story of the soup that began with a stone and everybody added something from their cupboard? This is a good catchall for winter vegetables and pantry shelf items.

10 TO 12 SERVINGS

1 small rutabaga, peeled and cut into ½-inch dice
1 medium white turnip, peeled and cut into ½-inch dice
1 large onion, thinly sliced
2 celery ribs, thinly sliced
3 cups sliced fresh mushrooms
½ cup dried porcini or imported (Polish) wild mushrooms
3 garlic cloves, quartered
1 (28-ounce) can crushed tomatoes
1 teaspoon dried tarragon
2 teaspoons salt
¼ teaspoon crushed hot pepper flakes
6 cups beef broth
1 (15-ounce) can kidney beans, drained

1. In a large soup pot, mix rutabaga, turnip, onion, celery, fresh mushrooms, dried mushrooms, garlic, tomatoes, tarragon, salt, and hot pepper flakes. Cover and cook over medium-low heat for 15 minutes, stirring often.

2. Add beef broth and kidney beans. Bring to a boil. Cook, uncovered, over medium heat, stirring occasionally, for 30 minutes, or until vegetables are tender. Serve hot.

MEAT

LOW-FAT VEGETABLE SOUP

*T*his satisfying soup of white winter vegetables, thickened with lentils or barley, contains absolutely no fat. If you can't find nonfat chicken broth in your supermarket, make up a batch with chicken bouillon cubes or granules. By using vegetable broth, you can also make this soup parve to serve with a dairy meal.

6 SERVINGS

1 medium onion, sliced
2 medium white turnips, cut into ½-inch dice
1 cup sliced fresh fennel bulb (about 4 ounces)
3 medium celery ribs, thinly sliced
1 small parsnip, diced
6 cups canned nonfat chicken broth
½ cup lentils
½ cup chopped dill
Pinch of cayenne
Salt and pepper

1. In a large nonstick saucepan, combine onion, turnips, fennel, celery, and parsnip with ¼ cup of chicken broth. Cover and cook over medium-low heat, stirring occasionally, until vegetables are tender but still firm, 20 to 25 minutes.

2. Add lentils, remaining 5¾ cups chicken broth, dill, and cayenne. Cook until lentils are soft, 20 to 30 minutes. Season with salt and pepper to taste. Serve hot.

INSTANT BUTTERMILK BORSCHT

*H*ere's a quick, tangy borscht made with canned beets without any added sugar. It provides a refreshing but quite substantial summer soup when served over warm baked or boiled potatoes.

2 TO 3 SERVINGS

2 teaspoons vegetable bouillon granules
1 (16-ounce) can sliced beets, drained
1 scallion, cut up
1 garlic clove, crushed through a press
1 tablespoon olive oil
3 tablespoons cider vinegar
2 teaspoons grated orange zest or ½ teaspoon dried grated
  orange rind
1½ cups buttermilk
Freshly ground pepper

1. Dissolve vegetable bouillon granules in 3 tablespoons hot water. Pour into a food processor.

2. Add beets to vegetable bouillon along with scallion, garlic, olive oil, vinegar, orange zest, and buttermilk. Whirl until smooth. Season to taste with pepper. Serve at room temperature.

DAIRY

CAULIFLOWER-ONION SOUP

When we were stranded in our house during the blizzard of '96, one of the vegetables in my refrigerator was a large head of cauliflower. Half was cooked and served as a vegetable, and the remainder was made into this creamy, delicious soup.

6 SERVINGS

2 tablespoons olive oil
2 large onions, sliced
4 cups small cauliflower florets
6 cups vegetable broth
4 ounces cream cheese (nonfat is fine), cut into ½-inch dice, at room temperature
¼ cup horseradish cream sauce
Salt
Minced fresh chives or scallion greens

1. Heat olive oil in a large saucepan over medium heat. Add onions and cook, stirring occasionally, until soft and golden, about 10 minutes.

2. Add cauliflower and broth to saucepan. Bring to a boil; reduce to a simmer, cover, and cook until cauliflower is soft, 15 to 20 minutes.

3. Add cream cheese to soup and stir until melted and blended in. Stir in horseradish sauce and season with salt to taste.

4. Ladle hot soup into bowls and serve garnished with chives.

DAIRY

CREAM OF CAULIFLOWER AND FENNEL SOUP

Goat's milk, now available in low-fat form and with kosher certification, gives this soup a lovely nutty flavor. It's also a terrific alternative for people who are lactose-intolerant of cow's milk. To speed preparation, purchase already cut-up cauliflower florets in the produce section of your supermarket.

4 TO 6 SERVINGS

1½ tablespoons butter
2 medium onions, sliced
1 garlic clove, sliced
1 small fennel bulb, sliced
1½ tablespoons flour
4 cups vegetable broth
¼ cup coarsely chopped fresh dill
Pinch of cayenne
1 pound cauliflower florets
2 cups milk, preferably goat's milk
Salt

1. Melt butter in a large soup pot or flameproof casserole. Add onions, garlic, and fennel. Cook over medium heat, stirring occasionally, until softened, about 10 minutes.

2. Add flour and cook, stirring, for 1 minute. Add broth, dill, and cayenne. Bring to a boil. Add cauliflower, cover, and reduce heat to medium-low. Cook until cauliflower is soft, 15 to 20 minutes. Remove from heat and let cool slightly.

3. In batches if necessary, puree soup in a blender or food processor until smooth. Return soup to pot and stir in milk. Heat until hot but do not allow to boil. Season with salt and additional cayenne to taste. Serve hot.

DAIRY

CHILLED CUCUMBER-DILL SOUP

*I*like the coarse texture and color of the unpeeled cucumber, but if you prefer, it may be peeled. Serve this soup ice cold with toasted pita bread or crackers.

2 SERVINGS

1 cucumber, scrubbed
½ cup plain yogurt
½ cup buttermilk
½ cup chopped fresh dill
Salt and white pepper

1. Cut cucumber into chunks. Chop coarsely in a food processor. Add yogurt and buttermilk and puree until fairly smooth.

2. Pour into a bowl and stir in dill. Season to taste with salt and pepper. Cover and refrigerate until cold. Serve chilled.

MILK SOUP

*T*his simple soup is a close runner-up to chicken soup for helping to cure winter coughs and colds.

2 TO 3 SERVINGS

1½ cups mashed potatoes
1½ cups milk
Salt and white pepper
Chives (optional)

1. In a medium saucepan, blend potatoes and milk. Bring to a simmer over medium-high heat, stirring until smooth.

2. Season with salt and white pepper to taste. Pour into bowls, sprinkle with a few chopped chives, and serve hot.

DAIRY

COOL KIRBY CUKE SOUP

*I*f you use nonfat plain yogurt, you'll end up with a refreshing creamy soup that is fat-free. The peel left on the kirby cukes makes this a lovely pale green.

4 TO 6 SERVINGS

1 small baking potato (5 to 6 ounces)
3 cups vegetable broth
2 cups plain yogurt
6 small kirby cucumbers, scrubbed and sliced
¼ cup coarsely cut-up fresh dill
Salt and white pepper

1. Peel potato and cut into 1-inch chunks. Place in a saucepan with water to cover by at least 1 inch. Bring to a boil over high heat. Cook for 15 to 20 minutes, until potato is soft; drain.

2. Place cooked potato, broth, yogurt, and sliced cucumbers in a blender or food processor. Puree until fairly smooth.

3. Add dill and process until it is chopped. Season soup with salt and white pepper to taste. Serve chilled.

DAIRY

GOLDEN GARLIC AND TURNIP SOUP

Garlic and turnips appear with regularity in Eastern European Jewish cooking. By using frozen mashed turnips thawed in the microwave, this creamlike soup can be made in minutes. Nondairy creamer can be substituted for light cream to make this parve.

4 SERVINGS

4 garlic cloves, thinly sliced
1 tablespoon olive oil or other vegetable oil
1 (11-ounce) package frozen mashed turnips, thawed
1 tablespoon Dijon mustard
2 cups vegetable broth
¼ cup light cream or nondairy creamer
Salt and pepper

1. In a medium saucepan, cook garlic in oil over medium heat until golden at edges, about 2 minutes. Add turnips, mustard, and broth. Bring to a boil, stirring to blend in mustard.

2. Remove from heat and stir in cream. Season with salt and pepper to taste. Serve hot.

DAIRY

SEPHARDIC GARLIC BREAD SOUP

*T*his lusty peasant soup thickened with challah probably came to Jewish cooking via the Sephardic Jews of Spain.

4 TO 6 SERVINGS

1 medium onion, sliced
10 good-sized garlic cloves, peeled and quartered
2 tablespoons extra-virgin olive oil
1 tablespoon fresh thyme leaves or 1 teaspoon dried
4 drops of hot pepper sauce, such as Tabasco
1 bay leaf
2 (14½-ounce) cans vegetable broth
4 cups cubed (1-inch) challah
¼ cup grated Parmesan cheese
2 tablespoons heavy cream

1. In a large saucepan, cook onion and garlic in oil over medium heat, stirring occasionally, until soft but not brown, 8 to 10 minutes. Add thyme, hot sauce, bay leaf, and broth. Cover and simmer for 10 minutes.

2. Remove and discard bay leaf. Stir in challah, remove from heat, and let soup stand for 10 minutes.

3. In batches if necessary, puree soup in a food processor or blender until smooth. Return to pot and reheat. Stir in cheese and cream and serve at once.

DAIRY

EVERYDAY COOKING FOR THE JEWISH HOME

SOUR CREAM SCHAV

4 SERVINGS

3 cups vegetable broth
6 cups sorrel leaves, shredded
¼ cup fresh dill sprigs
3 tablespoons fresh lemon juice
About 2 teaspoons sugar
½ cup sour cream
1 medium cucumber, peeled and diced
8 to 10 radishes, thinly sliced
4 scallions, thinly sliced

1. Bring broth to a boil in a medium nonreactive saucepan. Add sorrel and dill and return to a boil over high heat. Cook for 3 minutes.

2. Remove from heat and stir in lemon juice and 2 teaspoons sugar. Let cool slightly. Whisk in sour cream.

3. Pour soup into a food processor or blender and puree until smooth. Add more sugar to taste, if desired. Transfer to a bowl, cover, and refrigerate until cold.

4. To serve, ladle chilled soup into bowls. Sprinkle cucumber, radishes, and scallions on top.

DAIRY

CREAMY GAZPACHO WITH ALMONDS AND ARTICHOKES

With its white sour cream base and toasted almonds, this cool soup is deliciously different from the usual gazpacho. I first tasted it in a little mom-and-pop restaurant in a trendy neighborhood in Tel Aviv.

4 SERVINGS

⅓ cup slivered almonds
2 medium cucumbers, peeled
1 cup vegetable broth
1 cup sour cream
2 tablespoons fresh lemon juice
½ teaspoon salt
1 (6½-ounce) jar marinated artichokes, drained and quartered
8 cherry tomatoes, quartered
¼ cup coarsely chopped parsley

1. Preheat oven to 350°F. Spread almonds in a small baking dish and bake for 5 to 7 minutes, until lightly toasted. Transfer to a plate and let cool. Alternatively, put almonds on a microwave-safe plate and microwave on High for 1½ to 2 minutes.

2. Cut cucumbers in half lengthwise, then cut into chunks. Pulse in a food processor until coarsely chopped.

3. Add broth, sour cream, lemon juice, and salt to processor. Process briefly to blend. Transfer to a bowl, cover, and refrigerate until cold, at least 2 hours, or overnight.

4. In a small bowl, toss artichokes with tomatoes and parsley. Stir soup to blend and ladle into bowls. Spoon vegetables into center of soup. Sprinkle toasted almonds on top. Serve well chilled.

DAIRY

CHAPTER THREE

Fish

*K*osher fish must have fins and scales, so most fish are permitted, though eels, catfish, sturgeon, and all shellfish, of course, are excluded. Regional spices and seasonings have given a unique identity to Jewish fish cookery, which includes dishes from all over the world. Sweet-and-sour sauces, as in Halibut with Rhubarb Sauce, are typical of the fish dishes of Polish and German Jews. Middle Eastern-inspired recipes, such as Egyptian Poached Sea Bass, cooked with turmeric and lemon juice, and Roasted Red Snapper with Dates, spiced with cinnamon and ginger, have their own unique palate of seasonings.

Many distinctly Jewish fish dishes, such as gefilte fish, are made ahead and served chilled or at room temperature, so they're perfect for celebrations and for Shabbat, when no cooking is allowed. To Eastern and Central European Jews living inland, the only fish available were freshwater varieties, such as carp and pike, from lakes and streams. Gefilte fish (Yiddish for stuffed fish) is a prime example of the Jewish cook's thriftiness. Fish "meat" was chopped, using a *hack-messer* (large-bladed, wooden-handled knife), mixed with bread or matzoh meal, and stuffed back into the skin before cooking. Today, good-quality prepared gefilte fish, both raw and cooked, is readily available. You can fix either of these up to taste homemade—I've included several ways—or make your own from scratch using a classic recipe like Sylvia Daskell's Gefilte Fish or my decorative Gefilte Fish Mold; the food processor does the hard work in seconds.

Fish is highly perishable and is best used on the day of purchase. Fresh fish is displayed on ice, should have no odor, and absolutely should not smell "fishy." Beware of fish packaged in plastic wrap; it's impossible to tell how fresh it is.

MUSTARD-FRIED CARP STEAKS

*T*his kind of fish can be served in place of gefilte fish, especially on Shabbat. Other fish steaks, such as halibut or tuna, can be used.

4 SERVINGS

¼ cup salad mustard
4 carp steaks, cut ¾ inch thick
⅓ cup matzoh meal
1 teaspoon ground celery seed
2 tablespoons chopped parsley
1 teaspoon salt
Vegetable oil for frying
Lemon wedges

1. Brush mustard evenly over both sides of carp steaks.

2. Mix matzoh meal, celery seed, 1 tablespoon parsley, and salt in a shallow dish. Coat carp lightly on both sides with seasoned matzoh meal.

3. Heat ¼ inch of oil in a large skillet. Fry fish over medium-high heat for about 4 minutes on each side, or until nicely browned outside and opaque in center when flakes are separated. Drain on paper towels.

4. Serve warm or at room temperature. Garnish with remaining 1 tablespoon chopped parsley and pass lemon wedges on the side.

LEMON-BROILED FLOUNDER

*F*lounder is a delicate, low-fat fish that needs little embellishment. Serve hot from the broiler.

4 SERVINGS

1½ pounds flounder fillets
1 tablespoon Dijon mustard
2 tablespoons fresh lemon juice
1 teaspoon minced garlic
2 tablespoons chopped black olives or parsley

1. Preheat broiler. Coat broiler pan with nonstick vegetable spray. Place flounder on pan in a single layer.

2. In a small cup or bowl, whisk together mustard, lemon juice, and garlic. Spread mustard mixture over top of fish fillets.

3. Broil about 4 inches from heat without turning for 7 minutes, or until fish flakes are opaque when separated with a knife. Scatter olives or parsley over fish and serve at once.

SYLVIA DASKELL'S GEFILTE FISH

My friend and colleague, Myra Chanin, who inherited her mom's talent for perfect Jewish cooking, generously shared this recipe with me. Myra says that the broth and vegetables that remain after the fish is cooked can be served hot as a side dish with pieces of matzoh soaking in the broth.

8 TO 10 SERVINGS

3 celery ribs, sliced
2 large onions, sliced, plus 3 medium onions, coarsely chopped
2 carrots, sliced ½ inch thick
3 pounds carp fillet, plus bones, skin, and head
3 tablespoons salt
4 teaspoons black pepper
1 tablespoon sugar
3 medium eggs
3 slices of challah, soaked in water
Chrain (page 73)

1. Spread celery, sliced onions, and carrots in bottom of a large soup pot. Rinse carp bones, skin, and head well and add to vegetables in pot. Sprinkle with 1 tablespoon salt, 1 teaspoon pepper, and 1 teaspoon sugar. Set aside.

2. Chop carp fillet in a food processor for 20 seconds (you may need to do this in 2 batches, depending on size of processor bowl). Transfer to a large bowl. Add eggs, coarsely chopped onions, and challah with water squeezed out. Stir in the remaining 2 tablespoons salt, 1 tablespoon pepper, and 2 teaspoons sugar.

3. With wet hands, shape fish into 12 oval patties. Place in pot on top of vegetables. Add 1 cup water and bring to a boil over medium heat. Reduce to lowest heat, cover, and cook gently for about 3 hours, adding more water to keep moist, if necessary. Adjust seasoning after 2 hours by tasting. Let cool, then refrigerate and serve cold with Chrain.

GEFILTE FISH MOLD

*T*his pale green and orange-striped mold makes a lovely way to present gefilte fish for a special dinner, such as Shabbat. Prepare a day or two ahead and refrigerate. Do not freeze, or the texture will be mushy. Carp, whitefish, or, less traditionally, haddock or cod, or a mixture of these may be used.

8 TO 10 SERVINGS

2 pounds fish fillet
1 small onion, cut up
1 egg
3 tablespoons matzoh meal
2 tablespoons ice water
1 tablespoon prepared white horseradish
1 teaspoon sugar
1½ teaspoons salt
¼ teaspoon white pepper
1 carrot, grated
2 tablespoons chopped dill
Mayonnaise, black olives, and dill sprigs, for garnish
Chrain (recipe follows)

1. Preheat oven to 325°F. Line a 1½-quart bowl with 2 strips of wax paper long enough to allow a generous overhang. Coat with nonstick cooking spray.

2. In a food processor, chop fish and onion coarsely. Turn into a mixing bowl. Add egg, matzoh meal, ice water, horseradish, sugar, salt, and white pepper.

3. Transfer one-third of fish mixture to a separate bowl. Add carrot and mix well. Fold dill into remaining fish mixture.

4. Spoon half of dill mixture into lined bowl and smooth top with a spoon. Add a layer using all of carrot mixture and top with remaining dill mixture.

5. Bring excess wax paper up over fish to cover. Set bowl in a pan of hot water and bake in preheated oven for 1½ hours.

6. Let cool for 5 minutes; then, holding bowl with 2 kitchen mitts, carefully invert to unmold onto a round platter. Spoon a swirl of mayonnaise on top of gefilte fish and garnish with black olives and dill. Serve hot, at room temperature, or cold, cut into wedges. Pass a bowl of Chrain on the side.

CHRAIN

*I*deally, for full strength, this pungent horseradish should be made no more than 4 hours ahead. Custom dictates the fumes should be strong enough to make your eyes water. Serve chilled with gefilte fish or brisket.

MAKES 1¼ TO 1½ CUPS

¾ to 1 pound horseradish root
¼ cup cooked or canned sliced beets
1 teaspoon coarse kosher salt
2 tablespoons fresh lemon juice

1. Peel horseradish root with a sharp paring knife. Cut into ¼-inch slices. In a food processor, finely chop horseradish with beets.

2. Transfer to a mixing bowl and stir in salt, lemon juice, and ¼ cup water. Cover and refrigerate until cold. Serve chilled.

HOMESTYLE GEFILTE FISH

*T*his is the recipe to use when you don't have time to make gefilte fish from scratch and want to "doctor up" the jarred variety so no one will know. This starts with a jar of gefilte fish, simmered on top of the stove to absorb the juices and flavor from the onions and carrots. The peeled baby carrots available in a bag save a lot of preparation time.

8 SERVINGS

1 (24-ounce) jar gefilte fish
¼ cup coarsely chopped dill
1 large onion, sliced
8 baby carrots
1 teaspoon sugar

1. Pour jelly off fish. Place fish in a 2½-quart saucepan with dill, onion, carrots, and sugar.

2. Add enough cold water to almost cover gefilte fish. Bring to a boil. Reduce heat to low and simmer uncovered about 1 hour, until liquid has almost all evaporated.

3. Serve hot or cold. Garnish each piece with a baby carrot and a spoonful of onions.

PICKLED GEFILTE FISH

I often prepare this very simple dish on Shabbat, when no cooking is allowed. If you like it enough for Passover, use "kosher for Passover" products. Serve with crisp greens and pumpernickel rolls or matzoh.

3 OR 6 SERVINGS

1 (24-ounce) jar gefilte fish
⅓ cup Italian salad dressing
1 tablespoon wine vinegar
1 teaspoon minced garlic

1. Drain all jelly from gefilte fish. Arrange pieces in a shallow glass or ceramic serving dish.

2. Combine dressing, vinegar, and garlic. Pour over fish.

3. Marinate for 30 minutes at room temperature or for 1 hour in the refrigerator.

BAKED GEFILTE FISH WITH RED PEPPERS

*I*t's not always necessary to make gefilte fish from scratch. There are many ways to turn the jarred variety into your own creation. Here is one of them. It may be iconoclastic, but instead of horseradish, I like to serve this with tomato salsa.

6 TO 8 SERVINGS

⅓ cup coarsely chopped fresh dill plus dill sprigs, for garnish
1 (24-ounce) jar gefilte fish
1 medium red bell pepper, cut into 8 chunks

1. Preheat oven to 350°F. Spread half of chopped dill over bottom of a medium-size casserole or baking dish.

2. Arrange gefilte fish in casserole in a single layer. Pour fish jelly from jar over fish. Tuck red pepper around fish. Sprinkle remaining chopped dill on top. Cover loosely with foil.

3. Bake for 35 minutes. Remove foil and bake 10 minutes longer, basting fish with pan juices. Serve hot, garnished with sprigs of dill.

FRIED GEFILTE FISH BRITISH-STYLE

*T*his recipe comes from Marlene Morrison, who is co-owner of Michael Morrison's of Glasgow, the oldest kosher deli in Scotland. These patties have been sold there for seventy-five years.

4 TO 6 SERVINGS

1 pound haddock fillets
½ pound cod fillets
1 small onion, cut into chunks
2 eggs
2 teaspoons salt
⅛ teaspoon pepper
½ to ¾ cup matzoh meal, plus more to coat
Vegetable oil for frying
Egg and Lemon Sauce (recipe follows)

1. Cut haddock and cod into 2-inch pieces. Place in a food processor. Add onion and pulse until coarsely chopped. Transfer to a mixing bowl.

2. Stir in eggs, salt, pepper, and enough matzoh meal to form a soft but workable mixture. With wet hands, shape into oval patties about 3 by 2 inches and ¾ inch thick. Dredge in additional matzoh meal to coat on both sides.

3. Heat 1 inch of oil in a large heavy skillet. Fry patties over medium heat, turning once, until nicely browned on both sides, about 6 minutes total. Drain on paper towels. Serve hot, with Egg and Lemon Sauce.

EGG AND LEMON SAUCE

MAKES 1 1/2 CUPS

1 cup vegetable broth or fish broth
1 tablespoon cornstarch
2 eggs
Juice of 2 lemons
Pinch of cayenne
1/4 teaspoon salt

1. In a small saucepan, heat 3/4 cup broth over medium heat, until simmering.

2. In a bowl, blend cornstarch with remaining cold broth. Whisk in eggs, lemon juice, cayenne, and salt. Gradually whisk 1/4 cup hot broth into egg mixture in bowl.

3. Whisk egg mixture into broth remaining in saucepan. Cook over medium-high heat, stirring constantly, until thickened to consistency of thick cream, 3 minutes. Remove from heat immediately. Do not let sauce boil.

NOTE: To reheat if chilled, place in double boiler and whisk over low heat until heated through.

GEFILTE FISH CROQUETTES

*I*nspired by the football-shaped croquettes served at Grahames Sea Fare, a kosher-style London restaurant, this version is made with cooked fish and a handful of ground almonds. Serve as an appetizer or as a main dish with Cucumber and Red Onion Salad (page 173).

4 TO 6 SERVINGS

1 tablespoon vegetable oil, plus more for frying
1 medium onion, finely chopped
4 cups cooked, flaked fish
½ cup mashed potatoes
3 tablespoons finely ground almonds
2 eggs, beaten
½ to ¾ cup matzoh meal
½ teaspoon salt
¼ teaspoon pepper

1. Heat 1 tablespoon oil in a medium-size skillet over medium-high heat. Add onion and cook until lightly browned, about 5 minutes. Scrape into a mixing bowl.

2. Add fish, mashed potatoes, almonds, eggs, ½ cup matzoh meal, salt, and pepper to onion. Mix well. Mixture should be firm enough to shape. Add a little extra matzoh meal if needed.

3. If you have time, chill for half an hour. If not, don't worry. With an ice cream scoop, form mixture into balls.

4. In a large, deep saucepan or deep-fryer, heat about 2 inches of oil over medium-high heat to 350°F. on a deep-fat thermometer. (A piece of white bread should brown nicely in 60 seconds.)

5. Gently slide fish croquettes into hot oil. Fry, turning, until browned all over. If croquettes start to brown too fast, reduce heat to medium. Drain on paper towels and serve while hot.

HALIBUT WITH RHUBARB SAUCE

*T*his is a marvelously tart Eastern European Passover dish that defies the rule of white wine with fish. Springtime rhubarb grew wild in the old country, and fish was cheap in coastal areas; hence, this slightly unusual pairing.

4 SERVINGS

1 tablespoon vegetable oil
1 large tomato, coarsely chopped
2 cups sliced (½ inch) rhubarb
¼ cup dry red wine
3 tablespoons honey
½ teaspoon salt
¼ teaspoon lemon pepper seasoning
4 halibut steaks, cut ¾ to 1 inch thick
Small bunch of watercress, tough stems removed

1. Heat oil in a large skillet. Add tomato and rhubarb and cook over high heat, stirring, for 2 minutes to soften slightly. Add wine and honey.

2. Cover, reduce heat to medium-low, and simmer for 10 minutes, or until rhubarb is tender. Season with salt and lemon pepper.

3. Add halibut steaks to skillet in a single layer. Spoon sauce up over fish. Cover and cook for 10 minutes, or until halibut is white and opaque in center. Serve at once, garnished with watercress.

PICKLED MACKEREL

*A*t the crack of dawn, my father would meet the fishing boats in the harbor and come home with a "fry" of freshly caught mackerel or herring: 6 fish strung together. My mother fixed them the way her Lithuanian grandmother did. This dish is even better reheated the next day. Serve with boiled potatoes.

6 SERVINGS

2 medium onions, sliced
2 pounds mackerel fillets
1 teaspoon salt
½ teaspoon pepper
1 cup distilled white vinegar
3 to 4 bay leaves
6 to 8 peppercorns

1. Preheat oven to 350°F. Spread half of onions over bottom of a deep 1½-quart baking dish. Season mackerel fillets with salt and pepper and roll up, skin side out.

2. Place mackerel rolls tightly together on top of onions. Spread remaining onions over fish. Pour vinegar and ½ cup water into dish. Add bay leaves and peppercorns.

3. Cover loosely with aluminum foil. Bake in preheated oven for 45 minutes. Remove foil and bake 15 minutes longer. Serve hot or cold.

ROASTED RED SNAPPER WITH DATES

*F*ish and fruit may sound unusual to us, but this is a typical Moroccan New Year's dish. The head is always left on the fish in the hope that the family will be successful leaders in the coming year. Dates in the stuffing symbolize sweetness; pomegranate seeds are for fertility.

6 TO 8 SERVINGS

1 whole red snapper (about 4 pounds), scaled and cleaned
½ lemon
1 cup cooked white rice
½ cup pitted dates, halved lengthwise
¼ cup pine nuts
4 teaspoons cinnamon sugar
½ teaspoon ground ginger
½ teaspoon pepper
1 medium onion, chopped
3 tablespoons margarine
Pomegranate seeds, for garnish (optional)

1. Preheat oven to 400°F. Coat a large baking pan with nonstick vegetable spray. Place fish in pan, diagonally if need be to fit. Rub cavity with lemon, squeezing in juice.

2. In a bowl, mix rice, dates, pine nuts, 2 teaspoons of cinnamon sugar, ginger, and pepper. Stuff into fish cavity. Spoon onion around outside of fish and pour ⅓ cup cold water into pan.

3. Dot with margarine. Sprinkle remaining cinnamon sugar over fish. Cover loosely with foil.

4. Bake in preheated oven for 30 minutes. Remove foil and continue baking 25 to 30 minutes longer, until almost all liquid has evaporated, skin is crisp and browned, and fish is white and opaque next to bone. Serve hot or at room temperature, garnished with pomegranate seeds.

ROSA'S ROASTED SALMON

*T*his Russian dish by way of Israel cooks the fish slowly at a low temperature in juices extracted from carrot and onion. Serve with rice or bulgur pilaf.

4 SERVINGS

1 large carrot, peeled and thinly sliced
1 large onion, thinly sliced
Salt and pepper
4 salmon steaks (6 ounces each)

1. Preheat oven to 275°F. Spread half of carrot and onion over bottom of a shallow 9-by-12-inch baking dish. Sprinkle with salt and pepper.

2. Place salmon steaks on top in a single layer. Season lightly with salt and pepper. Cover fish with remaining carrot and onion.

3. Cover tightly with foil. Bake 2½ hours.

SALMON SCHNITZEL

Here's a Norwegian Chanukah dish, which illustrates how local ingredients are incorporated into Jewish cooking.

4 SERVINGS

2 pounds salmon fillet, cut 1 inch thick
1 scallion, finely chopped
1½ cups chopped mushrooms (about 4 ounces)
¼ cup minced parsley
1 tablespoon fresh lemon juice
3 tablespoons walnut oil
1 tablespoon coarse kosher salt
1 teaspoon pepper

1. Preheat oven to 400°F. Coat a baking sheet with nonstick spray. Cut salmon into 8 equal pieces. With a sharp knife, cut a pocket in each almost all the way through.

2. In a small bowl, mix scallion, mushrooms, parsley, and lemon juice. Stuff salmon pockets with mushroom mixture. Place on prepared baking sheet. Brush generously with walnut oil. Season with salt and pepper.

3. Bake in preheated oven until salmon is opaque throughout and skin is crisp, about 15 minutes. Serve hot.

POACHED SALMON

*S*imple poached salmon can be served by itself with lemon wedges or topped with mayonnaise, or it can form the base for any number of salads or fish cakes.

4 SERVINGS

Boiling water
¼ cup cider vinegar
½ teaspoon dried tarragon
1 bay leaf
4 salmon steaks, cut ¾ inch thick

1. Pour about 1 inch of boiling water into a large heavy skillet or flameproof casserole. Add vinegar, tarragon, and bay leaf.

2. Arrange salmon in skillet in a single layer. Add more boiling water to almost cover if needed. Bring to a simmer.

3. Cover and simmer over medium-low heat for 10 minutes, or until salmon is opaque in center when separated with a knife.

4. With a wide, flat spatula, transfer salmon steaks to a serving dish, pouring a little poaching liquid around fish to keep it moist. Serve warm, at room temperature, or chilled.

EGYPTIAN POACHED SEA BASS

*I*n Egypt, there were only communal ovens, and all home cooking was done on a stove-top burner. Plenty of herbs and spices are added here to perk up the taste. As in all Sephardic cooking, olive oil, not schmaltz is used.

6 SERVINGS

3 tablespoons fresh lemon juice
2 tablespoons olive oil
1 celery rib with leaves, coarsely chopped
¼ cup coarsely chopped parsley
1 small red bell pepper, cut into thin strips
1 tablespoon turmeric
1 teaspoon salt
2 pounds sea bass, cut into 1-inch steaks

1. Pour about ½ inch of water into a large, deep skillet or flameproof casserole. Add lemon juice, olive oil, celery, parsley, bell pepper, turmeric, and salt. Bring to a boil over high heat; reduce heat to medium.

2. Place fish steaks in skillet in a single layer. Cover and simmer for 10 to 15 minutes, until fish is opaque in center.

3. Remove fish steaks to a serving platter. Boil liquid in skillet uncovered over high heat until reduced by about half. Pour reduced pan liquid and vegetables over fish steaks. Serve cold or at room temperature.

FRIED SMELTS ISRAELI-STYLE

*T*ypical of the assimilation of cultures, these funny little fish coated with aromatic spices take on a decidedly Yemenite flavor. Restaurants at the port in Jaffa serve them like this.

4 SERVINGS

1 egg
¾ cup all-purpose flour
2 teaspoons lemon pepper seasoning
2 teaspoons ground cumin
½ teaspoon ground cardamom
1 teaspoon salt
24 medium-size smelts (about 2 pounds total)
Vegetable oil for frying
Lime wedges

1. Whisk egg in a shallow dish. In a separate shallow dish, combine flour, lemon pepper, cumin, cardamom, and salt.

2. Dip smelts first in beaten egg. Then dredge in seasoned flour to coat all over.

3. Heat about ¼ inch of oil in a large skillet until hot but not smoking. (Oil is hot enough when a 1-inch piece of bread browns in 60 seconds.)

4. Add smelts in batches without crowding and fry over medium-high heat for about 3 minutes on each side, until crisp and nicely browned. Drain on paper towels. Reduce heat slightly if fish start to brown too quickly. Add a little more oil if pan becomes dry.

5. Drain smelts briefly on paper towels. Serve hot with lime wedges.

SEARED SURIMI AND SNOW PEAS

*S*urimi is ready-to-eat Alaskan pollack, formed into the shape of lobster chunks or shrimp. Supermarket surimi is often flavored with shellfish broths and therefore isn't kosher. To be sure, buy from a kosher market or in sealed bags with the kosher certification.

4 TO 6 SERVINGS

3 tablespoons peanut oil
3 tablespoons cider vinegar
1 teaspoon Asian sesame oil
2 teaspoons brown sugar
1 teaspoon ground ginger
1 (8-ounce) package frozen baby corn, thawed
2 (10-ounce) packages frozen snow peas, thawed
2 tablespoons finely chopped chives or scallion greens
¼ cup coarsely chopped red bell pepper
1½ pounds surimi
Salt and pepper

1. In a large bowl, whisk together 1 tablespoon oil with vinegar, sesame oil, brown sugar, and ginger. Add corn, snow peas, chives, and red pepper; toss to coat vegetables well. Set aside.

2. Heat remaining 2 tablespoons peanut oil in a wok or large skillet over high heat. Add surimi and stir-fry 1 to 2 minutes to heat through.

3. Add corn and snow pea mixture and cook, tossing, until hot, 2 to 3 minutes longer. Season with salt and pepper to taste. Serve warm or at room temperature.

EIN GEV TILAPIA

*I*first tasted fresh tilapia, St. Peter's fish, at Kibbutz Ein Gev on the shores of Lake Galilee. The tender, bland flesh readily absorbs the herb-flavored tomato sauce in which it is baked. Serve with couscous or rice to sop up the sauce.

4 SERVINGS

1 cup marinara sauce
1 tablespoon fresh lemon juice
4 tilapia fillets (3 to 4 ounces each)
1 cup sliced mushrooms

1. Preheat oven to 400°F. Stir together marinara sauce and lemon juice. Spread ½ cup sauce over bottom of a shallow baking dish just large enough to hold fish in a single layer.

2. Arrange tilapia in dish. Cover with sliced mushrooms and pour remaining sauce over all.

3. Bake in preheated oven 20 minutes, or until fish is opaque in center and flakes when tested with a knife.

MIDDLE EASTERN GRILLED TROUT

*S*esame and lemon are common in Israel as well as all over the Middle East. Paired, they add just the right amount of flavor to delicate grilled trout.

4 SERVINGS

4 whole trout, cleaned
Coarse kosher salt and pepper
2 tablespoons tahini (stirred well before using)
2 tablespoons fresh lemon juice
Pinch of cayenne
Lemon wedges

1. Preheat an outdoor grill. Season insides of trout with salt and pepper. Stir together tahini, lemon juice, and cayenne. Dip trout in mixture to coat outsides.

2. Place fish on an oiled grill rack. Grill trout about 5 minutes on each side, basting once or twice with any remaining sauce, until opaque near bone. Serve garnished with lemon wedges.

GOLDERS GREEN FRIED FISH

*T*hink of this as Jewish fish and chips without the chips. In the 1960s, Jewish London was concentrated in an area called Golders Green, which was crammed with delis and kosher restaurants. Melt-in-the-mouth fresh fish, like this haddock, was cooked to order at restaurants or prepared at home for high tea. Any firm white fish fillets, such as cod or halibut, can be substituted for the haddock. Pass small dishes of olives and pickles with the fish.

4 SERVINGS

1½ pounds haddock fillets
⅓ cup matzoh meal
1½ teaspoons coarse kosher salt
½ teaspoon pepper
Pinch of ground mace
¼ cup milk
Vegetable oil for frying
⅓ cup cider vinegar

1. Rinse fish fillets in cold water. Pat dry with paper towels.

2. In a shallow dish, mix matzoh meal, salt, pepper, and mace. Pour milk into a separate shallow dish.

3. Dip haddock first into milk and then in seasoned matzoh meal to coat both sides.

4. Heat ¼ inch of oil in a large skillet over medium-high heat until hot but not smoking. (Oil is hot enough when a 1-inch piece of bread browns in 60 seconds.) Fry fish in batches for 3 to 4 minutes on each side, until crisply browned and crisp outside and opaque in center. If fish starts to brown too quickly, reduce heat to medium.

5. Drain on paper towels. Serve fish hot or at room temperature, sprinkled lightly with vinegar.

DAIRY

ONION-BAKED HALIBUT STEAKS

*F*ish steaks baked in this oniony custard come out soft and tender. This recipe is a favorite of British Jews, who probably added the onions. Serve hot, with toasted crumpets or English muffins and Garlic Tomato Wedges (page 189).

4 SERVINGS

1 medium onion, coarsely chopped
4 halibut steaks (6 to 8 ounces each)
¾ teaspoon salt
½ teaspoon pepper
2 tablespoons grated Parmesan cheese
2 eggs
1 cup milk
1 tablespoon butter or margarine
Paprika

1. Preheat oven to 350°F. Spread half of onions in a baking dish large enough to hold halibut in a single layer.

2. Place halibut over onions. Season fish with salt and pepper. Sprinkle Parmesan cheese on top. Cover with remaining onions.

3. Whisk together eggs and milk. Pour over fish. Dot with butter and dust lightly with paprika. Cover loosely with foil.

4. Bake in preheated oven for 30 minutes. Remove foil and bake 10 minutes longer. Serve hot.

DAIRY

EGGS BENJAMIN

*T*his recipe is the brainchild of my friend and colleague, Myra Chanin. Smoked salmon takes the place of the Canadian bacon in Eggs Benedict.

4 SERVINGS

1 tablespoon butter
4 slices of smoked salmon
2 English muffins, split, toasted, and buttered
4 poached eggs
Almost-Instant Hollandaise Sauce (recipe follows)

1. Heat butter in a medium skillet over medium heat. Add salmon. Turn heat to medium-high and cook until browned at edges, about 3 minutes.

2. Top each toasted muffin half with a salmon slice, then a poached egg.

3. Coat with 2 tablespoons Almost-Instant Hollandaise Sauce. Serve at once.

ALMOST-INSTANT HOLLANDAISE SAUCE: Warm ½ cup prepared hollandaise sauce in a double boiler over low heat. Whisk in a pinch of cayenne, 1 teaspoon chopped chives, and 1 tablespoon fresh lemon juice.

DAIRY

TUNA BAKED IN RED SAUCE

Quick, spicy, and tasty with marinara sauce, pesto, and sweet peppers. Serve small portions as a Friday night appetizer instead of gefilte fish. For Shabbat lunch, serve at room temperature. For a parve dish, use nondairy pesto.

4 MAIN-COURSE OR 8 APPETIZER SERVINGS

¾ cup marinara sauce
1 tablespoon prepared basil pesto sauce
4 tuna steaks (about 1½ pounds total), cut 1 inch thick
1 small yellow bell pepper, cut into 8 chunks
1 small red bell pepper, cut into 8 chunks
½ teaspoon coarse kosher salt

1. Preheat oven to 400°F. In a medium baking dish, mix marinara sauce and pesto.

2. Add tuna steaks to dish and spoon sauce over fish to cover. Arrange peppers around tuna. Season peppers lightly with salt.

3. Bake in preheated oven for 30 minutes, or until cooked to desired degree of doneness. Serve hot.

DAIRY

CHAPTER FOUR

Poultry

*K*osher poultry includes farm-raised chickens, turkeys, Cornish hens, ducks, and geese. In the old country, chicken was not an everyday food. Poultry was served on special occasions, and every part of the bird was used. The fat was rendered with pieces of skin to make *schmaltz* (chicken fat) and *griebens* (crisp cracklings). Giblets made a good, strong broth, and even the neck was stuffed with a savory mixture (*helzl*). For American Jewish families, chicken is eaten in many forms during the week, and it often stars at the traditional Friday night dinner.

Chickens and turkeys are eaten frequently in Israel, where beef is expensive. Israeli and Middle Eastern-influenced recipes, such as Moroccan B'Steeya and Roasted Pomegranate Chicken, are boldly spiked with sweet spices, oranges, lemons, olives, cumin, and cilantro. Eastern European dishes, such as Gedempte Chicken and Chicken Fricassee, are slowly cooked with simple old-world seasonings like onion, parsley, and paprika, but they'll still fill your kitchen with appetizing aromas.

Kosher chickens and turkeys are in great demand, not just by home cooks but by chefs and restaurateurs who prefer the superior flavor and appearance. At Empire Kosher Poultry in Pennsylvania, chickens roam free, and no hormones or artificial ingredients are added to the feed. In contrast to the practice of nonkosher poultry processors, no hot or heated water is used during processing, and all rinsing and washing is done in cold running water, 52° to 55°F., which is believed to minimize cross-contamination and bacterial growth. Kosher certification requires yearly site inspections, usually unannounced. Nonetheless, before preparing any poultry, especially whole birds, always rinse well under cold running water, then pat dry with paper towels.

SCHMALTZ AND GRIEBENS

*S*chmaltz, rendered chicken or goose fat, was the Eastern European kosher cook's olive oil. Every part of the fowl was used. Most prized was goose fat; the bird was roasted at Chanukah, and the fat was kept for Passover. *Griebens,* the crisp cooked skin, or cracklings, were added to chopped liver and kugels, or enjoyed as a snack with rye bread or matzoh (assuming, of course, you're not worried about cholesterol).

MAKES 1 CUP SCHMALTZ AND ½ CUP *GRIEBENS*

Fat and fatty skin from 3 large fryer chickens or 1 goose
1 small onion, chopped

1. Cut fat into 2-inch chunks. Cut skin with some fat attached into 1-inch pieces.

2. Place fat and skin in a heavy medium-size skillet with ¼ cup cold water. Bring to a boil over medium heat. Cover and cook for 20 minutes. Reduce heat to low, uncover, and cook, stirring often so skin doesn't stick to bottom of pan, until all water has evaporated, 20 to 30 minutes.

3. Add onion and continue cooking over low heat until all fat is rendered, skin is brown and crisp, and onion is nicely browned but not burned, 25 to 30 minutes longer.

4. Let cool slightly, then strain fat into a covered jar. Store in refrigerator for up to 3 weeks or in freezer for up to a year. Use wherever schmaltz is called for.

5. Serve crisp, brown skins (*griebens,* or cracklings) at room temperature. If not eaten soon, store in refrigerator for up to 3 days. Reheat in a preheated 350°F. oven for 5 to 10 minutes to crisp. Watch carefully to avoid scorching onion.

MEAT

GEDEMPTE CHICKEN

*G*edempte means braising, or long, slow cooking in liquid, which draws out the flavors to make a delicious gravy. Though it contains only basic seasonings, this dish will fill your kitchen with the most appetizing aromas. Serve with fluffy kasha to sop up the pan juices.

4 SERVINGS

2 large onions, sliced
1 (3½-pound) chicken, cut into 8 pieces, neck and giblets reserved; liver reserved for another use
1 tablespoon paprika
1 teaspoon salt
½ teaspoon pepper

M E A T

1. Preheat oven to 325°F. In a heavy Dutch oven, spread half the onions. Add ¼ cup water.

2. Sprinkle chicken all over with paprika, salt, and pepper. Place in pot with neck and giblets. Cover with remaining onions.

3. Cover pot tightly and place in preheated oven. Bake 1½ hours.

CHICKEN FRICASSEE

*A*lmost every Jewish grandmother has a recipe for chicken fricassee. In the old days, giblets, wings, and even chicken feet, all bought cheaply, were cooked together to a savory richness. For festive occasions, tiny meatballs were added. I've included everything but the feet to make a contemporary stew, which is what a fricassee really is. Serve with noodles, rice, or couscous.

4 TO 6 SERVINGS

1 tablespoon rendered schmaltz or vegetable oil
1 (3½-pound) fryer, cut into 8 pieces, giblets (but not liver) reserved
2 medium onions, sliced
1½ teaspoons salt
½ teaspoon pepper
½ pound ground turkey
¼ cup soft challah crumbs
1 egg, lightly beaten
2 tablespoons dry onion soup mix
¼ cup coarsely chopped parsley

MEAT

1. Heat oil in a large, deep skillet or flameproof casserole. Add chicken and cook over medium heat, turning, until lightly browned, about 7 minutes.

2. Add giblets and onions to pan. Season with salt and pepper. Pour 1½ cups hot water over all. Cover and simmer over low heat for 45 minutes.

3. Combine ground turkey with challah crumbs, egg, and onion soup mix. Shape into 12 small balls about 1 inch in diameter. Place on top of chicken in skillet.

4. Cover, raise heat to medium, and cook 20 minutes longer. Transfer chicken and gravy to warm serving dish. Garnish with chopped parsley.

NOTE: If you prefer a thicker gravy, transfer chicken and meatballs to serving dish with a slotted spoon. Blend 2 teaspoons flour with 3 tablespoons cold water. Stir into liquid in pan. Bring to a boil, stirring constantly. Cook 2 minutes, then pour over chicken.

MOROCCAN B'STEEYA

This a Jewish adaptation of the classic Moroccan pigeon pie, made with chicken and flavored heavily with sweet spices. Admittedly, it does take time, but much of it can be prepared in stages ahead. It makes a wonderful party dish and can be frozen after baking.

8 SERVINGS

3 large onions, sliced
1 bunch of fresh cilantro, rinsed, tough stems removed
1 tablespoon ground cinnamon
1 tablespoon ground cumin
1 tablespoon ground coriander
1 (3½-pound) chicken, quartered
1 teaspoon salt
½ teaspoon pepper
1 lemon, sliced
3 eggs
½ cup ground almonds
¼ cup cinnamon-sugar
10 leaves of filo dough
6 tablespoons margarine, melted

MEAT

1. Spread onion slices and cilantro over bottom of a large deep skillet or flameproof casserole. In a small bowl, combine cinnamon, cumin, and coriander. Rub spices all over chicken. Place chicken on top of onions and cilantro in pan and season with salt and pepper. Top with lemon slices.

2. Pour in enough hot water to barely cover chicken. Cover skillet and cook over medium heat for 1 hour, or until meat is falling off bones. Remove chicken and set aside. Strain cooking liquid and return to pot. Skim off fat. Boil until reduced to about ¾ cup; remove from heat and set aside to cool. As soon as chicken is cool enough to handle, remove and discard skin and bones. Tear meat into shreds.

3. Whisk eggs and beat into cooled liquid in skillet. Cook over medium heat, stirring constantly, until thick and creamy, 5 minutes. Do not let boil, or sauce will curdle.

4. In a small bowl, mix almonds with 2 tablespoons of cinnamon-sugar.

5. To assemble b'steeya, place 1 sheet of filo dough in an oiled 10-inch pie dish, letting edges overhang rim. Brush with melted margarine. Repeat with 4 more leaves. Spread chicken shreds evenly over filo. Sprinkle almond mixture over chicken. Pour egg mixture into pie.

6. Fold overhanging filo sheets over filling around rim. Cover top of pie with remaining filo, adding 1 sheet at a time and brushing each with margarine. Fold over edges to enclose pie. Brush with remaining margarine. Sprinkle 1 tablespoon cinnamon-sugar evenly over top.

7. Preheat oven to 400°F. Bake pie for 30 minutes, or until filo is golden on top. Invert onto a cookie sheet so that bottom of pie is on top. Sprinkle with remaining 1 tablespoon cinnamon-sugar and bake 20 to 30 minutes longer, until filo is golden brown. Serve hot or at room temperature.

NOTE: To reheat if frozen: Thaw in refrigerator overnight. Cover lightly with foil and bake in a preheated 350°F. oven for 25 minutes, or until heated through.

ZA'ATAR BAKED CHICKEN WITH GREEN TOMATOES

MEAT

My Aunt Sherry, who lived in Israel, was an "experimental" cook. Having bought a basket of green tomatoes from the *shouk*, or "open-air market," because they were cheap, she made this wonderful chicken jazzed up with *za'atar* (Arab spice) for Shabbat.

4 TO 6 SERVINGS

4 medium-size green tomatoes, cut into wedges
1 medium red onion, thinly sliced
1 tablespoon Za'atar Seasoning (page 15)*
1 (3½-pound) chicken, cut up
½ cup bottled lemon pepper salad dressing

1. Preheat oven to 375°F. Place tomatoes and red onion in a shallow 3-quart baking dish. Sprinkle with za'atar and toss to mix.

2. Arrange chicken pieces on top. Pierce each piece 6 to 8 times with tip of a sharp knife. Pour salad dressing over chicken and spread with spoon to coat evenly. Cover loosely with foil.

3. Bake in preheated oven for 30 minutes. Remove foil. Increase heat to 400°F. and bake 15 minutes longer, or until skin is brown and crisp and juices run clear when a chicken thigh is pierced with a fork.

*Or substitute a mixture of 1 teaspoon dried marjoram, 1 teaspoon sesame seeds, ½ teaspoon dried thyme, and ½ teaspoon coarse kosher salt.

ROASTED POMEGRANATE CHICKEN

*T*his is a favorite Rosh Hashanah dish with Moroccan Jews. Because of their many seeds, pomegranates symbolize the hope that in the year ahead, Jews will be able to perform many worthy deeds, or *mitzvahs*.

4 SERVINGS

¼ cup olive oil
1 tablespoon minced garlic
1 (3½- to 4-pound) chicken, quartered
1 pomegranate, halved
¼ cup dry white wine
Juice of 1 lemon
1 tablespoon cinnamon-sugar
Salt and pepper

MEAT

1. Preheat oven to 375°F. In a cup, mix oil and garlic. Brush garlic oil over chicken.

2. Place chicken in a shallow baking dish. Drizzle any remaining oil over chicken. Bake in preheated oven for 45 minutes, basting several times with pan juices, until skin is browned and juices run clear when a thigh is pierced at thickest part with a fork.

3. Remove 1 tablespoon seeds from pomegranate. Set aside for garnish. Squeeze juice from remaining pomegranate through a sieve into a small bowl.

4. In a small nonreactive saucepan, mix pomegranate juice, wine, lemon juice, and cinnamon-sugar. Bring to a boil over high heat. Reduce heat to low and cook 5 minutes. Season sauce with salt and pepper to taste.

5. Transfer roasted chicken to a serving platter and pierce each piece several times. Pour sauce over chicken. Garnish with pomegranate seeds and serve at room temperature.

INDIAN JEWISH CHICKEN

*I*n the 1970s almost all of the dark-skinned Black Jews of Cochin in southwest India emigrated to Israel, where their cuisine remains alive and well. Kosher tandoori seasoning is available in many supermarkets. Serve with fluffy, hot bulgur.

4 SERVINGS

1 (3½-pound) chicken, cut into 8 pieces, skin removed
¼ cup tandoori seasoning
3 tablespoons oil
1 (14½-ounce) can stewed tomatoes
2 tablespoons cider vinegar
8 small red potatoes (1½ pounds), scrubbed and quartered
¼ cup dark raisins

M E A T

1. Rub chicken all over with tandoori seasoning. Heat oil in a large deep skillet or flameproof casserole over medium-high heat. Add chicken and cook, turning, until browned all over, 6 to 8 minutes. Drain off any fat.

2. Mix stewed tomatoes with their juices, vinegar, and ¼ cup cold water. Pour over chicken. Tuck potatoes around chicken and sprinkle with raisins.

3. Cover and cook over low heat for 45 minutes, or until chicken is tender.

BRAISED CHICKEN WITH BLACK OLIVES

*T*his is a Moroccan Jewish dish. For authentic taste, be sure to use briny kalamata or black Greek olives.

4 TO 6 SERVINGS

3 tablespoons olive oil
1 (3½-pound) chicken, cut into 8 serving pieces
6 to 8 whole garlic cloves
2 tablespoons distilled white vinegar
¼ teaspoon salt
½ teaspoon pepper
1½ cups pitted kalamata or black Greek olives
¼ cup Chardonnay or other dry white wine
½ cup fresh coriander or parsley sprigs

M
E
A
T

1. In a large skillet or flameproof casserole, heat olive oil. Add chicken and cook over medium-high heat, turning, until browned all over, 5 to 7 minutes.

2. Add garlic and cook until slightly browned, 1 to 2 minutes. Pour on vinegar and season with salt and pepper. Add olives and wine, reduce heat to low, and cook for 2 to 3 minutes, until almost all wine has evaporated.

3. Pour 1 cup warm water over chicken. Cover pan and simmer 45 minutes, or until chicken is tender. Garnish with coriander before serving.

BOMBAY CHICKEN CUTLETS

*U*nsweetened coconut milk, available canned, is parve. Here it offsets the hot, fiery spices used by the Bene Israel Jews of Bombay. Serve with hot steamed rice and chutney.

4 SERVINGS

4 chicken cutlets (4 to 5 ounces each)
2 tablespoons vegetable oil
¼ cup bottled garlic salad dressing
½ cup unsweetened coconut milk
1 fresh serrano or jalapeño pepper, seeded and minced
1 teaspoon ground cardamom
½ teaspoon turmeric
Salt
2 medium tomatoes, cut into wedges

MEAT

1. In a large skillet, preferably nonstick, cook chicken cutlets in oil over medium-high heat, turning once, until lightly browned, about 2 minutes per side.

2. Add garlic dressing, coconut milk, serrano pepper, cardamom, and turmeric. Mix well.

3. Cover and bring to a simmer. Cook for 15 minutes. Season to taste with salt. Add tomatoes, cook 5 minutes longer, and serve.

ZA'ATAR GRILLED CHICKEN BREAST

*A*n Israeli—Arab—style glaze creates the most succulent roast. Boneless breast of a roaster is just enough for a family or a small dinner party. Serve with Honeyed Baby Carrots (page 171) and couscous.

4 TO 6 SERVINGS

2 tablespoons Za'atar Seasoning (page 15)*
2 tablespoons olive oil
2 tablespoons frozen orange juice concentrate, thawed
1 teaspoon coarse kosher salt
1½ pounds skinless, boneless roaster chicken breast

1. Mix together za'atar, olive oil, orange juice concentrate, and salt. Spread over all surfaces of roaster breast. Cover and marinate in refrigerator for at least 30 minutes or overnight.

2. Light a hot fire in a barbecue grill or preheat broiler. Grill about 4 inches from hot coals or broil, turning once, for 8 minutes on each side, or until white throughout but still juicy.

3. Let cool slightly before slicing.

*Or substitute 2 teaspoons dried marjoram, 2 teaspoons sesame seeds, 1 teaspoon dried thyme, 1 teaspoon ground cumin, and 1 teaspoon coarse kosher salt.

MEAT

OLD CITY CHICKEN

Infused with the flavors of Israel, all easily available in any market, this makes a fine Friday night dinner. Serve with couscous, carrots, and a salad of Israeli tomatoes or Marrakesh Relish (page 190).

4 SERVINGS

1 (3½- to 4-pound) chicken
2 teaspoons ground cumin
¾ teaspoon salt
¼ teaspoon pepper
1 orange, skin on, cut into 8 wedges
1 medium onion, cut into 1-inch chunks
2 tablespoons olive oil

1. Preheat oven to 350°F. Rinse chicken under cold running water. Pat dry.

2. Sprinkle large cavity of chicken with half of cumin, salt, and pepper. Place orange and onion inside. Use toothpicks to close or tie legs together with white kitchen string. Brush all over with olive oil and dust with remaining 1 teaspoon cumin, salt, and pepper.

3. Place chicken in a shallow roasting pan. Roast in preheated oven 1½ hours, or until juices run clear when thigh is pierced at thickest part.

MEAT

SHULAMA

*I*f you thought chicken à la king was an American classic, see what you think of this Romanian version.

4 TO 6 SERVINGS

1¼ pounds skinless, boneless chicken breasts
1 teaspoon distilled white vinegar
1¼ teaspoons salt
3 tablespoons vegetable oil
1 large sweet onion, sliced
3 cups sliced mushrooms
2 tablespoons flour
1⅔ cups chicken broth
½ cup diced (¼-inch) pimiento
⅓ cup chopped fresh parsley
¼ teaspoon pepper
4 kaiser rolls, split and toasted, or baked puff pastry shells

M E A T

1. Place chicken in a saucepan and add vinegar, 1 teaspoon salt, and enough boiling water to cover. Cover pan and simmer for 10 to 15 minutes, until chicken is white and opaque all the way through. Drain and tear or cut chicken into ¼-inch-wide strips.

2. Heat oil in a large skillet. Add onion and mushrooms and cook over medium-high heat until mushrooms are tender and onion lightly browned, 5 to 7 minutes. Sprinkle with flour and cook, stirring, for 1 minute.

3. Add broth and bring to a boil over medium heat, stirring constantly. Boil for 1 minute, until liquid is thickened and smooth. Add chicken, pimiento, parsley, pepper, and remaining ¼ teaspoon salt. Bring to a simmer over medium heat. If too thick, add a little more broth.

4. Spoon over hot toasted rolls or, for an elegant supper, over baked puff pastry shells.

POTATO-CHICKEN CUTLETS

When I first visited Russian cousins living outside of Tel Aviv, they served these cutlets as just one part of an enormous meal. Chicken first cooked for soup is fine to use here or leftover roast or rotisserie chicken. Serve with a tossed salad for lunch.

2 TO 3 SERVINGS

1 small onion, chopped
1 tablespoon vegetable oil, plus more for frying
1½ cups chopped cooked chicken
1½ cups mashed potatoes
1 egg, lightly beaten
1 teaspoon salt
1 teaspoon pepper

1. In a medium skillet, cook onion in oil over medium-high heat until softened and translucent, about 3 minutes. Transfer to a mixing bowl.

2. Add chopped chicken, mashed potatoes, egg, salt, and pepper. Mix well. Shape into 6 oval cutlets about ½ inch thick.

3. Heat about ¼ inch of oil in a large skillet, preferably nonstick. Fry cutlets over medium heat, turning once carefully with a wide spatula, until browned and crisp, 3 to 4 minutes on each side. Drain on paper towels. Serve hot.

CHICKEN PILAF CASSEROLE

Sweet and spicy mango chutney pares preparation for this popular Rosh Hashanah dish to a minimum. Any homemade or prepared kosher fruit chutney you have on hand can be substituted for the mango I suggest.

4 TO 6 SERVINGS

2 tablespoons olive oil
1 medium onion, sliced
3 cups cooked noodles
2 cups cooked rice
2 teaspoons Asian sesame oil
4 cups diced cooked chicken
⅓ cup mango chutney
¼ cup chopped fresh cilantro
Salt and pepper

MEAT

1. Preheat oven to 375°F. In a large skillet, heat olive oil over medium heat. Add onion and cook until golden, 5 to 7 minutes.

2. Stir in noodles, rice, sesame oil, chicken, chutney, and cilantro. Season to taste with salt and pepper.

3. Transfer to an oiled 1½-quart baking dish. Bake for 20 minutes, or until crisp on top.

NOTE: If you're short on time, serve without baking. To make ahead, prepare to end of step 2 and refrigerate; slip into oven 20 minutes before needed.

SEPHARDIC CHICKEN PILAF

*P*ersian Jews created pilafs redolent with herbs and fruits. You'd never guess that this is made with leftovers.

4 TO 6 SERVINGS

¼ cup olive oil
1 large onion, coarsely chopped
½ cup golden raisins
½ cup dried apricots, quartered
4 cups cooked rice
3 to 4 cups diced cooked chicken
2 teaspoons ground sumac or 2 teaspoons grated lime zest
    and ½ teaspoon ground cumin
½ cup bottled sesame seed salad dressing
Salt and pepper

1. Preheat oven to 375°F. In a large ovenproof skillet, heat 1½ tablespoons oil. Add onion and cook over medium heat, stirring occasionally, until golden, 8 to 10 minutes.

2. Stir in raisins, apricots, rice, chicken, sumac, and salad dressing. Season with salt and pepper to taste.

3. Drizzle remaining 2½ tablespoons olive oil over top. Bake in preheated oven for 20 minutes, or until crusty on top.

MEAT

ORANGE-BAKED SHABBOS CHICKEN

*R*oast chicken is the star of the Friday night dinner, the beginning of Shabbat. If you want a traditional dinner and have no time to cook—pick up a roasted or barbecued chicken from the market and follow the directions below.

4 SERVINGS

1 barbecued (rotisserie) chicken, quartered
¼ cup orange marmalade
⅓ cup raisins
½ to 1 teaspoon garlic powder, to taste

1. Preheat oven to 350°F. Place chicken in a baking dish.

2. Brush all over with marmalade and sprinkle with raisins and ½ teaspoon garlic powder or to taste.

3. Cover tightly with foil. Bake for 30 minutes, or until heated through.

MEAT

SHERRY-GLAZED ROASTED CAPON

A capon is a castrated rooster, fattened and brought to market before it is 10 months old. Prized by Jewish immigrants in the early 1900s and still served on special occasions, capon meat is particularly juicy and tender. Serve with crisp potato latkes or cherry latkes.

6 TO 8 SERVINGS

¼ cup packed brown sugar
¼ cup dry sherry
2 tablespoons soy sauce
5- to 6-pound capon
2 teaspoons coarse kosher salt
1½ teaspoons lemon pepper seasoning

M E A T

1. Preheat oven to 400°F. In a small bowl, mix brown sugar, sherry, and soy sauce.

2. Pour 2 to 3 tablespoons mixture inside large cavity of capon; then season cavity with 1 teaspoon salt and ½ teaspoon lemon pepper seasoning.

3. Place on a rack in a roasting pan. Brush with remaining sherry mixture. Sprinkle with remaining 1 teaspoon salt and 1 teaspoon lemon pepper seasoning.

4. Roast in preheated oven for 15 minutes. Reduce heat to 350°F. Cover capon loosely with foil and continue roasting 1½ hours longer, basting often with remaining sherry mixture and pan juices. Capon is done when juices run clear when a thigh is pierced near bone.

TANDOORI CORNISH HENS

*Y*es, there were Jews in India, and while preserving their culture, they adapted Indian cooking methods. Instead of calling for a mix of spices, this dish is greatly simplified, with little more than tandoori seasoning, which can be found in major spice lines at supermarkets. Serve with couscous and mango or other fruit chutney.

4 SERVINGS

Juice of 3 limes
⅓ cup olive oil
2 garlic cloves, minced
1 tablespoon paprika
1 tablespoon tandoori seasoning
¼ teaspoon red food coloring
2 large Cornish hens (1½ pounds each), split in half down backbone

1. In a large shallow glass dish, combine lime juice, olive oil, garlic, paprika, tandoori seasoning, and food coloring.

2. Prick each hen half several times in breast and thigh. Place in lime marinade; then brush with marinade to coat all over. Cover and refrigerate for 6 hours, or overnight.

3. Preheat oven to 375°F. Transfer Cornish hens, skin side up, and liquid to a roasting pan and roast for 45 minutes, basting occasionally. When ready, juices will run clear when a thigh is pierced with a fork at thickest part.

CITRUS-ROASTED TURKEY BREAST

*C*itrus are the national fruits of Israel, and here, along with the ubiquitous Middle Eastern olive, they add zesty taste and moisture to white meat turkey, which can be bland. Be sure to warn your guests that the olives have pits in them. Serve with fresh sliced oranges and more olives on the side.

8 TO 10 SERVINGS

1 juicy orange, peel on, cut into 1-inch chunks
½ pickled lemon (page 24), sliced, or ½ lemon, sliced and sprinkled with ¼ teaspoon coarse kosher salt
1 cup oil-cured black olives, such as Niçoise
2½-pound boneless turkey breast
1½ teaspoons lemon pepper seasoning
1 teaspoon ground cumin
2 tablespoons olive oil

1. Preheat oven to 400°F. In a roasting pan, toss orange, pickled lemon, and olives.

2. Place turkey breast in pan, folding thin sides under to make a pocket. Tuck some of orange-olive mixture into pocket. Sprinkle with lemon pepper and cumin and drizzle oil over turkey. Tent with foil.

3. Roast in preheated oven for 30 minutes. Reduce heat to 350°F. and continue cooking 1 hour longer, basting once or twice, until juices run clear at thickest part.

4. Let stand for 10 minutes before slicing. Serve with pan juices and olives.

MEAT

THREE-BEAN TURKEY CHILI

*S*erve this low-fat chili over corn bread or toasted whole wheat rolls.

6 TO 8 SERVINGS

1½ tablespoons vegetable oil
1 pound ground turkey
1 large onion, thinly sliced
1 (32-ounce) can Italian-style crushed tomatoes
1 (8-ounce) can tomato sauce
1 tablespoon chili powder
1 tablespoon chopped garlic
1 teaspoon salt
⅛ teaspoon crushed hot pepper flakes
1 (15-ounce) can kidney beans, drained
1 (15-ounce) can black beans, drained
1 (8-ounce) can chickpeas, drained
¼ to ½ cup tomato juice or chicken broth

M E A T

1. Heat oil in a large, heavy saucepan over medium heat. Add ground turkey and onion slices and cook, stirring occasionally, until lightly browned, 7 to 10 minutes.

2. Stir in crushed tomatoes, tomato sauce, chili powder, garlic, salt, and hot pepper flakes. Cover and simmer for 15 minutes.

3. Add kidney beans, black beans, and chickpeas. Bring to a boil. If too thick, thin with a little tomato juice or broth. Season with additional salt to taste and serve.

LEMON-TAHINI BROILED DUCK BREASTS

*S*kinless, boneless duck breasts can be purchased from a fine butcher, or you can buy a couple of whole ducks and bone out the breasts yourself. Make a stew or roast the rest of the bird. Prepared this way, duck is meaty, elegant, and surprisingly lean. Serve with wild rice and roasted red and yellow peppers.

4 SERVINGS

2 duck breasts, about 1 pound each
2 tablespoons all-purpose flour
⅓ cup tahini (stir well before using)
1½ tablespoons fresh lemon juice
2 teaspoons grated lemon zest
Salt and cayenne

1. Light a hot fire in a barbecue grill or preheat broiler. Rub duck breasts all over with flour. In a small bowl, mix together the tahini, lemon juice, lemon zest, and 2 tablespoons water, or enough water to dilute to a thick pouring consistency. Season with salt to taste and a dash of cayenne. Brush some of the lemon tahini sauce over duck meat to coat lightly.

2. Grill or broil for 6 minutes on each side, basting breasts with remaining lemon-tahini sauce just before turning them. Meat should be tender and slightly pink in middle.

3. Transfer to a carving board and let stand for 5 minutes, then cut crosswise against grain into thin slices.

ROAST GOOSE

In Germany and Poland, geese fattened during the summer were cooked for the Chanukah table. The fat was stored for Passover.

6 TO 8 SERVINGS

1 (6- to 8-pound) goose
Savory Potato Stuffing (recipe follows)
¼ cup all-purpose flour
1 teaspoon paprika
1 teaspoon salt
½ teaspoon pepper

M
E
A
T

1. Preheat oven to 325°F. Loosely fill large cavity of goose with Savory Potato Stuffing or stuffing of your choice. Truss by tying legs together with string. Prick skin all over with tines of a fork.

2. In a small bowl, mix together flour, paprika, salt, and pepper. Rub over goose.

3. Place goose on a rack in a large roasting pan. Roast in preheated oven about 2½ hours (25 minutes per pound), until skin is crisp and juices run clear when a thigh is pierced near bone. Baste often with hot water and use a bulb baster or large spoon to remove most fat as it is rendered from goose so you don't smoke up your kitchen.

4. Remove goose to a carving board and let stand 10 minutes. Meanwhile, spoon stuffing into a serving bowl. Carve goose and serve with stuffing.

SAVORY POTATO STUFFING

MAKES ABOUT 5 CUPS; ENOUGH FOR A 6-POUND BIRD

3 large baking potatoes, cut into 2-inch chunks
1 medium onion, cut into 2-inch chunks
4 scallions, cut into 1-inch pieces
1 teaspoon garlic powder
1 teaspoon salt
½ teaspoon pepper
2 tablespoons schmaltz or melted margarine

1. In a food processor or on large holes of a hand grater, shred potatoes. Transfer to a bowl.

2. Change to steel blade. Coarsely chop onion and scallions. Add to potatoes.

3. Stir in garlic powder, salt, pepper, and schmaltz. Spoon into goose, capon, or large chicken and roast as directed. As soon as bird is done, scoop out stuffing and transfer to a serving bowl.

MEAT

CHAPTER FIVE

Meats

*I*n the Torah, kosher animals are identified as those who chew their cud and have split hooves. That means beef, veal, and lamb are kosher, though even then, the hind quarters cannot be eaten. Pork and the by-products of pork are not kosher. Farm-raised game animals, such as venison, are kosher if ritually slaughtered.

Kosher meat has been salted and soaked to remove as much blood as possible. Consequently, kosher meats are drier than nonkosher, and to prepare them so that they are juicy and tender, they must be cooked by slow, moist methods. Cholents, the overnight one-pot meals prepared for Shabbat, are often based on tough but flavorful cuts of meat that cook up beautifully tender when left in a warm oven overnight. Marinating can also add flavor and act as a tenderizer, especially for meats that are grilled or broiled relatively quickly, like Galilee Beef Steak or Garlicky London Broil.

Beef brisket, the boned breast, is a popular cut in the Jewish kitchen. I've included several succulent recipes for it: Roasted Beer Brisket, Sweet-and-Sour Brisket, and Brisket in Wine Sauce. It is economical and traditional for holiday dinners, but top round, bottom round, or chuck may be substituted. Here you'll also find recipes for ground beef, tongue, veal, and lamb. Ashkenazic meat dishes, like Weeknight Pot Roast, are generously seasoned with garlic and embellished with sturdy root vegetables, while Sephardic dishes, such as Lamb Tagine with Seven Vegetables, tend to be sweeter, flavored with dried fruits, cinnamon, and the aromatic herbs of warmer climates.

To save time during the week, I often combine frozen and ready-to-cook fresh vegetables. For quick flavor-boosters, I never hesitate to use kosher convenience foods, such as salsas, salad dressings, and pestos. Prepared pastry, such as filo dough and puff pastry, make savory pies quick and easy—even for beginners.

GALILEE BEEF STEAK

The olive-lemon marinade used here tenderizes tough meats in one hour. It is practically effortless. Olive Sprate, a mixture of olives, garlic, and olive oil, is available in stores under The Peaceworks, Inc., label. Serve with grilled vegetables and couscous.

4 SERVINGS

2 tablespoons Olive Sprate*
Juice of 2 lemons
1½ pounds round steak, cut ½ inch thick, then into 4
    equal pieces

1. In a glass pie plate or shallow dish, mix Olive Sprate and lemon juice. Add steak and turn to coat on both sides with mixture. Marinate in pie plate in refrigerator for at least 1 hour.

2. Preheat broiler. Set steak on rack in baking pan. Broil 2 minutes on each side for medium-rare, or longer for desired doneness.

*If Olive Sprate is not in available in your market, substitute 2 tablespoons pitted kalamata olives, 2 crushed garlic cloves, and 1½ tablespoons extra-virgin olive oil whirled to a paste in a mini-processor or crushed with a mortar and pestle.

MEAT

GARLICKY LONDON BROIL

Tenderized by steeping in a pungent sauce and studded with mild elephant garlic, London broil is delicious whether barbecued or broiled. Serve hot with grilled vegetables and baked potatoes. Leftovers are delicious in sandwiches.

4 TO 6 SERVINGS

1½ pounds London broil, cut about 1½ inches thick
3 garlic cloves, cut into slivers
1½ cups dry red wine
½ cup soy sauce
1 onion, thinly sliced

1. Trim any visible fat from meat. With a sharp knife, make tiny cuts over surface of London broil. Press a garlic sliver into each.

2. In a shallow, nonmetal dish, mix wine, soy sauce, and onion. Add London broil to wine mixture and turn to coat both sides. Spoon some of marinade over top of steak. Cover and refrigerate 2 hours or overnight, turning after 1 hour or before you go to bed.

3. Remove from marinade. Broil or grill about 5 minutes on each side for medium-rare. Slice thinly across the grain.

MEAT

GRILLED MARINATED FLANK STEAK

6 TO 8 SERVINGS

1½ to 2 pounds flank steak
1½ cups dry red wine
½ cup soy sauce
1 medium onion, sliced
1 teaspoon dried thyme
½ teaspoon pepper
1 garlic clove, crushed

1. Place steak in a shallow baking dish. Pour wine and soy sauce over meat and add onion, thyme, pepper, and garlic. Marinate in refrigerator 8 hours or overnight, turning at least once for flavor and tenderizing.

2. Light a hot fire in a barbecue grill or preheat broiler. Remove steak from marinade. Grill or broil 5 to 6 minutes per side for medium-rare.

3. Remove to a carving board and let stand 5 minutes. Slice thinly across the grain. Serve hot or at room temperature.

MEAT

WEEKNIGHT POT ROAST

*A*s with many braised meats, this *gedempte fleisch* is best served the next day, which makes it ideal for the busy cook.

6 TO 8 SERVINGS

2 tablespoons vegetable oil
3-pound beef chuck roast
1 tablespoon paprika
1½ teaspoons salt
¼ teaspoon pepper
2 large onions, cut into 1-inch chunks
16 garlic cloves, peeled
1 small turnip, cut into ½-inch dice
2 cups peeled baby carrots
2 medium leeks, split lengthwise in half, rinsed well, and
    cut into 4-inch lengths

MEAT

1. Heat oil in a large, heavy oval pot over medium-high heat. Add chuck roast and cook, turning, until nicely browned all over, 7 to 10 minutes. Sprinkle paprika, salt, and pepper over meat.

2. Add onions and whole garlic cloves to pot along with ¾ cup hot water. Cover, reduce heat to medium-low, and simmer for 1½ hours.

3. Add turnip, carrots, and leeks to pot. Cover and cook 1 hour longer, or until meat is fork-tender.

4. To serve, slice chuck across the grain. Arrange on a heated platter and spoon vegetables around meat. Ladle a little of pan juices over meat. Pass remainder in a gravy boat.

BRISKET IN WINE SAUCE

Brisket was, and in some homes still is, the classic Jewish holiday dish. The three secrets: marinate the meat first, braise it slowly in a well-seasoned sauce, and let it rest overnight in the cooking gravy before reheating and serving. All this is made especially easy by cooking the brisket in a disposable oven-roasting bag—a kitchen tool Grandma never had.

6 TO 8 SERVINGS

1 tablespoon all-purpose flour
1 cup kosher dry red wine
1 cup ketchup or ½ cup marinara sauce
1 large onion, thinly sliced
2 tablespoons chopped garlic
3½- to 4-pound brisket, trimmed of excess fat

1. Prepare a large-size oven roasting bag according to directions; dust inside with flour.

2. Pour wine, ketchup, onion, and garlic into bag and mix. Add brisket and spoon wine mixture over meat. Tie bag and place in a roasting pan large enough to hold brisket bag without it flopping over the sides. Marinate in refrigerator 2 to 4 hours.

3. Preheat oven to 325°F. Bake brisket in bag 2½ to 3 hours, or until a fork easily pierces thickest part of meat. Let cool slightly, then slice and arrange in a baking dish. Pour gravy from bag over meat, cover with foil, and refrigerate overnight in sauce.

4. Shortly before serving, skim any fat from top of meat and sauce. Cover tightly with foil and bake in a preheated 375°F. oven until warmed through, 20 to 25 minutes. Alternatively, reheat the meat in a shallow pot over medium heat, covered, for 15 to 20 minutes.

SWEET-AND-SOUR BRISKET

*F*or really fabulous flavor, let the cooked sliced brisket marinate in its own gravy overnight. You won't believe how good it is when reheated.

12 TO 16 SERVINGS

6-pound brisket
1 (12-ounce) bottle chili sauce
¾ cup packed dark brown sugar
3 tablespoons red wine vinegar
1 (2.8-ounce) can fried onion rings

1. Line a large roasting pan with enough heavy-duty aluminum foil to fold over brisket. Place brisket in pan.

2. Mix chili sauce with brown sugar and vinegar. Pour over brisket, turning meat to coat all surfaces with sauce. Cover and marinate 12 hours in refrigerator.

3. Preheat oven to 350°F. Scatter onion rings over brisket. Fold foil over to seal tightly and bake for 3 hours. Let cool before slicing across grain.

4. Transfer slices to a heatproof serving dish. Pour gravy over meat. Cover and refrigerate for at least 6 hours or overnight. To serve, heat through, covered, in a preheated 375°F. oven, 20 to 30 minutes.

MEAT

GRILLED LAMB CHOPS

My recipe tester, Meredith Deeds, came up with this deliciously simple "barbecue rub." Refrigerate at least 6 hours to allow the flavors to penetrate. Cooked on the outdoor barbecue, these chops are aromatic, juicy, and fork-tender.

6 SERVINGS

6 lamb shoulder chops, cut about ¾ inch thick
2 to 3 tablespoons olive oil
2 tablespoons chopped fresh rosemary or 2 teaspoons dried
1 tablespoon ground cumin
1 tablespoon ground cinnamon
1 tablespoon dried coriander

1. Lay lamb chops on a cutting board. Drizzle olive oil over both sides and smear with your fingers to coat.

2. In a cup or small bowl, mix rosemary, cumin, cinnamon, and coriander. Rub into both sides of chops. Cover and refrigerate for at least 6 hours or overnight. Let stand at room temperature for 1 hour before cooking.

3. Prepare a hot fire in a barbecue grill or preheat your broiler. Grill or broil 6 to 8 minutes per side for medium-rare to medium or longer for whatever degree of doneness you prefer.

MEAT

ROASTED BEER BRISKET

*T*his fine, robust dish, big enough for a holiday crowd, can conveniently be made ahead. Leftovers freeze beautifully.

12 TO 15 SERVINGS

2 tablespoons olive oil
5- to 6-pound brisket
1 pound small white boiling onions, peeled
1 medium rutabaga, cut into 2-inch chunks
1 (16-ounce) bag peeled baby carrots
3 bay leaves
1½ teaspoons salt
½ teaspoon black peppercorns
1 cup beer
1 pound button mushrooms, halved or quartered

1. Preheat oven to 325°F. Heat oil in a large Dutch oven over high heat. Add brisket and cook, turning, until nicely browned on all sides, 6 to 8 minutes.

2. Remove from heat. Add onions, rutabaga, carrots, bay leaves, salt, and peppercorns. Pour beer over brisket and cover pot tightly. Bake in preheated oven 2 hours.

3. Stir in mushrooms. Cook 1 to 1½ hours longer, or until brisket and vegetables are tender. A fork should slide out easily when inserted in thickest part of brisket.

4. Let stand 10 minutes before slicing. Serve on a warm platter with vegetables spooned around brisket. Skim fat off surface of gravy and pass in a sauceboat on the side.

MEAT

CARROT-SWEET POTATO TZIMMES WITH MEAT

*T*his mishmash of tender meat and sweet vegetables, symbolic of a year of happiness, is served at Rosh Hashanah. Carrot tzimmes is most popular with Jews of Russian and Polish descent.

4 TO 6 SERVINGS

2 tablespoons schmaltz or vegetable oil
1½ pounds brisket or boneless chuck, cut into 2-inch
   pieces
1 large onion, cut into 1-inch chunks
4 medium carrots, sliced ½ inch thick
3 large sweet potatoes (about 1½ pounds), cut into
   1-inch chunks
2 teaspoons salt
¼ teaspoon pepper
8 ounces mixed dried fruits
¼ cup packed dark brown sugar
1 teaspoon ground ginger
1 tablespoon all-purpose flour (optional)

1. In a large Dutch oven, heat schmaltz over medium heat. Add meat in 2 or 3 batches and cook over medium-high heat, turning, until browned all over, about 7 minutes per batch.

2. Add onion, carrots, sweet potatoes, salt, and pepper. Pour enough hot water over to cover, about 4 cups. Cover, reduce the heat to medium-low, and simmer 1 hour.

3. Add dried fruits, brown sugar, and ginger. Stir gently to mix. Cover and continue cooking over medium-low heat 45 minutes longer, or until meat and vegetables are fork-tender.

4. If the sauce is thin, blend flour in a small bowl with 3 tablespoons cold water. Slowly whisk ½ cup cooking liquid into flour paste. Stir into tzimmes. Bring to a boil, reduce heat, and simmer 5 to 10 minutes to thicken. Serve hot.

SHABBAT CHOLENT

Since the observant do not cook on Shabbat, one-pot meals are often placed in a slow oven to cook overnight. The family can then have a hot, hearty meal of dumpling, meat, and vegetables when they come home from synagogue.

4 TO 6 SERVINGS

2 eggs
2 tablespoons schmaltz
2 teaspoons salt
½ teaspoon plus ⅛ teaspoon pepper
½ to ¾ cup matzoh meal
2 large onions, cut into 1-inch chunks
1½ to 2 pounds brisket or boneless beef chuck
3 large potatoes, cut into 2-inch chunks
1 medium parsnip, sliced ½ inch thick
2 large carrots, cut into 1-inch chunks
1 small green cabbage, cut into 2-inch-thick wedges

1. Preheat oven to 225°F. In a bowl, whisk eggs, schmaltz, ½ teaspoon salt, and ⅛ teaspoon pepper together. Stir in enough matzoh meal to make a soft dough. Refrigerate 15 minutes to firm up.

2. Spread onions over bottom of a Dutch oven or large ovenproof casserole. Season brisket on both sides with remaining 1½ teaspoons salt and ½ teaspoon pepper and lay on top of onions.

3. Form matzoh meal dough into a ball and place at side of brisket. Tuck in potatoes, parsnip, carrots, and cabbage wherever they'll fit.

4. Pour enough boiling water over to barely cover (about 3 cups). Bring to a boil. Cover tightly and place in preheated oven. Bake overnight or until ready to eat at lunch.

MEAT

BRAISED BEEF WITH KASHA AND LIMA BEANS

Kasha, or buckwheat groats, the broken, hulled kernels of the buckwheat plant, is native to Russia. Added to stews and soups and eaten as a cereal, it was belly filling . . . and cheap. This rib-sticking recipe combines kasha with beef and beans for a really hearty winter one-dish meal. Serve with a spoon as well as a fork. Note: Instead of dried lima beans, frozen or drained canned beans may be added just before serving.

6 TO 8 SERVINGS

1 cup dried lima beans
¼ cup vegetable oil
3 pounds beef chuck, cut into 1½-inch cubes
2 medium onions, thickly sliced
4 garlic cloves, cut into slivers
2 teaspoons paprika
1½ teaspoons salt
½ teaspoon pepper
½ cup kasha

1. Place lima beans in a large saucepan with enough cold water to cover the beans by about 1 inch. Bring to a boil, cover, and cook over medium heat ½ hour; drain. (The beans will finish cooking later.)

2. Heat oil in a large heavy pot over medium heat. Add beef, onions, garlic, and paprika and stir to mix. Cook, stirring, until beef has lost its redness, 8 to 10 minutes. Season with salt and pepper.

3. Add kasha, lima beans, and 3 cups water. Cover, reduce heat to medium-low, and simmer for 2 hours, until beef and beans are tender. Stir occasionally. Add a little hot water if needed.

MEAT

BARBECUED SHORT RIBS

*T*o retain their juiciness on the barbecue, these ribs are partially cooked first. Serve with coleslaw and roasted or mashed potatoes.

4 SERVINGS

4 pounds beef short ribs
1 cup tomato sauce
⅓ cup salad mustard
2 tablespoons fresh lime juice
1½ teaspoons dried sage

1. Place ribs in a large pot and cover with water. Bring to a boil over high heat. Reduce heat to medium-low and cook 45 minutes.

2. Drain off water. Pat dry with paper towels and place in a shallow dish.

3. In a small bowl, combine tomato sauce, mustard, lime juice, and sage. Spoon generously over ribs, making sure all surfaces are coated.

4. Cook ribs over medium-hot coals. Cook 30 minutes, basting and turning frequently, or until cooked to desired doneness.

MEAT

SWEET AND SPICY BEEF RIBS

*S*hort ribs come from the first seven ribs of a kosher animal. These are oven roasted, sweet, spicy, and sticky—guaranteed to be irresistible. Serve hot, with plenty of napkins.

4 SERVINGS

1 cup barbecue sauce
¼ cup applesauce
2 tablespoons warm molasses
4 pounds beef short ribs, trimmed of fat

1. Preheat oven to 350°F. Line a roasting pan with enough foil to leave a 6-inch overlap.

2. Combine barbecue sauce, applesauce, and molasses. Brush ribs generously with sauce mixture. Place on a rack in prepared roasting pan.

3. Pour 3 tablespoons water around meat. Fold aluminum foil over to cover ribs.

4. Bake in preheated oven 1 hour. Unfold foil slightly to expose ribs and roast 30 minutes longer, basting often with pan juices and remaining sauce mixture. If needed to keep moist, add ¼ cup more water during cooking.

MEAT

MAMA'S MEAT LOAF

*A*s a child, I never knew a meat loaf could be made with bread crumbs. My mother used only matzoh meal and plenty of chopped onions. I use scallions instead of onions and add barbecue sauce for extra seasoning. I also divide the mixture into two small loaves for quicker cooking.

4 TO 6 SERVINGS

1 pound lean ground beef
3 scallions, chopped
½ cup barbecue sauce
1 egg
⅓ cup matzoh meal
½ teaspoon salt
¼ teaspoon pepper

1. Preheat oven to 375°F. Coat a large baking dish with nonstick vegetable spray.

2. In a medium bowl, combine ground beef, scallions, ¼ cup of barbecue sauce, egg, matzoh meal, salt, and pepper. Mix until well blended. Divide mixture in half and shape into 2 loaves.

3. Place meat loaves in baking dish and bake in preheated oven for 10 minutes. Reduce heat to 350°F. Drizzle remaining ¼ cup barbecue sauce over loaves and continue cooking for 25 minutes longer, or until juices run clear when a loaf is pierced with a fork.

M E A T

SHEPHERD'S PIE

*H*ere's an easy Monday night supper, using leftover meats and mashed potatoes from the weekend. If you don't have any leftover potatoes, this simple savory pie is worth whipping up a batch for.

6 SERVINGS

3 cups cooked roast beef, shredded
¼ cup steak sauce
¼ cup ketchup
2 scallions, thinly sliced
1 (10-ounce) package frozen peas and carrots, thawed
3 to 4 cups mashed potatoes
Paprika

1. Preheat oven to 375°F. In a medium bowl, combine roast beef, steak sauce, ketchup, scallions, and peas and carrots. Stir to mix. Turn into a 10-inch glass pie dish. Spread mashed potatoes over top to edge of dish and swirl surface with a fork. Dust with paprika.

2. Bake in preheated oven 25 to 30 minutes, or until potato topping is browned and pie is hot throughout.

KOKLETIN

Meat croquettes were as popular in German-Jewish homes as hamburgers are in America. These onion-studded beef croquettes are cooked until well done, never rare. For a change, I sometimes pour stewed tomatoes over these croquettes. Serve with Dilled Potatoes (page 183) and Easy Sweet-and-Sour Green Beans (page 178).

6 SERVINGS

1 medium onion, cut up
1 egg
¼ cup matzoh meal
2 teaspoons lemon pepper seasoning
1 teaspoon salt
1½ pounds lean ground beef
¼ cup vegetable oil

1. In a food processor, place onion, egg, 2 tablespoons water, matzoh meal, lemon pepper, and salt. Process to coarsely chop onion.

2. Add ground beef and process to mix well and form a ball. With wet hands, form into 6 oval shapes (croquettes) about ¾ inch thick.

3. Heat oil in a large skillet. Fry croquettes over medium heat for 10 minutes on each side, or until browned outside and well done inside.

MEAT

STUFFED CABBAGE

*T*his Russian-Polish main dish was versatile in that it could be stretched with bread crumbs, rice, or bulgur when little meat was available. Nowadays we have plenty of meat, but know that nutritionally it is best to stretch it anyway. As with many tomatoey preparations, this dish is even better reheated the next day. *Tip: If the softer Savoy cabbage is used, there's no need to soak the leaves first.*

6 TO 8 SERVINGS

16 large cabbage leaves (Savoy or regular green)
1½ pounds ground beef or turkey
4 medium onions—2 chopped, 2 sliced
⅔ cup bulgur (cracked wheat)
6 tablespoons steak sauce
1 (28-ounce) can crushed tomatoes
⅓ cup cider vinegar
⅓ cup brown sugar
6 gingersnap cookies

M E A T

1. Preheat oven to 350°F. Soften cabbage leaves by soaking in a bowl of very hot water for 5 minutes. Drain and pat dry.

2. In a medium bowl, combine beef, chopped onions, bulgur, and steak sauce. Mix with your hands to blend thoroughly.

3. Place about ⅓ cup mixture in center of each cabbage leaf. Beginning at stem end, roll up bottom, fold in sides, and roll up. Place seam side down in a 9-by-12-inch baking dish. Scatter sliced onions over cabbage rolls.

4. Combine crushed tomatoes, vinegar, and brown sugar. Crumble in gingersnaps. Pour over cabbage rolls. Cover loosely with foil. Bake in preheated oven 1½ hours.

GROUND BEEF PATTIES WITH LEEKS AND CHICKPEAS

Leeks, a symbol of good fortune, are eaten by Greek and Turkish Jews, especially during the Days of Awe, the days between Rosh Hashanah and Yom Kippur.

6 SERVINGS

4 leeks (white and tender green parts), split lengthwise in half and washed well
2 tablespoons olive oil
1 medium onion, chopped
2½ teaspoons salt
¾ teaspoon pepper
1 (15-ounce) can chickpeas, drained
1½ pounds lean ground beef
½ cup fresh soft bread crumbs
1 egg
1 teaspoon turmeric
2 teaspoons ground cumin
2 tablespoons chopped chives

MEAT

1. Cut 3 leeks into 2-inch lengths. Heat olive oil in a large skillet over medium-low heat. Add leeks, onion, 1½ teaspoons salt, and pepper. Cover and cook until very soft but not brown, 10 to 15 minutes. Remove from heat and stir in chickpeas. Set aside.

2. Cut remaining leek into 1-inch lengths. Chop finely in a food processor. Add ground beef, bread crumbs, egg, turmeric, cumin, and remaining 1 teaspoon salt. Process to mix.

3. Shape into 6 patties about 1 inch thick. Lay beef patties on top of leek and chickpea mixture in skillet. Add ½ cup water. Cover and simmer over medium-low heat for 30 minutes. Juices should run clear when pierced with a knife. Before serving, sprinkle chives on top. Serve hot.

SHABBAT BEEF AND EGGS

This is the North African Jewish equivalent of Eastern European cholent, a slow-cooked stew prepared just before Shabbat. My version was inspired by Copeland Marks's recipe in his book *Sephardic Cooking* (Donald I. Fine).

6 SERVINGS

1 pound lean ground beef
1 tablespoon ground cumin
1 teaspoon salt
1 teaspoon lemon pepper seasoning
7 eggs (6 in the shell)
½ cup chopped fresh cilantro
9 small white potatoes (about 1½ pounds), scrubbed and quartered
9 dried figs
9 pitted prunes

1. Preheat oven to 225°F. Combine ground beef, cumin, salt, and lemon pepper. Crack 1 egg and add to meat. Blend well. Shape into a loaf about 6 by 3 inches.

2. Place meat loaf in a Dutch oven or large ovenproof casserole and sprinkle cilantro over top. Arrange potatoes, remaining 6 eggs in their shells, figs, and prunes around loaf. Pour in enough hot water to cover loaf completely.

3. Bring to a boil. Cover with a tight-fitting lid. Place in oven and cook overnight.

NOTE: This can also be made in an electric slow cooker. Arrange ingredients as above. Cover and cook on low overnight.

SALAMI AND EGGS

Sunday morning is often a day for a more substantial breakfast in the Jewish home. If it's not lox and bagels, there's a good chance it's salami and eggs. Here's a tasty breakfast (or brunch) for two, whipped up in minutes. Serve with toasted rye bread.

2 SERVINGS

4 slices of salami, cut ¼ inch thick
2 plum tomatoes, cut into ½-inch dice
¼ cup coarsely chopped green bell pepper
4 eggs
2 tablespoons water
¼ teaspoon black pepper

MEAT

1. Cut salami into ¼-inch strips. In a large nonstick skillet, fry salami over medium heat until browned at edges, 2 to 3 minutes.

2. Add tomatoes and bell pepper and cook just until pepper starts to soften, about 2 minutes.

3. Whisk eggs, water, and black pepper. (You probably won't need any salt because salami is salty.) Pour over salami. Cook, still over medium heat, stirring from center to edges, until eggs are set, 3 to 5 minutes. Serve at once.

FRANKS AND SAUERKRAUT

*T*raditionally franks are cooked with the sauerkraut, but I prefer them crisply grilled and set on top; so that's how I've presented them here.

6 SERVINGS

2 tablespoons vegetable oil
1 large onion, sliced
1 pound sauerkraut, drained
1 large baking potato (about ½ pound), peeled and shredded
1 tablespoon caraway seeds
1 teaspoon salt
¼ teaspoon pepper
6 jumbo frankfurters
2 to 3 tablespoons Dijon mustard

1. Heat oil in a large saucepan. Add onion and fry over medium heat until browned, 5 to 7 minutes.

2. Stir in sauerkraut and potato. Cover and cook 10 minutes, until potato is soft. Season with caraway seeds, salt, and pepper.

3. While sauerkraut is cooking, preheat broiler. Make several slashes on top of each frankfurter and smear generously with mustard. Broil about 5 minutes, turning, until browned.

4. Place on top of sauerkraut and serve while hot.

BOILED TONGUE

4 pounds fresh beef tongue
8 peppercorns
3 bay leaves
4 to 6 whole cloves
¼ cup distilled white vinegar
Creamy Horseradish Sauce (recipe follows) or Raisin Sauce
(page 147)

1. Rinse tongue under cold running water. Place in a large, deep pot. Add peppercorns, bay leaves, cloves, vinegar, and enough water to cover by at least 2 inches.

2. Bring to a boil over medium-high heat. Reduce heat to low, cover, and simmer 3 to 4 hours, or until a fork penetrates easily at thickest part. Leave tongue in water until cool enough to handle.

3. With a sharp, pointed knife, peel off thick outer skin. Trim and cut out tough end portion. Slice remaining tongue and serve with Creamy Horseradish Sauce or Raisin Sauce.

MEAT

CREAMY HORSERADISH SAUCE

MAKES 1 CUP

¾ cup mayonnaise
2 tablespoons cider vinegar
2 tablespoons prepared white horseradish

In a small bowl, whisk together mayonnaise, vinegar, and 1 tablespoon cold water until smooth. Stir in horseradish. Cover tightly and refrigerate. Serve chilled with sliced tongue or poached fish.

TONGUE WITH SWEET-HOT CRANBERRY SAUCE

*C*alves' tongues weigh about one pound each: a perfect size for family menus. Serve with mashed potatoes and peas or green beans.

4 SERVINGS

2 fresh calves' tongues (about 1 pound each)
2 teaspoons salt
3 bay leaves
8 peppercorns
1 (8-ounce) can whole cranberry sauce
½ cup bottled chili sauce

1. Wash tongues and place in a deep kettle with salt, bay leaves, and peppercorns. Add enough water to cover tongues by 2 inches. Bring to a boil, cover pot, and cook 1¼ hours, or until tender; drain.

2. As soon as tongues are cool enough to handle, use tip of a sharp knife to cut away part of thick outer skin. The rest should peel off easily. Slice both tongues.

3. In a small saucepan, mash down cranberry sauce. Add chili sauce and cook over medium heat, stirring, until melted and blended, 3 to 5 minutes. Serve slices of tongue hot. Spoon a little sauce over meat. Pass the remainder on the side.

PICKLED TONGUE

*T*his recipe makes enough for a crowd. Pickled tongues are available in every kosher meat market. Serve with rice or noodles.

15 TO 20 SERVINGS

1 (3½- to 4-pound) pickled tongue
4 bay leaves, crumbled
8 whole peppercorns
Raisin Sauce (recipe follows)

1. Place tongue in a large, deep saucepan. Cover with cold water and bring to a boil.

2. Pour off water. Pour enough fresh cold water over to cover tongue by about 2 inches. Add bay leaves and peppercorns. Cover pot and bring to a boil. Reduce heat to medium-low and simmer for 3 to 3½ hours, or until tongue is tender.

3. Drain, reserving 2 cups liquid. Remove skin from tongue with a sharp knife. After 1 cut, the skin is easily pulled off.

4. Cut tongue crosswise into ¼-inch-thick slices. Arrange on a warm platter. Pour ½ cup reserved liquid over meat to keep it moist. Use the remainder to prepare the Raisin Sauce. Pour hot sauce over tongue and serve. (Or tongue can be covered and refrigerated at this point. When needed, reheat in Raisin Sauce over medium-low heat.)

MEAT

RAISIN SAUCE

MAKES 1 1/2 CUPS

2 tablespoons vegetable oil
1 medium onion, chopped
¼ cup distilled white vinegar
⅓ cup packed dark brown sugar
1½ cups cooking broth reserved from Pickled Tongue
   (preceding recipe)
1 teaspoon salt
1 teaspoon lemon pepper seasoning
3 to 4 crushed gingersnap cookies
½ cup golden raisins

1. Heat oil in a medium saucepan. Add onion and cook over medium heat, stirring, until softened and translucent, 3 to 5 minutes.

2. Stir in vinegar, brown sugar, reserved broth, salt, and lemon pepper. Add 3 gingersnaps and the raisins. Cook over medium-low heat until gingersnaps are dissolved and sauce is slightly thickened, 2 to 3 minutes. Add another gingersnap if needed for taste.

MEAT

GEDEMPTE VEAL CHOPS

*G*edempte means "braised," in this case in tomato juice, aromatics, and vegetables, for succulent, tender chops that are as satisfying to eat as they are simple to cook. Veal chops are meaty, lean, and relatively low in cholesterol. Serve with potato kugel.

4 SERVINGS

4 veal chops
¼ teaspoon salt
⅛ teaspoon pepper
3 tablespoons olive or other vegetable oil
2 medium onions, sliced
2 celery ribs, sliced
¼ cup julienned carrots
½ cup tomato juice

M E A T

1. Season veal chops with salt and pepper. Heat oil in a large skillet over medium heat. Add veal chops and cook, turning, until browned on both sides, 3 to 4 minutes per side.

2. Add onions, celery, carrots, and tomato juice. Cover and simmer over low heat for 45 minutes, or until veal is tender.

KARNATZLACH

Geri Etter, food editor at *The Philadelphia Inquirer*, described this old Romanian dish from his childhood to me. Originally, the ground veal, highly seasoned with garlic and black pepper, was stuffed into a sausage casing. I form the mixture into sausage-shaped rolls and bake them. Serve with a kugel.

4 SERVINGS

1 pound ground veal
2 tablespoons matzoh meal
2 tablespoons minced garlic
1 tablespoon pepper
1 teaspoon salt
Paprika

M E A T

1. Preheat oven to 350°F. Coat a roasting pan with nonstick vegetable spray.

2. Combine veal, matzoh meal, garlic, pepper, and salt. Mix thoroughly.

3. With wet hands, shape into rolls about 4 inches long and 1 inch thick. Place in prepared pan. Dust with paprika.

4. Bake 25 minutes, or until meat rolls are cooked through and juices run clear. Serve hot.

SAUTEED VEAL STEAKS

While this is similar to wiener schnitzel, I use thick slices of veal cut from the shoulder in steaks. If you prefer to use thin scaloppine from the leg, prepare the recipe the same way through step 2 only; the veal should be cooked through and tender at that point.

4 SERVINGS

⅓ cup flour or matzoh meal
½ teaspoon dried thyme
½ teaspoon salt
¼ teaspoon pepper
4 veal shoulder steaks, cut ¾ to 1 inch thick
1 egg, beaten
¼ cup vegetable oil
Paprika
2 tablespoons chopped fresh parsley

1. In a shallow dish, mix flour or matzoh meal with dried thyme, salt, and pepper. Dredge steaks in mixture to coat both sides, then dip floured steaks in beaten egg, letting excess drip back into bowl.

2. Heat oil in a large skillet over medium heat. Place coated veal steaks in skillet in a single layer. Fry to a golden brown, about 5 minutes on each side.

3. Reduce heat to lowest setting and add 3 tablespoons water to skillet. Cover and cook 25 to 30 minutes, or until steaks are tender. Transfer to a heated platter. Sprinkle with paprika and parsley and serve at once.

MEAT

HERBED VEAL SCALOPPINE

With scaloppine, thin veal cutlets, and salad dressing mix, dinner can be on the table in minutes. Stuffed into Italian rolls and topped with coleslaw, these make great sandwiches.

4 SERVINGS

½ cup matzoh meal
1 tablespoon dry garlic-onion salad dressing mix
¼ cup liquid Italian salad dressing
1 pound thin veal cutlets
Olive or vegetable oil for frying
Thin lemon slices and chopped parsley (optional)

1. In a shallow dish, combine matzoh meal and dry salad dressing mix. Pour Italian dressing into a separate shallow dish.

2. Dip each cutlet on both sides first in Italian dressing, then in matzoh meal mixture to coat.

3. Heat ⅛ inch of oil in a large, nonstick skillet over medium heat. Fry cutlets, in batches if necessary, 3 to 4 minutes per side, until golden. Drain on paper towels.

4. Serve hot, with thin slices of lemon and chopped parsley as garnish.

MEAT

BRAISED VEAL BREAST WITH PARSLEY STUFFING

*A*sk your butcher to bone the veal breast, which will give you a natural pocket.

10 TO 12 SERVINGS

¼ pound lean ground beef
½ cup cooked rice
1 cup coarsely chopped fresh parsley
1 teaspoon allspice
1 teaspoon salt
¼ teaspoon pepper
4-pound veal breast, boned
¼ cup olive oil
3 celery ribs, sliced
1 medium onion, coarsely chopped

1. In a medium bowl, combine ground beef, rice, parsley, allspice, salt, and pepper. Mix until well blended.

2. Lay veal cut side up on a flat surface. Spread parsley mixture over veal to within 1½ inches of edges. Roll up as for a jelly roll. Tie neatly with string to secure.

3. Heat oil in a large, heavy saucepan or flameproof casserole over medium-high heat. Add veal and cook, turning, until browned all over, 8 to 10 minutes. Add celery, onion, and 1 cup warm water.

4. Cover, reduce heat to medium-low, and simmer 2½ hours, or until veal juices run clear when pierced. Add a little more water during cooking if needed.

5. Transfer to a cutting board, remove string, and let stand 5 to 10 minutes. Carve into ½-inch-thick slices.

MEAT

VERMOUTH-BRAISED VEAL KIDNEYS

I use kitchen scissors to trim off any fat from the kidneys. Serve these in their delicate, savory sauce with rice and steamed asparagus.

2 SERVINGS

½ pound veal kidneys, fat removed
2 tablespoons flour
½ teaspoon dried thyme
½ teaspoon dried basil
¼ teaspoon salt
⅛ teaspoon pepper
2 tablespoons vegetable oil
¼ cup dry vermouth
4 slices of toasted French bread
Chopped parsley

1. Cut kidneys into 1½-inch pieces. In a shallow dish, mix flour, thyme, basil, salt, and pepper. Toss kidney pieces in seasoned flour to coat.

2. Heat oil in a medium nonstick skillet over medium-high heat. Add kidneys and cook, tossing, until browned, 2 to 3 minutes.

3. Add vermouth and bring to a boil over high heat, stirring constantly. Gravy will be smooth, light, and slightly thickened. Reduce heat to low, cover, and simmer until kidneys are tender and just pale pink in center, 4 to 5 minutes. Spoon kidneys and sauce over toasted French bread. Sprinkle parsley on top and serve at once.

ROASTED LAMB SHOULDER WITH GARLIC

Spring lamb is plentiful in the Middle Eastern countries, where the Sephardim from Spain settled. Roast lamb at Passover is a Sephardic tradition, granted, however, that the salsa is my own innovation. For easy preparation, ask your butcher to bone the lamb shoulder and to cut a pocket for you.

6 TO 8 SERVINGS

2 tablespoons oil
20 garlic cloves, peeled
½ cup thawed frozen chopped spinach, squeezed dry
½ cup finely chopped fresh mint
½ cup finely chopped parsley
½ cup crumbled mandlen, homemade (page 144) or purchased
¼ teaspoon grated nutmeg
½ teaspoon salt
¼ teaspoon pepper
4-pound boned lamb shoulder roast with a pocket
1½ cups mild salsa

1. Preheat oven to 375°F. In a large skillet, heat oil over medium heat. Reduce heat to low. Add whole garlic cloves and cook, stirring often, until soft and golden, 15 to 20 minutes. Stir in spinach, mint, parsley, mandlen, nutmeg, salt, and pepper. Remove from heat. Mash garlic to a paste.

2. Stuff spinach mixture into lamb pocket and press lightly to close. Don't worry if some stuffing seeps out. Place stuffed lamb in roasting pan. Spoon ¾ cup salsa over meat. Tent with foil. Roast 1¾ hours, basting often with remaining salsa and pan juices. Remove foil for last 20 minutes of cooking time. Lamb is ready when juices run clear when pierced in thickest part.

3. Transfer roast to a carving board and let stand for 10 minutes. Skim fat off pan juices and pour into a gravy boat. Carve lamb across grain into slices and arrange on a platter. Spoon a little sauce over meat. Pass remainder on the side.

MEAT

LAMB STEW WITH TOMATOES AND PEPPERS

*F*or speedy preparation, have the butcher cut up the lamb for you. Be sure to tell him that you want it well trimmed. This stew is particularly good ladled over Noodles with Poppy Seeds and Dill (page 231).

6 SERVINGS

1½ pounds boneless lamb shoulder, cut into 1½-inch pieces
1 tablespoon sweet paprika
2 tablespoons olive oil
1 large onion, cut into 1-inch chunks
1½ teaspoons dried marjoram
1 teaspoon lemon pepper seasoning
1 teaspoon salt
1 (14½-ounce) can stewed tomatoes
2 medium red bell peppers, cut into ¼-inch-wide strips
1 medium green bell pepper, cut into ¼-inch-wide strips

1. Dust lamb with paprika. In a large, flameproof casserole, heat oil over medium-high heat. Add lamb and cook, turning, until browned all over, 5 to 7 minutes.

2. Reduce heat to medium-low and add onion. Cook 2 to 3 minutes, or until onion is translucent. Sprinkle with marjoram, lemon pepper seasoning, and salt. Stir in stewed tomatoes with their liquid and ⅓ cup hot water.

3. Bring to a simmer, reduce heat to medium-low, cover, and cook for 1 hour.

4. Add red and green pepper strips and cook 10 to 15 minutes longer, or until lamb is tender.

MEAT

LAMB RAGOUT WITH BRANDIED DRIED FRUITS

*P*opular in Israel and typical of Middle Eastern food in general, this mouthwatering stew is sweetened with dried fruits and honey. I steep the dried fruits in Sabra, the orange-flavored liqueur produced in Israel. Serve over couscous.

6 SERVINGS

½ cup coarsely chopped dried pears
½ cup quartered dried apricots
¼ cup Sabra or other orange-flavored liqueur
3 tablespoons vegetable oil
1½ pounds boneless lamb shoulder, cut into 1½-inch pieces
2 medium red onions, cut into 1-inch chunks
1 (14½-ounce) can stewed tomatoes
1 tablespoon honey
1½ teaspoons ground cumin
1½ teaspoons ground coriander
½ teaspoon cinnamon
Salt and pepper

1. In a small bowl, mix pears, apricots, and liqueur. Set aside while you brown meat.

2. In a large skillet, heat oil over medium heat. Add lamb pieces and cook, stirring often, until browned all over, 8 to 10 minutes. Add onions and cook 5 minutes longer.

3. Stir in stewed tomatoes with their juices, honey, cumin, coriander, cinnamon, dried fruits with liqueur, and ¼ cup water. Bring to a boil over high heat. Reduce heat to low, cover, and simmer 1 hour, or until lamb is tender. Season with salt and pepper to taste.

MEAT

LAMB TAGINE WITH SEVEN VEGETABLES

With its Moorish spices and large variety of vegetables, this makes a wonderful Sephardic main dish to celebrate the harvest festival of Succoth. Serve with couscous or rice.

6 SERVINGS

3 pounds lamb shanks or cut-up shoulder
2 carrots, sliced 1 inch thick
½ pound pumpkin, cut into 2-inch chunks
4 small white turnips, peeled and quartered
2 onions, sliced
2 small zucchini, cut into 1-inch chunks
1 bunch of Swiss chard, cut into ½-inch-wide pieces
1 medium leek, washed, trimmed, and sliced 1 inch thick
¼ cup olive oil
¼ teaspoon saffron
1 tablespoon cumin
½ teaspoon salt
¼ cup sugar
1 tablespoon cinnamon

M E A T

1. Preheat oven to 350°F. In a large Dutch oven, place lamb, carrots, pumpkin, turnips, onions, zucchini, chard, and leek.

2. Stir in oil, saffron, cumin, and salt. Pour in enough cold water just to cover. Bring to a boil.

3. Cover and bake in preheated oven for 1 hour 15 minutes. Remove lid and bake 15 minutes longer.

4. Raise oven heat to 425°F. Sprinkle sugar and cinnamon over top of stew and continue baking, uncovered, until cinnamon-sugar is slightly caramelized, 20 to 30 minutes.

RUSSIAN SHASHLIK

*T*he Russian version of grilled lamb is marinated in an uncomplicated vinegar mixture, then cooked on the barbecue or under the broiler. I marinate it in a sealed plastic bag, which takes up less room in the refrigerator and is airtight. Serve the meat hot, with pita bread lightly toasted on the grill.

4 SERVINGS

¼ cup extra-virgin olive oil
3 tablespoons red wine vinegar
1 tablespoon soy sauce
1 tablespoon chopped garlic
1 teaspoon oregano or marjoram
½ teaspoon salt
¼ teaspoon pepper
1 pound lean boneless lamb shoulder, cut into 2-inch pieces
2 medium onions, quartered
1 large green bell pepper, cut into 8 pieces

MEAT

1. In a shallow dish, combine olive oil, vinegar, soy sauce, garlic, oregano, salt, and ¼ teaspoon pepper.

2. Add lamb cubes and turn to coat all lamb surfaces. Cover and refrigerate overnight.

3. Preheat broiler or barbecue. Thread one-fourth of lamb cubes and 2 pieces onion and pepper onto each of 4 long metal skewers.

4. Cook over medium coals or 4 inches from preheated broiler, 10 to 15 minutes, turning often, until onion is tender and lightly browned around edges and lamb is browned outside but still pink in center.

LEBANESE LAMB PIE

*S*lightly sweet and aromatic with the spices used in shash-lik, the barbecued lamb that is Israeli street food, this savory pie makes a nice lunch or picnic dish—easily served or packed. Buy the pastry crust or make your own using margarine or vegetable shortening.

6 TO 8 SERVINGS

1 tablespoon olive oil
1 medium onion, chopped
1 garlic clove, minced
1 pound lean ground lamb
1½ teaspoons ground cinnamon
1 teaspoon ground cumin
1 teaspoon dried mint
½ teaspoon salt
¼ teaspoon pepper
2 eggs, lightly beaten
Pastry for a 2-crust, 9-inch pie

1. Heat olive oil in a medium saucepan. Add onion. Cook over low heat until golden, about 10 minutes.

2. Add garlic and lamb and cook over medium heat, stirring, until all the pink has disappeared. Stir in cinnamon, cumin, mint, salt, and pepper. Let cool slightly.

3. Preheat oven to 400°F. Line a 9-inch pie pan with pastry. Spoon in lamb mixture. Pour eggs over meat. Place pastry over top and press to seal.

4. Cut 3 (2-inch) slits in crust. Bake in preheated oven for 20 minutes, or until crust is nicely browned. Serve warm or at room temperature, cut into wedges.

CHAPTER SIX

Vegetables and Salads

✡

*T*his is where Sephardic Jewish cuisine, the Jewish cooking of the Mediterranean, really shines. After their expulsion from Spain in 1492, Jews settled in the warm climates of the Near East, North Africa, and even Italy, where an incredible variety of fresh fruits and vegetables grew abundantly. Drawing on the cooking methods and foods of their adopted countries but keeping to the laws of kashruth, they created dishes like Sweet Carrot and Date Dome and Minted Aubergine Salad. For cooking, locally produced olive oil was used. Today this Sephardic cuisine is growing in popularity with Jews all over the world as it happens to be right in step with today's nutritional recommendations.

For the Ashkenazim, who lived in the harsh climates of Central and Eastern Europe, hardy root vegetables and cabbage were harvested in the fall to store for winter eating. Recipes such as Sweet-and-Sour Cabbage Slaw and Erminia's Potato-Onion Casserole are typical of the tasty vegetable dishes made from a limited variety of ingredients. New World vegetables, such as pumpkin and peppers, were totally unfamiliar to Ashkenazic Jews. Today they are an integral part of everyone's diet. I've included treatments of them, as well as many other familiar vegetables, in this chapter. Also here are several dressings that are Jewish in character—Poppy Seed Dressing, Sweet-and-Sour Citrus Dressing, and Garlic and Sesame Dressing, which can be used over any salad of your choice.

One final note: I've put my grandmother's chopper and wooden bowl up on the top shelf. In the modern everyday Jewish kitchen, the food processor is a necessity when it comes to slicing, chopping, and grating vegetables and mincing large quantities of fresh herbs. I also keep a pair of kitchen scissors on hand to snip smaller amounts of herbs.

WHITE ASPARAGUS VINAIGRETTE

White asparagus was a luxury item in the 1920s and 1930s, when many German Jews emigrated to this country. It is still a favorite in many families.

4 TO 6 SERVINGS

2 (15-ounce) cans white asparagus spears, drained
¼ cup white wine vinegar
¼ cup fresh lemon juice
¼ cup peanut oil
½ teaspoon salt
¼ teaspoon pepper
1 shallot, minced

1. Place asparagus in a shallow serving dish.

2. In a small bowl, whisk together vinegar, lemon juice, peanut oil, salt, and pepper. Stir in shallot.

3. Pour dressing over asparagus and turn spears to coat. Cover and refrigerate until chilled.

BABY BEETS

*N*aturally sweet beetroots are traditionally served at Rosh Hashanah as a symbol of an abundant and sweet year to come. Save the beet greens here and cook them up as a vegetable as suggested on the following page.

4 SERVINGS

16 baby beets (about 1½ pounds)
2 tablespoons margarine
Salt and pepper

1. Rinse beets under cold running water. Cut off leafy tops to within ½ inch of beets.

2. Place beets in a large saucepan. Pour in enough boiling water to cover by about 2 inches. Cover pan and cook over medium-high heat for 40 to 45 minutes, or until beets are tender. Test by lifting 1 out of water, let cool slightly, and press with your fingers. Don't pierce with a knife, or the color will bleed.

3. Drain and set aside until cool enough to handle, 5 to 10 minutes. Remove skins (they will slip off easily) and slice beets ¼ inch thick or leave whole.

4. Melt margarine in a saucepan over medium heat. Add beets and toss to coat. Season with salt and pepper to taste. Serve hot.

PARVE

SKILLET STEAMED BEET GREENS

*B*eets are not just for borscht. The leafy green tops are delicious and rich in vitamin A and calcium.

4 TO 6 SERVINGS

Leafy green tops from 2 large bunches of beets
1 teaspoon salt
½ teaspoon pepper
3 tablespoons garlic-flavored oil

1. Rinse beet greens well in cold water. Do not dry. Coarsely shred greens and place in a large skillet. Season with salt and pepper.

2. Cover and cook over medium heat, tossing occasionally, until greens are wilted, about 5 minutes.

3. Drizzle with oil and serve hot.

MICROWAVE BROCCOLI RABE

*U*ntil recently, broccoli rabe was a little-known peppery Italian vegetable. Prepared as it is here, it's a lusty dish—with plenty of garlic and balsamic vinegar, the latter now available with kosher certification. For a dairy meal, top this dish with slivers of Parmesan cheese.

4 SERVINGS

1 bunch of broccoli rabe, trimmed and thinly sliced
2 tablespoons finely chopped garlic
3 tablespoons olive oil
3 tablespoons balsamic vinegar
1 teaspoon salt
¾ teaspoon pepper

1. Spread half of broccoli rabe in a shallow nonmetal serving dish. Sprinkle 1 tablespoon garlic, 1½ tablespoons olive oil, and 1½ tablespoons balsamic vinegar over broccoli rabe. Season with half of salt and pepper.

2. Spread remaining broccoli rabe in dish and repeat with remaining ingredients. Toss to mix.

3. Cover lightly with microwave-safe plastic wrap. Microwave on High for 3 minutes.

GARLICKY BRUSSELS SPROUTS

4 SERVINGS

2 (10-ounce) packages frozen baby brussels sprouts, thawed
3 tablespoons olive oil
1 tablespoon chopped garlic
Salt and pepper

1. Pat brussels sprouts dry on paper towels. In a large skillet, cook sprouts in olive oil over medium heat, stirring often, for 5 minutes. Cover and cook 10 minutes, shaking pan several times, until tender.

2. Stir in garlic, reduce heat to medium-low, and cook 2 minutes longer.

3. Season with salt and plenty of pepper to taste. Serve hot.

JACKIE'S BUTTERNUT SQUASH CASSEROLE

*S*quash makes a smooth, creamy side dish that goes well with meats, poultry, and fish. For everyday convenience, I suggest the already cooked and mashed frozen variety. To serve at a dairy meal or dairy buffet, substitute butter for the margarine and milk for the nondairy creamer.

4 TO 6 SERVINGS

1 (10-ounce) package thawed frozen mashed butternut squash
1 stick (4 ounces) margarine, melted
½ cup all-purpose flour
½ cup sugar
3 eggs, beaten
2 cups nondairy creamer
1 teaspoon cinnamon

1. Preheat oven to 350°F. Coat a 1½-quart casserole with nonstick vegetable spray.

2. In a large bowl, mix squash, margarine, flour, sugar, eggs, creamer, and cinnamon.

3. Pour into prepared casserole. Bake in preheated oven until set in center, about 1 hour. Serve hot.

SWEET-AND-SOUR CABBAGE SLAW

*R*ed cabbage adds color, and caraway seeds, popular in German Jewish dishes, impart a nutty, anise flavor to this slaw. For convenience, buy cabbage ready shredded in a bag from the supermarket.

4 SERVINGS

¼ cup cider vinegar
¼ cup mayonnaise
1 tablespoon honey, warmed
2 teaspoons salt
1½ teaspoons pepper
6 cups shredded red cabbage
1 medium sweet onion, chopped
2 tablespoons caraway seeds

1. In a small bowl, mix vinegar and mayonnaise until blended. Stir in honey, salt, and pepper.

2. In a large bowl, toss red cabbage with onion and caraway seeds. Pour dressing over cabbage and toss to mix. Serve chilled.

SAVORY BRAISED CABBAGE

In Russia, they add caraway seeds to cabbage; in Poland, it's apples. Jewish immigrants who came here cook this year-round vegetable with the all-American condiment: ketchup.

4 TO 6 SERVINGS

1 (1½-pound) head of green cabbage
¼ cup ketchup
1 tablespoon fresh lemon juice
1½ teaspoons salt
½ teaspoon pepper

1. Cut cabbage into quarters and remove core. Shred finely in a food processor or on the large holes of a hand grater.

2. Place cabbage in a large nonreactive pot. Add ketchup, lemon juice, salt, pepper, and ¼ cup water. Stir to mix.

3. Cover tightly and cook over medium heat, stirring occasionally, until cabbage is tender, about 20 minutes. Serve hot as a side dish.

INDIAN-STYLE COLESLAW

*F*resh ginger and cilantro, typical Indian-Jewish seasonings, pack a punch into this crunchy coleslaw. For convenience, use packaged, shredded cabbage and carrots.

4 SERVINGS

6 cups mixed shredded cabbage and carrots
1 cup vinaigrette salad dressing
½ cup chopped fresh cilantro
2 tablespoons grated fresh ginger
¼ cup toasted sesame seeds

1. Place cabbage and carrots in a mixing bowl. In a small bowl, combine salad dressing, cilantro, ginger, and 3 tablespoons sesame seeds. Pour over shredded cabbage and carrots. Toss to mix.

2. Spoon into a serving bowl. Sprinkle with remaining sesame seeds and serve.

NOTE: Sesame seeds may be purchased toasted. To toast at home: Spread on a small baking sheet and toast under preheated broiler for 1 minute. Stir several times. Watch carefully to avoid scorching.

HONEYED BABY CARROTS

*H*oney, a symbol of sweetness, is used extensively in cooking for the High Holy Days. This may be served at Rosh Hashanah or at the meal before the Yom Kippur fast. Use a bag of cleaned fresh carrots from the supermarket.

4 TO 6 SERVINGS

1 tablespoon vegetable oil
1 small onion, chopped
1 (16-ounce) bag baby carrots
2 tablespoons honey
2 teaspoons grated fresh ginger or ½ teaspoon ground
1 tablespoon minced fresh parsley

1. Heat oil in a medium saucepan. Add onion and carrots. Fry over high heat until onions are beginning to brown, 3 to 4 minutes. Reduce heat to medium.

2. Stir in honey and ginger. Cover and cook, stirring occasionally, until carrots are tender, about 15 minutes.

3. Before serving, garnish with parsley. Serve hot.

SWEET CARROT AND DATE DOME

A doubly sweet Persian dish served at Rosh Hashanah and festive celebrations. Substitute a bag of frozen Parisian-style carrots (round balls) instead of carrot coins, if you see them in your market.

4 SERVINGS

½ cup long-grain white rice
2 tablespoons walnut oil
4 cups carrot coins
1 teaspoon salt
½ cup chopped pitted dates
2 tablespoons thawed frozen orange juice concentrate
½ teaspoon turmeric
¼ cup chopped fresh mint

1. In a large saucepan, cook rice in walnut oil over medium-high heat, stirring, for 2 minutes. Add carrot coins, salt, and 1½ cups water. Bring to a boil, cover, reduce heat to low, and cook 20 minutes, or until rice is tender and water is absorbed.

2. Stir in dates, orange juice, and turmeric. Turn out onto a warm platter and shape into a dome. Serve at once, garnished with fresh mint.

CUCUMBER AND RED ONION SALAD

*S*alads like this one with a piquant dressing are traditionally served with steaks or roasts to cut the heavy textures and tastes. It is equally delicious as part of a vegetarian meal or as a side dish for poultry and fish.

6 SERVINGS

2 cucumbers, peeled if desired and thinly sliced
1 large red onion, halved and thinly sliced
⅓ cup sugar
⅓ cup cider vinegar
3 whole cloves
2 teaspoons salt
1 teaspoon pepper

1. Place cucumbers and red onion in a heatproof serving bowl.

2. In a small nonreactive saucepan, combine sugar, vinegar, cloves, salt, pepper, and ⅓ cup water. Bring to a boil over medium heat, stirring to dissolve sugar. Reduce to low, cover, and cook 5 minutes.

3. Pour vinegar mixture over cucumbers and onions. Stir to mix. Cover and refrigerate at least 2 hours before serving.

STUFFED BABY EGGPLANTS

Baby eggplants don't have the bitterness of the large variety, so there's no need to go through the tedious process of salting and draining. These go especially well with roast chicken or lamb.

4 SERVINGS

8 baby eggplants
1 cup walnuts
1 small sweet onion, cut into 1-inch chunks
2 large garlic cloves, quartered
½ large red bell pepper, cut into 1-inch chunks
½ cup parsley sprigs
½ teaspoon salt
¼ teaspoon pepper
3 tablespoons olive oil

1. Preheat oven to 375°F. Coat a shallow baking dish, just large enough to hold eggplants in a single layer, with nonstick vegetable spray.

2. Cut eggplants in half lengthwise. Starting ½ inch below stem end, cut 3 slits across the cut side of each eggplant half, without cutting all the way through the skin. Arrange the 8 halves, cut sides up, in prepared baking dish.

3. In a food processor, combine walnuts, onion, garlic, red bell pepper, parsley, salt, and pepper. Pulse to coarsely chop.

4. Divide mixture evenly over each eggplant half in baking dish. Lightly press remaining 8 halves on top to resemble whole eggplants. Brush with oil. Cover lightly with aluminum foil.

5. Bake in preheated oven until eggplants are tender and a sharp pointed knife slips easily into vegetable, about 45 minutes. Serve hot or at room temperature.

MINTED AUBERGINE SALAD

Sephardic and North African Jews have created literally hundreds of recipes for aubergines, or eggplants. This is one of my favorites. Serve cold as a salad or relish with warm pita bread.

4 TO 6 SERVINGS

6 baby eggplants
½ cup all-purpose flour
¼ cup olive oil
1 large red bell pepper, cut into thin strips
½ cup chopped fresh mint
3 tablespoons balsamic vinegar
1 teaspoon pepper

1. Trim eggplants but do not peel. Cut lengthwise into ½-inch-thick strips. Toss in flour to coat.

2. Heat oil in a large skillet, preferably nonstick. Add eggplants and fry over medium heat, tossing often, until tender, about 10 minutes. Reduce heat to low, add bell pepper, and cook 10 minutes longer.

3. Transfer to a shallow serving dish. Gently stir in mint.

4. Mix vinegar with pepper and 2 tablespoons water. Pour over eggplant and toss gently to mix. Refrigerate until chilled, at least 2 hours or overnight, before serving.

GRAPEFRUIT SALAD WITH PARSLEY AND MINT

*I*sraelis make use of the local cultivated fruit in hundreds of dishes. Try this for a quick, refreshing snack.

4 SERVINGS

2 grapefruits, peeled
Red lettuce leaves
⅓ cup chopped fresh parsley
2 tablespoons chopped fresh mint
¼ teaspoon lemon pepper seasoning

1. Slice grapefruits horizontally into large rounds about ¼ inch thick.

2. Line 4 plates with lettuce leaves. Arrange grapefruit slices on lettuce, overlapping as necessary.

3. In a small bowl, toss parsley, mint, and lemon pepper seasoning. Sprinkle over grapefruits. Serve at room temperature.

GREEN BEANS IN GARLIC TOMATO SAUCE

4 TO 6 SERVINGS

1 (20-ounce) bag frozen French-style green beans
1 tablespoon olive oil
2 garlic cloves, minced
¼ cup tomato sauce
1 tablespoon fresh lemon juice
Salt and pepper

1. Place green beans and olive oil in a medium saucepan. Cover and cook over low heat, stirring often, until beans are tender, 15 to 20 minutes.

2. Stir in garlic, tomato sauce, lemon juice, and ½ cup water. Partially cover and cook over medium heat until liquid is almost absorbed, about 10 minutes. Season with salt and pepper to taste. Serve hot.

EASY SWEET-AND-SOUR GREEN BEANS

3 TO 4 SERVINGS

⅓ cup bottled sweet-and-sour salad dressing
2 teaspoons grated lemon zest
2 (10-ounce) packages frozen green beans
1 tablespoon chopped pimiento

In a large nonreactive saucepan, combine salad dressing and lemon zest. Add frozen green beans and cook over medium heat, stirring occasionally, until beans are thawed and heated through, about 10 minutes. Serve hot, garnished with pimiento.

MOUNTAIN GREENS AND BERRIES

*T*he Nissimovs, who escaped from Chechnya to Israel, remember how in springtime the whole family would hike to the mountains near their home in Grozny to gather young, wild greens for salads. Dandelion greens, from farmers' markets, are pleasantly bitter and best combined with mild lettuces, such as Boston or Bibb. Serve with crusty bread and goat cheese.

4 TO 6 SERVINGS

2 cups young dandelion greens or arugula
4 cups torn Boston lettuce
1 cup fresh mint leaves
1½ cups strawberries, quartered
¼ cup olive oil
¼ cup fresh lemon juice
1 teaspoon paprika
½ teaspoon salt
¼ teaspoon pepper

1. Toss together greens, lettuce, mint, and berries.

2. Whisk oil with lemon juice, paprika, salt, and pepper.

3. Pour dressing over greens and berries. Toss gently to mix. Serve at once.

BRAISED LEEKS WITH EGGS

*I*n this Jewish dish from Chechnya, egg is poured over vegetables to make a crust. Serve as a main dish with warm, crusty bread.

4 SERVINGS

4 medium leeks
2 tablespoons olive oil
Juice of 2 lemons
6 large garlic cloves, quartered
1½ teaspoons salt
½ teaspoon pepper
3 eggs

1. Trim leeks by cutting off root base and fibrous part of green leaves. Split lengthwise down center and rinse under cold running water until all grit is removed.

2. Cut into 3-inch pieces. Place in a large skillet. Add olive oil, lemon juice, garlic, and ¼ cup water. Sprinkle with 1 teaspoon salt and ¼ teaspoon pepper.

3. Cover and bring to a boil. Reduce heat to medium-low and cook until leeks are tender, 15 to 20 minutes.

4. Beat eggs with remaining ½ teaspoon salt and ¼ teaspoon pepper. Pour over leeks. Cover and cook over medium heat until eggs are set, about 5 minutes. Serve hot.

BRAISED LEEKS WITH SUN-DRIED TOMATOES

*L*eeks are a common European winter vegetable. When braised in broth, leeks are mellow and silky. I add a splash of dry white wine for a light, fruity flavor.

4 SERVINGS

3 large leeks (white and tender green)
2 tablespoons olive oil
3 garlic cloves, minced
¼ cup vegetable broth
2 tablespoons dry white wine, preferably Chardonnay
¼ cup chopped fresh parsley
1 teaspoon salt
¼ teaspoon pepper
¼ cup chopped sun-dried tomatoes

1. Trim leeks, cut lengthwise into quarters, and rinse thoroughly under cold running water. Cut crosswise into 3-inch lengths.

2. Heat oil in a large skillet. Add leeks, garlic, broth, wine, parsley, salt, and pepper.

3. Cover and cook over medium heat for 15 minutes. Add sun-dried tomatoes and continue cooking until leeks are softened, 10 minutes longer. Serve hot.

GLAZED WHITE ONIONS

*T*his quick and easy vegetable makes a tasty side dish or terrific-looking garnish for meat and chicken dishes. It starts off in the microwave and finishes in minutes on top of the stove.

4 TO 6 SERVINGS

2 pounds white boiling onions (10 to 12), peeled and cut in half
3 tablespoons olive oil
1 tablespoon sugar
Pepper

1. Place onions in a shallow microwave dish. Cover with moistened microwave-safe paper towels and cook on High for 3 to 4 minutes, until onions yield to gentle pressure.

2. Heat olive oil in a large skillet over medium-high heat. Add onions, sprinkle with sugar, and cook 2 to 3 minutes on each side to brown.

3. Season with a grinding of pepper and serve hot.

DILLED POTATOES

*T*raditionally served as a filler alongside borscht, these tasty potatoes, spiked with garlic and fresh dill, are good also with fish or chicken.

4 TO 6 SERVINGS

6 medium boiling potatoes
1 medium onion, peeled
2 tablespoons vegetable oil
2 garlic cloves, minced
¼ cup chopped fresh dill
Salt and pepper

1. Peel potatoes and cut into 1½-inch chunks. Place in a large saucepan with whole onion and pour in enough boiling water to cover by 1 inch.

2. Cover pan and bring to a boil. Cook over medium heat until a knife inserted in a potato comes out easily, 20 to 25 minutes. Drain well.

3. Return potatoes to pan and shake over heat for 1 to 2 minutes to dry out.

4. Remove from heat. Slice cooked onion and add to potatoes along with oil, garlic, and dill. Stir gently to mix. Season with salt and pepper to taste. Serve hot.

ERMINIA'S POTATO-ONION CASSEROLE

6 SERVINGS

3 large baking potatoes (about 1½ pounds total)
¼ cup olive oil
¼ cup dry unseasoned bread crumbs
1 teaspoon salt
½ teaspoon pepper
1 large onion, peeled and thinly sliced

1. Preheat oven to 350°F. Coat a shallow, medium baking dish or 9- or 10-inch pie plate with nonstick cooking spray.

2. Peel potatoes and thinly slice on a diagonal. Arrange half of potatoes over bottom of dish, overlapping slices slightly. Drizzle on 2 tablespoons olive oil. Sprinkle 2 tablespoons bread crumbs, ½ teaspoon salt, and ¼ teaspoon pepper over potatoes.

3. Spread all of onion slices over potato layer and drizzle on 1 tablespoon olive oil. Top with remaining potatoes. Drizzle remaining 1 tablespoon oil over casserole. Sprinkle remaining 2 tablespoons bread crumbs, ½ teaspoon salt, and ¼ teaspoon pepper on top.

4. Cover lightly with foil and bake in preheated oven for 45 minutes. Remove foil and continue to bake until potatoes are browned on top and tender, about 15 minutes longer. (A sharp, pointed knife should slide in easily.) Serve hot.

HOT BAKED POTATO SALAD

On Israeli kibbutzim, nothing is wasted. Baked potatoes from yesterday's dinner are spiked with lemon juice and fresh herbs to make this simple salad.

4 SERVINGS

2 medium onions, halved and thinly sliced
2 tablespoons olive oil
3 large baked potatoes, skins on, cut into ½-inch dice
3 tablespoons fresh lemon juice
½ cup chopped fresh parsley
1 tablespoon chopped fresh rosemary or 1 teaspoon dried
Salt and pepper

1. In a large skillet, cook onions in oil over medium heat, until soft and golden, about 10 minutes.

2. Add potatoes, lemon juice, parsley, and rosemary. Cook, tossing, until heated through, about 5 minutes.

3. Season with salt and pepper to taste. Serve hot or at room temperature.

GOLDEN SPICED PUMPKIN

Pumpkins are in season at Rosh Hashanah, and this aromatic dish, akin to a carrot tzimmes, is a holiday favorite in Israel. Serve hot as a side dish or sweeten with sugar or honey and offer as a dessert.

4 TO 6 SERVINGS

3 tablespoons margarine
6 cups peeled and seeded fresh pumpkin cut into 2-inch
   pieces (from a 4- to 6-pound pumpkin)
1 cup orange juice
½ cup sugar
1 teaspoon ground cardamom
½ cup golden raisins

1. Melt margarine in a large saucepan. Add pumpkin, orange juice, and sugar. Bring liquid to a simmer over medium heat. Cover and cook until pumpkin is soft and pulpy, about 20 minutes. Remove from heat.

2. Add cardamom and mash with a fork. Stir in raisins. If mixture is too liquid, return to pan and cook, uncovered, until liquid is almost absorbed.

LEAN ROTACH

Black-skinned winter radishes may weigh a pound or more and may be cooked or served raw as in this salad. This Russian salad is my friend Jackie's lighter, healthier version of one that was handed down to her by her father. Serve with fresh rye bread.

4 SERVINGS

1 tablespoon margarine
1 tablespoon olive oil
1 (1-pound) black radish, peeled
1 small sweet onion
1½ teaspoons salt
½ teaspoon pepper

1. Melt margarine and mix with olive oil

2. Grate radish coarsely in a food processor. Transfer to a mixing bowl.

3. Chop onion finely in a food processor. Add to grated radish.

4. Stir in oil mixture, salt, and pepper. Serve at room temperature.

ARMEKO

A Sephardic onion-tomato stew from the Greek islands. Thin down leftovers with broth to make a tasty instant soup. Serve hot as a side dish with meat or dairy dishes.

4 TO 6 SERVINGS

2 medium onions, halved and sliced
1 large red bell pepper, cut into ½-inch dice
1 (14½-ounce) can Italian-style stewed tomatoes
¼ cup long-grain white rice
2 tablespoons chopped fresh cilantro

1. In a medium saucepan, combine onions, bell pepper, stewed tomatoes with their juices, rice, and ⅓ cup water.

2. Bring to a simmer over medium heat. Cover and cook, stirring occasionally, until rice is tender, 20 to 25 minutes.

3. Stir in cilantro and serve.

GARLIC TOMATO WEDGES

*T*hese crunchy, garlic-topped tomato segments brighten any meat or dairy platter.

4 TO 6 SERVINGS

3 beefsteak tomatoes
2 tablespoons extra-virgin olive oil
Pepper
2 tablespoons chopped garlic

1. Preheat oven to 400°F. Coat a broiler pan with nonstick vegetable spray.

2. Cut each tomato into 8 wedges and arrange on prepared pan. Drizzle oil lightly over tomatoes and season sparingly with pepper. Sprinkle chopped garlic over tomato wedges.

3. Bake in preheated oven until edges are browned and sizzling but wedges still hold their shape, 12 to 15 minutes. Serve hot.

MARRAKESH RELISH

Moroccan-born Esther Press McManus, who maintains that simplest is best, gave me this recipe. Be sure to use ripe, flavorful tomatoes.

MAKES 4 CUPS

2 pounds tomatoes, cut into ¼-inch dice
6 garlic cloves, minced
⅔ cup extra-virgin olive oil
1½ teaspoons salt
¼ teaspoon pepper

1. Place tomatoes, garlic, and olive oil in a heavy saucepan. Bring to a boil over medium heat, stirring often.

2. Reduce heat to low. Cook, stirring often, until relish is thickened, 50 to 60 minutes.

3. Season with salt and pepper. Serve at room temperature with meats, poultry, or fish.

ISRAELI SALAD

*T*his is a healthful salad that you will find on every Israeli table, both at home and in restaurants.

4 TO 6 SERVINGS

4 tomatoes, diced
½ medium cucumber, scrubbed and cut into ½-inch dice
1 small green bell pepper, cut into ½-inch dice
2 scallions, thinly sliced
1 cup coarsely chopped fresh parsley
3 tablespoons fresh lemon juice
2 tablespoons extra-virgin olive oil
1 teaspoon celery seed
¾ teaspoon salt
¼ teaspoon pepper

1. In a bowl, mix tomatoes, cucumber, green pepper, scallions, and parsley.

2. Add lemon juice, olive oil, celery seed, salt, and pepper. Toss to mix. Serve chilled or at room temperature.

ALMOST INSTANT TZIMMES

*T*raditional tzimmes is a mishmash of sweet vegetables served at the New Year. This version of the mellow, meatless side dish requires no peeling or chopping.

6 TO 8 SERVINGS

1 (12-ounce) package pitted prunes
1 (17-ounce) can vacuum-packed sweet potatoes
1 (10-ounce) package frozen sliced carrots
¼ cup raisins
½ teaspoon salt
⅛ teaspoon pepper
1 (6-ounce) can frozen orange juice concentrate, thawed
1½ teaspoons ground ginger

1. Preheat oven to 325°F. Place prunes, sweet potatoes, carrots, and raisins in a 2½-quart baking dish. Sprinkle with salt and pepper.

2. In a bowl, mix orange juice, ¾ cup water, and ginger. Pour over prune mixture. Stir once or twice to combine.

3. Bake uncovered in preheated oven for 1 hour, stirring after 30 minutes. Add a little more juice and cover loosely with foil if dish becomes too dry. Serve hot.

VEGETARIAN CHICKEN LIVER

Sylvia Daskell was a wise lady. She concocted this vegetarian dish to tempt a daughter who hated vegetables and told her the mushrooms were really chicken livers, which she loved. I use the big portobello mushrooms, which cook up like juicy chunks of meat, and toss in a few sugarsnap peas for color.

4 SERVINGS

2 tablespoons olive oil
1 medium onion, chopped
1 portobello mushroom, cut into 1-inch pieces
1 large ripe tomato, chopped
½ small carrot, shredded
2 small red potatoes, cut into ½-inch dice
1 tablespoon Dijon mustard
1 teaspoon salt
⅛ teaspoon pepper
1 cup frozen sugarsnap peas

1. Heat olive oil in a medium saucepan. Add onion and mushroom pieces and cook over high heat, stirring often, until onion is beginning to brown, about 3 minutes.

2. Reduce heat to low. Cover and cook until some liquid is released from mushrooms, about 5 minutes.

3. Add tomato, carrot, potatoes, mustard, salt, and pepper. Cover and cook over medium heat until vegetables are tender, about 15 minutes longer.

4. Stir in sugarsnap peas and heat through. Taste for seasonings. Serve hot.

GARLIC AND SESAME DRESSING

*O*nce you make this and like it, double the quantity and store it in the refrigerator up to 2 weeks. It adds zest to salad greens or leftover cooked vegetables to be served chilled.

MAKES ABOUT ²/₃ CUP

½ cup balsamic vinegar
2 tablespoons Asian sesame oil
1 tablespoon minced garlic
2 teaspoons lemon pepper seasoning

Combine vinegar, 3 tablespoons water, sesame oil, garlic, and lemon pepper seasoning in a tight-lidded jar. Shake well. Refrigerate and use as needed.

SWEET-AND-SOUR CITRUS DRESSING

*U*se this for a nonmayonnaise cabbage slaw. Pour over 6 cups shredded red and green cabbage, toss, and refrigerate overnight.

MAKES ABOUT 1 CUP

¼ cup sugar
¼ cup distilled white vinegar
Juice and grated zest of 1 lemon
1½ teaspoons salt
1 teaspoon pepper
1 teaspoon paprika
½ cup vegetable oil

1. In a small nonreactive saucepan, mix sugar, vinegar, lemon juice, lemon zest, salt, pepper, and paprika. Cook over medium heat, stirring to dissolve sugar, for 2 to 3 minutes.

2. Remove from heat. Let cool about 5 minutes. Gradually whisk in oil in a slow, steady stream. Store, covered, in refrigerator. Use at room temperature.

POPPY SEED DRESSING

*U*se this sweet and simple dressing to brighten broiled grapefruit or to drizzle over fruit salads. It keeps for months in the refrigerator.

MAKES 1¼ CUPS

¼ cup sugar
¼ cup honey
¼ cup cider vinegar
1 teaspoon salad mustard
2 teaspoons poppy seeds
½ cup vegetable oil

1. In a small saucepan, mix sugar, honey, vinegar, mustard, and poppy seeds. Bring to a boil over high heat, stirring to dissolve sugar.

2. Remove from heat. Whisk in oil in a slow, steady stream. Let cool to room temperature before using.

ZUCCHINI FRITTATA WITH BASIL AND TOMATOES

*Y*ou could think of a frittata as an Ashkenazic kugel. Serve as a light supper or lunch dish or a tasty "brown-bag" meal to eat at work.

2 SERVINGS

3 tablespoons garlic-flavored oil
2 tablespoons chopped onion
1 medium zucchini, shredded
1 tablespoon chopped fresh basil or 1 teaspoon dried
½ teaspoon salt
Pepper
4 eggs, beaten
2 medium tomatoes, thinly sliced

1. Heat oil in a heavy 9-inch skillet with ovenproof handle. Add onion and zucchini. Cook over medium heat until onion is translucent and zucchini is tender, about 5 minutes. Season with basil, salt, and a pinch of pepper.

2. Pour eggs over zucchini and stir to mix. Arrange tomatoes on top, overlapping slices decoratively. Season lightly with a few grinds of pepper.

3. Cook over medium heat, carefully lifting cooked edges to allow uncooked mixture to run underneath, until frittata is set and underside is browned and firm, about 7 minutes.

4. Meanwhile, preheat broiler. Transfer skillet to broiler and cook to brown top, 1 to 2 minutes. Serve hot or at room temperature.

NOTE: If you don't have a skillet with ovenproof handle, cut frittata in half when underside is brown and firm. Flip each half over. Cook over medium-low heat to brown, 1 to 2 minutes.

QUICK SEPHARDIC SUPPER

*T*his is a typical, simple Israeli lunch or supper. Serve spooned over baked potatoes or couscous.

4 SERVINGS

1 tablespoon olive oil
1 medium onion, sliced ¼ inch thick
1 cup cut-up fresh green beans
1 (14½-ounce) can Italian stewed tomatoes
1 (7½-ounce) can Italian eggplant appetizer (caponata)
2 teaspoons ground cumin
4 eggs
Salt and pepper

MEAT

1. In a large skillet, heat olive oil over medium heat. Add onion and green beans and cook 7 to 8 minutes, until soft.

2. Add tomatoes, eggplant appetizer, and cumin. Stir and bring to a simmer over medium heat.

3. Make 4 indentations in vegetable mixture with back of a wooden spoon. Break an egg into each hollow. Season eggs lightly with salt and pepper. Cover and cook over medium heat for 5 to 8 minutes, or until whites are opaque and yolks are cooked to desired doneness.

BRAISED FENNEL WITH SOURI OLIVES

*U*se both the stems and feathery leaves of this licorice-flavored vegetable. Cook as the Israelis do, simmered to a buttery texture in olive oil with classic, small, tree-ripened olives from Galilee. Niçoise olives can be substituted. Either way, be sure to warn your guests that the olives have pits. Serve hot as a side dish with meats or fish.

4 SERVINGS

2 medium fennel bulbs
3 tablespoons olive oil
12 to 16 Souri or kalamata olives
1 teaspoon garlic powder
1 teaspoon salt
½ teaspoon pepper
¼ cup chicken broth*

1. Trim tough ends from fennel. Cut lengthwise into ¼-inch-thick slices.

2. Heat olive oil in a large skillet over medium heat. Add fennel and olives.

3. Sprinkle with garlic powder, salt, and pepper. Pour chicken broth over fennel. Cover and cook over medium heat until fennel is tender, about 10 minutes.

*To make this a parve vegetable, substitute vegetable broth or water for the chicken broth.

MEAT

ROTACH

*T*his is the real McCoy—grated black radishes mixed with melted chicken fat (schmaltz) and *griebens* (crisp-cooked chicken skin). Chicken and goose fat were the only cooking fats available to the Eastern European kosher cook, adding an indescribably delicious texture and flavor. Serve with fresh, crusty rye bread.

4 TO 6 SERVINGS

1 (1-pound) black radish, peeled
3 tablespoons schmaltz, melted
3 tablespoons *griebens* (page 97)
1 teaspoon salt
3 grinds of pepper

MEAT

1. Grate radish on grater blade of a food processor. Transfer to a medium bowl.

2. Pour chicken fat over radishes. Add *griebens,* salt, and pepper. Toss to mix. Serve at room temperature.

ARTICHOKES ITALIAN-STYLE

*T*his piquant vegetable recipe is said to have originated in the ghettos of Rome. It's a prime example of Jewish ingenuity in creating kosher dishes with local ingredients. Serve hot as an appetizer or side dish.

4 SERVINGS

2 tablespoons olive oil
2 (14-ounce) cans artichoke hearts, drained and patted dry
3 garlic cloves, minced
3 tablespoons fresh lemon juice
2 tablespoons grated Parmesan cheese

1. In a medium skillet, heat olive oil over high heat. Add artichokes and cook 2 minutes to heat through.

2. Reduce heat to low. Stir in garlic and lemon juice. Cook 5 minutes longer. Remove from heat and add Parmesan cheese. Stir gently to mix.

3. Transfer to an oiled broiling pan. Finish off under preheated broiler to brown at edges, 2 minutes.

NOTE: This can be made parve by omitting the cheese and seasoning with salt and pepper to taste.

DAIRY

CUCUMBERS AND RADISH SALAD WITH LIME YOGURT

*I*n Sephardic cooking, which was influenced by the cuisines of their adopted lands, such as Morocco and the Middle East, yogurt is used extensively. Here, it contrasts smoothly with peppery radishes.

4 TO 6 SERVINGS

1 cup plain yogurt
¼ cup fresh lime juice
1 teaspoon sugar
2 cucumbers, thinly sliced
1 bunch of radishes, thinly sliced
⅓ cup golden raisins

1. In a small bowl, mix together yogurt, lime juice, and sugar.

2. In a medium bowl, combine sliced cucumbers and radishes. Pour yogurt mixture over vegetables and toss gently. Sprinkle raisins on top.

3. Serve at room temperature, as accompaniment to fish or dairy dishes.

NOTE: Radishes will bleed into yogurt dressing if not served within an hour or so but this in no way affects the taste. Dressing and vegetables can be refrigerated separately and combined just before serving.

DAIRY

CREAMED MUSHROOMS ON TOAST

*I*n Lithuania, wild mushrooms were dried in summer for winter meals. My Florida friend Edith Flinkman remembers mopping up the rich, creamy sauce with crusty kaiser rolls.

4 SERVINGS

2 ounces imported dried mushrooms
2 tablespoons butter
1 medium onion, chopped
1½ cups sour cream
4 kaiser rolls, split and toasted

1. Place mushrooms in a medium bowl. Add enough warm water to cover by 2 inches. Let soak 30 minutes.

2. Drain well. Thinly slice mushrooms.

3. In a medium skillet, melt butter over medium heat. Add onion and cook until softened, about 5 minutes. Stir in mushrooms and cook 5 minutes longer.

4. Remove from heat and stir in sour cream. Serve over split, toasted kaiser rolls.

DAIRY

LIBYAN-STYLE PUMPKIN

*T*his Jewish-Libyan method of cooking pumpkin is marked by the flavors of Italy, which harks back to the early twentieth century, when Libya was an Italian colony. Serve as a side dish with a lentil or chicken curry.

4 SERVINGS

1 (16-ounce) can solid-pack pumpkin
1 tablespoon fresh lemon juice
1 tablespoon ground coriander
1 tablespoon grated fresh ginger
¼ cup sour cream
1 teaspoon salt

1. In a medium saucepan, mix pumpkin, lemon juice, coriander, ginger, sour cream, and salt.

2. Cook over medium-low heat, stirring several times, until heated through.

DAIRY

CHAPTER SEVEN

Beans, Grains, and Rice

*E*ven in the culinary world, irony has a place. What was once the humble peasant survival food of the *shtetls* in Russia and Eastern Europe is now recommended as healthy "complex carbohydrates" to our nutrition-conscious society as it heads into the twenty-first century.

Dried beans, peas, and lentils—all legumes and sometimes called "pulses"—as well as rice and grains made every dish go further and were incorporated into the most appetizing soups, stews, casseroles, and side dishes. Kasha, or buckwheat, a staple grain all over Poland, Russia, and the Ukraine, is very popular with Eastern European Jews, who often ate it as hot breakfast cereal moistened with milk and sweetened with sugar or honey. Kasha and Bow Ties (*kasha var-nishkes*), a favorite savory American Jewish side dish, combines buckwheat, cooked with egg or egg white to keep it fluffy, and bow tie-shaped egg noodles.

Recipes in this chapter reflect dishes planned around cheap staple ingredients. Eastern European immigrants prepared dishes like Barley Casserole with Mushrooms and Thyme, using the traditional dried mushrooms; and for English Jews, kedgeree, a breakfast rice dish dating back to British colonial times, fitted easily into their dairy menus. While many of the bean and grain dishes here are designed as "sides," some, such as Falafel, serve as healthful vegetarian main dishes.

Packaged, quick-cooking versions of cereals and grains, such as couscous, tapioca, and pearl barley, shorten preparation and cooking time. One important tip: To fluff rice and couscous, use a fork; a spoon mashes the tender grains together.

BARLEY CASSEROLE WITH MUSHROOMS AND THYME

Barley and mushrooms make a meaty combination, which is particularly good with sliced brisket.

4 TO 6 SERVINGS

3 tablespoons margarine
3 tablespoons peanut oil
1 large portobello mushroom, cut into ½-inch dice
12 ounces fresh white mushrooms, quartered
1¼ cups pearl barley
1 (1.25-ounce) envelope parve onion soup mix
½ teaspoon dried thyme

1. In a large saucepan, melt margarine with oil over medium-high heat. Add portobello and white mushrooms and cook, stirring often, until lightly browned, 3 to 5 minutes.

2. Add barley, 5½ cups water, onion soup mix, and thyme. Bring to a boil. Cover, reduce heat to low, and cook, stirring often, for 40 minutes, or until barley is tender. If liquid is not completely absorbed, remove lid and continue cooking over low heat for 10 minutes.

BULGUR WITH SUMMER HERBS

*T*his is one of those dishes where adding a bit more or less of one herb doesn't matter. It's bursting with the clean taste of mixed fresh herbs. To save time, use a mini food processor to chop all those herbs.

4 SERVINGS

1 cup bulgur
1 cup coarsely chopped fresh parsley
1 cup coarsely chopped fresh basil
1 cup coarsely chopped fresh mint
3 tablespoons extra-virgin olive oil
2 teaspoons coarse kosher salt
2 teaspoons lemon pepper seasoning

1. Place bulgur in a heatproof bowl and pour enough boiling water over it to cover. Soak for 10 minutes to soften. Drain well. Squeeze with your hands to remove as much moisture as possible.

2. Place bulgur in a medium bowl. Stir in parsley, basil, mint, olive oil, salt, and lemon pepper. Serve at room temperature.

CHICKPEA SALAD

*I*first tasted this piquant chickpea preparation in Florida, where it's a best-seller in kosher markets. Serve in small lettuce-lined bowls as a starter or side salad.

4 TO 6 SERVINGS

2 (16-ounce) cans chickpeas, drained
¼ cup chopped fresh parsley
2 tablespoons chopped red onion
2 tablespoons chopped pimiento
1 garlic clove, minced
3 tablespoons distilled white vinegar
Salt and pepper

1. In a medium bowl, combine chickpeas, parsley, red onion, pimiento, garlic, and vinegar. Gently stir together.

2. Season with salt and generously with pepper to taste. Serve at room temperature.

FALAFEL

*T*his is typical Israeli street food. Dished up hot in paper cups with tahini sauce or stuffed into pita bread with Israeli salad and Zhoug (recipe follows), a flaming hot Middle Eastern "salsa" spooned on top, it's always delicious.

MAKES 30 TO 32; 10 TO 12 SERVINGS

1 cup dried chickpeas, soaked overnight
1 slice of firm-textured white bread
½ small onion, cut up
3 garlic cloves, halved
¼ cup tightly packed fresh parsley
2 tablespoons flour
¾ teaspoon baking powder
1 egg
1 tablespoon ground cumin
2 teaspoons ground coriander
2 teaspoons lemon pepper seasoning
1 teaspoon salt
Vegetable oil for frying
Pita bread, Zhoug (recipe follows) or Harissa (page 212),
  and Israeli Salad (page 191)

1. Drain chickpeas. Place in a food processor and chop finely. Transfer to a mixing bowl.

2. Trim crusts off bread. Soak bread in a small bowl of water until soft. Squeeze to remove excess liquid.

3. In a food processor, combine onion, garlic, and parsley. Pulse until coarsely chopped. Add bread, flour, baking powder, egg, cumin, coriander, lemon pepper, and salt. Process until finely chopped. Add to chickpeas and knead with your hands to mix well.

4. Shape into 1-inch patties about ½ inch thick. Heat ½ inch of oil in a large, heavy skillet over medium-high heat (350°F. on a deep-fat thermometer). Gently slide patties into hot oil. Fry 2 to 3 minutes, turning often, until nicely browned. Serve in pita bread, with Zhoug or Harissa and Israeli Salad.

ZHOUG

This is a red-hot relish, popular to fire up Falafel and shish kebab, that you can watch babushka'd women in the old Yemenite quarter of Tel Aviv pound by hand. It's a cinch to make with the food processor, but wear gloves and don't rub your eyes while handling peppers. If the peppers are seeded and deveined, the Zhoug will be less hot.

MAKES ½ CUP

5 jalapeño peppers, quartered
½ cup fresh parsley
½ cup fresh cilantro
6 garlic cloves
1 teaspoon ground cumin
¼ teaspoon salt

1. In a food processor, combine peppers, parsley, cilantro, and garlic. Process until finely chopped. Add cumin and salt. Process to mix.

2. Store in a tightly lidded container in refrigerator. Use at room temperature.

HARISSA

*I*sraelis slather this fiery North African chili paste on falafel. Serve it as a relish, but warn guests—it's hot!

MAKES ²/₃ CUP

1 cup dried red chili peppers
3 garlic cloves
1 teaspoon salt
¼ cup olive oil

1. Pour enough hot water over chili peppers to cover. Let soak for 20 minutes and drain.

2. In a food processor, finely chop chili peppers, garlic, and salt.

3. Transfer to a bowl and stir in olive oil. Cover and refrigerate. Use at room temperature.

SAFED SALAD

6 SERVINGS

2 (16-ounce) cans chickpeas
½ cup chopped celery
1 medium carrot, peeled and cut into ¼-inch dice
⅓ cup finely chopped sweet onion
2 tablespoons chopped fresh basil
2 tablespoons minced fresh flat-leaf parsley
3 garlic cloves, minced
¼ cup olive oil
2 tablespoons cider vinegar
1 teaspoon salt
1 teaspoon lemon pepper seasoning

1. Dump chickpeas into a colander. Rinse well under cold running water. Drain well.

2. Transfer chickpeas to a large bowl. Add celery, carrot, sweet onion, basil, parsley, garlic, oil, vinegar, salt, and lemon pepper. Toss to mix. Serve at room temperature.

GOLDEN CHALLAH

*T*ry this food processor method just one time with kids helping and it will become a habit. A little saffron gives color; honey adds just a trace of sweetness. One-third cup raisins may be added before kneading.

MAKES 2 SMALL LOAVES OR 1 LARGE LOAF

½ cup tepid water (about 110°F.)
2 tablespoons honey, warmed
1 (¼-ounce) envelope rapid-rise dry yeast
2¾ cups flour
1½ teaspoons salt
¼ teaspoon saffron threads
¼ cup peanut oil
3 eggs
1 tablespoon sesame seeds

1. In a small bowl, mix tepid water and 1 tablespoon honey. Sprinkle on yeast and stir once or twice. Let stand at room temperature until foamy, 10 minutes.

2. In a food processor, mix flour, salt, and saffron. Add yeast mixture, oil, 2 beaten eggs, and remaining 1 tablespoon honey.

3. Process until mixture comes together in a ball, 30 seconds. Turn out onto a floured board. Knead for 2 minutes until smooth. Let rest 10 minutes. Punch down. Divide dough in half if desired for 2 small loaves.

4. If making 1 large loaf, press into a rectangle about 10 by 6 inches; if making 2 small loaves, press each half into an 8 by 4-inch rectangle. Cut rectangle into 3 strips lengthwise. Pinch together at one end. Braid by bringing right strip over center, then left over center, repeating until you come to the end. Pinch ends together and tuck under.

5. Place on oiled baking sheet. Cover lightly with a kitchen towel. Set in a warm, draft-free place until double in size, about 1 hour.

6. Preheat oven to 375°F. Beat remaining egg and brush over challahs. Sprinkle with sesame seeds.

7. Bake until deep golden and bread sounds hollow when tapped on bottom with fingers, 25 minutes for small loaves, 40 minutes for 1 large loaf. Let cool on wire rack. Serve at room temperature.

COCHIN SPICED COUSCOUS

Cochin, on the west coast of India, was one of the main Jewish centers of the spice trade. Though we normally think of couscous as a savory dish, this one is sweetened and mixed with fruit and is offered as a dessert.

4 TO 6 SERVINGS

1 cup couscous
1 tablespoon fresh lime juice
½ teaspoon ground cinnamon
¼ teaspoon ground cardamom
Pinch of grated nutmeg
2 tablespoons brown sugar
1 medium banana, chopped
1 (8-ounce) can crushed pineapple, drained
1 ripe mango, peeled and cut into ½-inch dice
2 tablespoons chopped pistachios
Nondairy whipped topping

1. In a medium saucepan, bring 1½ cups water to a boil over high heat. Remove from heat. Stir in couscous, lime juice, cinnamon, cardamom, nutmeg, and brown sugar. Cover and let stand 5 minutes.

2. In a large serving bowl, combine banana, pineapple, mango, and pistachios.

3. Fluff couscous with a fork. Add fruit mixture and fold gently to combine. Serve warm with nondairy whipped topping.

QUICK CURRIED COUSCOUS

Jews have lived in Calcutta, India, for 200 years. This marriage of Middle Eastern and Indian ingredients blends the spice and spirit of two cultures.

4 SERVINGS

3 tablespoons olive oil
1 (10-ounce) package couscous
2 teaspoons curry powder
¼ cup fruit chutney
¼ cup chopped peanuts
⅓ cup chopped fresh cilantro
½ teaspoon sumac or ¼ teaspoon nutmeg

1. In a medium saucepan, bring 2¼ cups water to a boil over high heat. Add olive oil. Stir in couscous, cover, and remove from heat. Let stand undisturbed for 5 minutes. Fluff with a fork.

2. Stir in curry powder, chutney, peanuts, and half of cilantro. Cook over medium-low heat for 5 minutes, stirring several times.

3. Spoon into a serving dish and sprinkle remaining cilantro and sumac or nutmeg over top.

KASHA AND BOW TIES

*I*n the poor soil of many Eastern European countries, kasha, or buckwheat, was one of the few grains to flourish. Combined with noodles, usually bow ties, it is a favorite of Ashkenazi Jews. Roasted walnut oil, chopped walnuts, and a pinch of ground cloves enhance the flavor of this hearty side dish.

4 TO 6 SERVINGS

2 cups bow ties
1 cup coarse kasha
1 whole egg or 2 egg whites, beaten
2 cups boiling water
1½ teaspoons salt
⅓ cup chopped walnuts
2 tablespoons walnut oil
Pinch of ground cloves
¾ teaspoon pepper

1. In a large saucepan of boiling salted water, cook bow ties until tender but still firm. Drain well.

2. In a large saucepan, mix kasha and egg. Cook over medium heat, stirring constantly, until grains are dry and separate, about 2 minutes.

3. Remove from heat. Carefully stir in boiling water and ¾ teaspoon salt. Cover and cook over medium heat until water is absorbed and grains are dry, 10 to 12 minutes. Fluff with a fork.

4. Add bow ties, walnuts, walnut oil, cloves, remaining ¾ teaspoon salt, and pepper. Stir over medium-low heat to heat through, 5 minutes. Season with pepper and remaining salt. Serve hot.

KASHA WITH CARROTS

*T*his one-pot side dish is refreshed with a generous handful of parsley. Kasha cooked this way is easy and delicious.

4 SERVINGS

½ cup whole kasha
1 egg white, lightly beaten
1⅓ cups hot vegetable broth
1 (16-ounce) bag frozen baby carrots, thawed
½ cup chopped fresh parsley
2 garlic cloves, minced
1 teaspoon salt
½ teaspoon pepper

1. In a medium saucepan, stir kasha and egg white with fork. Cook over high heat, stirring constantly, until kasha is slightly toasted and grains separate, 2 to 3 minutes.

2. Remove from heat. Carefully add vegetable broth (it can splatter), carrots, parsley, garlic, salt, and pepper.

3. Bring to a boil over medium heat. Reduce heat to low. Cover and cook 10 minutes, or until kasha is tender. Serve hot.

LEBANESE LENTIL SALAD

*L*entils, along with dried beans and pulses, have always been looked down as peasant food, but lentil dishes are served on festive occasions by Sephardic Jews. In fact, they are traditional on the "Meatless Days" that precede the fast day of Tisha B'Av, the day that commemorates the destruction of the Temples.

6 SERVINGS

1½ cups dried lentils
1 medium sweet onion, chopped
¾ cup currants
½ cup sweet-and-sour salad dressing
2 teaspoons brown sugar
1 tablespoon ground cumin
1 teaspoon salt
¼ teaspoon pepper
¼ cup chopped fresh cilantro

1. Rinse lentils and pick over to remove any grit. In a medium saucepan, bring 4 cups water to a boil. Add lentils, reduce heat to medium-low, and simmer, uncovered, stirring occasionally, until lentils are tender but still slightly chewy, 20 to 25 minutes; drain.

2. Transfer lentils to a bowl. Stir in onion, currants, salad dressing, brown sugar, cumin, salt, and pepper. Sprinkle cilantro on top. Serve at room temperature.

SMOKED SALMON KEDGEREE WITH SUN-DRIED TOMATOES

*I*was inspired to add chopped smoked salmon (lox) and dill instead of smoked haddock to this popular British breakfast dish. It's one of the first dishes to disappear at Sunday morning brunches in my house.

4 TO 6 SERVINGS

1 tablespoon olive oil
2 shallots, minced
1⅓ cups long-grain white rice
1 teaspoon turmeric
⅛ teaspoon grated nutmeg
1 teaspoon salt
Pinch of cayenne
2½ cups vegetable broth
1 tablespoon cider vinegar
3 to 4 ounces smoked salmon, chopped
3 tablespoons chopped sun-dried tomatoes
2 tablespoons chopped fresh dill or 1½ teaspoons dried
3 hard-cooked eggs

1. In a medium saucepan, heat oil over medium heat. Add shallots and cook until soft, 2 to 3 minutes.

2. Stir in rice, turmeric, nutmeg, salt, and cayenne. Add broth and vinegar. Bring to a boil over high heat. Stir once, cover, and reduce heat to medium. Cook 18 to 20 minutes. Rice should be slightly chewy.

3. Remove from heat. Stir in salmon, sun-dried tomatoes, and dill. Transfer to a serving dish. Chop egg whites and spoon around edge of dish. Press egg yolks through a sieve to garnish top. Serve hot.

WHEATBERRY SALAD

Wheatberries are whole, unprocessed kernels of wheat. They are a rich source of vitamins and fiber, are available in health food stores, and are an inexpensive source of protein.

4 SERVINGS

½ cup wheatberries
1½ tablespoons red wine vinegar
1 tablespoon Dijon mustard
1 tablespoon honey
¼ cup olive oil
1½ cups diced jicama
½ cup chopped fresh cilantro
½ cup dried cranberries
Salt and pepper

1. Place wheatberries in a bowl and add enough cold water to cover by about 1 inch. Refrigerate and soak overnight.

2. Drain wheatberries and place in a saucepan with 2 cups fresh cold water. Bring to a simmer over medium heat. Cover and cook until wheatberries are chewy, about 20 minutes; drain.

3. In a mixing bowl, whisk together vinegar, mustard, and honey. Gradually whisk in oil until blended. Add wheatberries and toss to coat.

4. Add jicama, cilantro, and dried cranberries and toss again. Season with salt and pepper to taste. Serve at room temperature.

WHEATBERRY, ONION, AND PEPPER PILAF

*W*ith all the current attention to good nutrition, Jewish cooks, like everyone else, are looking for new ways to incorporate more whole grains into their families' diets. Here's one: a fine side dish to serve with meat or chicken. If you don't see wheatberries in your supermarket, you'll find them at any health food store.

4 TO 6 SERVINGS

1½ cups wheatberries
2 tablespoons peanut or other vegetable oil
2 medium onions, cut into ½-inch dice
1 small red bell pepper, cut into ½-inch dice
1 garlic clove, minced
¾ teaspoon dried savory
1 teaspoon salt
½ teaspoon pepper

1. Place wheatberries in a bowl with enough cold water to cover by at least 1 inch. Cover bowl and refrigerate overnight.

2. Drain wheatberries and transfer to a medium saucepan. Pour 3 cups boiling water over wheatberries. Cook over medium heat, stirring often, until wheatberries are tender and chewy, about 20 minutes; drain.

3. Heat oil in a large skillet over medium heat. Add onions and cook over medium heat, stirring occasionally, until softened and translucent, about 3 minutes. Add bell pepper, garlic, and savory. Cook, stirring, until pepper is crisp-tender but still bright red, about 3 minutes longer.

4. Scrape contents of skillet over wheatberries. Add salt and pepper and mix well. Serve hot.

WILD RICE AND BULGUR SALAD WITH CURRANTS

*N*o need to cook bulgur. Just soak it in hot water to slightly tenderize but retain the nutty crunchiness. This is a nicely flavored side dish for poultry.

4 TO 6 SERVINGS

1 cup wild rice
½ cup bulgur
1 small red onion, minced
⅓ cup currants
¼ cup chopped fresh cilantro
3 tablespoons fresh lemon juice
¼ cup sweet-and-sour salad dressing
1 tablespoon cumin
Salt and pepper

1. Rinse wild rice. Place in pan with 4 cups water. Cover and bring to a boil over high heat. Reduce heat to medium. Cook rice until chewy-tender, about 30 minutes; drain.

2. While rice is cooking, cover bulgur with boiling water to about ½ inch above bulgur. Let stand 20 minutes, then drain.

3. Combine cooked wild rice, bulgur, red onion, currants, cilantro, lemon juice, salad dressing, and cumin. Season with salt and pepper to taste. Serve hot or at room temperature.

COUSCOUS WITH PRUNES AND ALMONDS

Here's a typical North African dish festive with glazed fruit and nuts that is served in Sephardic homes at Rosh Hashanah to symbolize a fruitful year. It goes well with lamb or chicken. You can make this parve by substituting water or vegetable broth for the chicken broth.

4 TO 6 SERVINGS

2¼ cups chicken broth
½ teaspoon salt
1 (10-ounce) package couscous
2 tablespoons vegetable oil
1 medium onion, minced
¼ cup whole almonds
16 pitted prunes
2 tablespoons cinnamon-sugar

1. In a medium saucepan, bring chicken broth and salt to a boil. Stir in couscous. Cover and remove from heat. Let stand 5 minutes. Press couscous into a dome shape in serving dish and keep warm.

2. In a small skillet, heat oil over medium heat. Add onion and cook for 3 to 4 minutes, until softened.

3. Add almonds and prunes. Cook over medium heat for 5 minutes, stirring often. Spoon around base of couscous dome.

4. Sprinkle with cinnamon-sugar. Serve hot.

LEMON-PARSLEY COUSCOUS WITH BULGUR

*T*his fragrant, pleasing combination of couscous and bulgur makes a lively side dish with roast chicken or fish. The two grains give it a sturdier texture than delicate couscous has alone. Use vegetable broth instead of chicken broth to make the dish parve.

4 SERVINGS

½ cup bulgur
Boiling water
1¼ cups chicken broth
1 tablespoon olive oil
2 teaspoons salt
¾ cup couscous
½ pickled lemon (page 24), chopped*
¼ cup chopped fresh flat-leaf parsley
1 teaspoon paprika
½ teaspoon pepper

M E A T

1. Place bulgur in a small heatproof bowl. Add enough boiling water to cover. Let soak 15 minutes to soften. Drain well.

2. In a medium saucepan, bring chicken broth, olive oil, and 1 teaspoon salt to a boil over medium-high heat. Stir in couscous. Remove from heat. Cover and let stand 5 minutes. Fluff with a fork.

3. Add drained bulgur, pickled lemon, parsley, paprika, pepper, and remaining 1 teaspoon salt. Stir to mix. Serve hot.

NOTE: To make a substitute for pickled lemon, place 4 thick lemon slices in a small saucepan of boiling water. Cook for 3 minutes, until skin has lost its raw look; drain. Chop and mix with 1 teaspoon olive oil.

CHAPTER EIGHT

Noodles and Kugels

*I*n my mother's house, *lokshen* was the collective word for all noodles and pasta, but unlike her mother—my grandmother—she never made them from scratch. There was no need. Noodles are inexpensive, they come in dozens of shapes and thicknesses, and those prepared without egg yolks are cholesterol-free. And don't forget, these days another word for noodles is pasta, an all-American favorite, even in Jewish homes.

Kugels, baked puddings usually made from potatoes or noodles and bound with eggs, were common eating for Eastern European Jews. Starch based, rich, and comforting, they packed in a lot of calories. Most important, they were warm and filling.

Creative cooks adapted the basics into well-seasoned hearty main dishes, such as Beef-Noodle Kugel, as well as delicate, luscious desserts, such as Apple and Almond Kugel, a favorite on Shavuot, when dairy dishes are appropriate. A distinctive feature of Jewish kugels is that they can be sweet or savory, and even mildly sweet kugels are usually served as a side dish along with the main course. But sweet kugels are also served as dessert, especially after a light meal, or as a substantial snack.

Look also in the Passover chapter for several kugels that are made with matzoh meal, designed especially for Passover, but which are, in fact, good all year-round.

FARFEL WITH PLUM TOMATOES AND PINE NUTS

*T*raditional and contemporary ingredients here actually represent a blending of Ashkenazic and Sephardic cultures. In winter, use Israeli tomatoes for sweetest flavor and ripeness. Serve as a side dish with brisket or roast chicken.

6 TO 8 SERVINGS

1 tablespoon olive oil
2 medium onions, thinly sliced
1 small celery rib, chopped
1½ cups farfel
3 cups boiling water
1 teaspoon salt
¼ teaspoon pepper
⅓ cup pine nuts
4 plum tomatoes, cut into 8 wedges each

1. In a medium saucepan, heat olive oil over medium-low heat. Add onions and celery and cook, stirring occasionally, until vegetables are softened, 8 to 10 minutes.

2. Add farfel, boiling water, salt, and pepper. Cover and bring to a boil over high heat, stirring a few times. Reduce heat to medium and cook, covered, for 10 minutes. Add pine nuts and tomatoes. Cook, uncovered, until farfel is soft and water is absorbed, 10 minutes.

VARIATION: This makes a delicious, nutty kugel. In step 2, after adding pine nuts and tomatoes, stir in 2 eggs, ½ cup diced red bell pepper or pimiento, and a handful of chopped fresh herbs, such as dill or parsley. Pour into a greased 9-inch square baking dish. Drizzle a couple of tablespoons olive oil on top. Bake in preheated 350°F. oven for 45 minutes, until browned and crisp on top.

FETTUCCINE WITH LEEKS

If you use a pesto sauce that contains cheese, the flavor will be lovely, but keep in mind the dish will then be dairy.

4 TO 6 SERVINGS

1 pound fettuccine
2 tablespoons olive oil
2 medium leeks (white and tender green), well rinsed and
   cut into 1-inch pieces
1 teaspoon oregano
1 teaspoon salt
¼ teaspoon pepper
3 tablespoons fresh lemon juice
1½ teaspoons grated lemon zest
⅓ cup parve basil pesto sauce
¼ cup toasted pine nuts*

1. In a large pot of salted boiling water, cook fettuccine until tender but still slightly firm, 10 to 12 minutes. Drain into a colander.

2. Meanwhile, in a large skillet, heat oil over medium heat. Add leeks, oregano, salt, pepper, and 3 tablespoons water. Cover and cook until leeks are soft, 10 to 15 minutes. Stir in lemon juice, lemon zest, and pesto.

3. Spoon over hot cooked fettuccine. Toss to mix well. Season with additional salt and pepper to taste. Transfer to a serving dish and sprinkle pine nuts on top.

*To toast pine nuts: Microwave on High for about 1 minute, until golden; check after 45 seconds. Or spread on a small baking tray and toast in a 375°F. oven or in a toaster oven for 5 to 7 minutes.

NOODLES WITH POPPY SEEDS AND DILL

*P*oppy seeds have long been used by Jews of Central and Eastern Europe in sweet and savory dishes. This is a deliciously pretty dish flecked with orange, green, and black.

4 TO 6 SERVINGS

3 tablespoons peanut oil
3 tablespoons poppy seeds
1 pound medium egg noodles, cooked and drained
1 small carrot, grated
¼ cup chopped fresh dill or 1 tablespoon dried
Salt and pepper

1. Heat oil in a small skillet over medium-high heat. Add poppy seeds and cook 1 minute, stirring constantly. Pour over cooked noodles.

2. Add carrot and dill and stir to mix. Season with salt and pepper to taste. Serve hot.

APPLE AND ALMOND KUGEL

10 TO 12 SERVINGS

1½ cups chopped dried pears
½ cup dried cranberries
¼ cup brandy
2 Granny Smith apples, cored and chopped
1 (21-ounce) can apple pie filling
1 pound small pasta shells (orecchiette), cooked and drained
3 eggs, beaten
1 tablespoon grated orange zest
2 teaspoons cinnamon
⅓ cup packed brown sugar
⅓ cup ground almonds

1. Preheat oven to 350°F. Coat a large baking dish with nonstick cooking spray.

2. Place dried pears and cranberries in a small bowl. Pour brandy over fruit. Stir and cover tightly with plastic wrap. Set aside for 30 minutes.

3. In a separate bowl, mix apples, apple pie filling, pasta, eggs, orange zest, and cinnamon. Stir in dried fruit and brandy mixture.

4. Transfer to prepared baking dish. Mix brown sugar and ground almonds. Sprinkle over top of kugel.

5. Bake in preheated oven for 1 hour, or until golden brown and set in center. Serve hot or at room temperature.

JERUSALEM KUGEL

*T*his unusual kugel is served at every *simcha* (celebration) in Mea Shearim, the strictly orthodox area in Jerusalem. I always add dates for mellow sweetness; they contrast nicely with the crisp, peppery dish. If you want to, double the recipe and bake it in a 10-inch springform pan.

6 SERVINGS

⅓ cup olive oil
⅓ cup sugar
8 ounces vermicelli, cooked and drained
¾ teaspoon salt
2 teaspoons lemon pepper seasoning
2 eggs, beaten
¼ cup chopped dates

1. Preheat oven to 350°F. Coat a 9-inch square baking dish with nonstick vegetable spray.

2. In a medium, heavy-bottomed saucepan, mix oil and sugar. Cook over medium heat, stirring constantly, until sugar turns golden, 7 minutes.

3. Remove from heat and immediately stir in vermicelli, salt, and lemon pepper. If sugar mixture becomes lumpy, stir over low heat until sugar melts.

4. Refrigerate 15 minutes to cool. Stir in eggs and dates.

5. Spoon into prepared baking dish. Bake in preheated oven until golden brown and crisp on top, 40 minutes. Serve warm or at room temperature.

ONE-STEP KUGEL

Mixed in one bowl so there's no messy cleanup, this is also convenient because it freezes well. It is terrific to have on hand for a meat or dairy meal.

6 TO 8 SERVINGS

½ pound medium egg noodles, cooked and drained
1 cup nondairy creamer
3 eggs
⅓ cup sugar
⅓ cup raisins
⅓ cup chopped walnuts
2 tablespoons chopped crystallized ginger
2 tablespoons fresh lemon juice
4 tablespoons margarine, melted

1. Preheat oven to 350°F. Coat a 9-inch square baking dish with nonstick vegetable spray.

2. In a large bowl, mix noodles with ½ cup water, nondairy creamer, eggs, sugar, raisins, walnuts, crystallized ginger, lemon juice, and melted margarine. Transfer to prepared baking dish.

3. Bake 1 hour in preheated oven, until crusty and firm in center. Serve warm.

ROASTED PEPPER KUGEL

*F*or Rosh Hashanah, I make this with yellow and red bell peppers and, to boost flavor, handfuls of fresh herbs. If you're not having a lot of people for dinner, make two small kugels and freeze one for the Yom Kippur breaking of the fast.

12 TO 15 SERVINGS

1 pound rotini noodles
1 (14-ounce) jar all-natural spaghetti sauce
3 eggs, lightly beaten
2 cups coarsely chopped loosely packed mixed fresh herbs, such as basil, parsley, and dill
1 teaspoon lemon pepper seasoning
1½ teaspoons coarse kosher salt
2 large red bell peppers, cut into 1½-inch pieces
1 large yellow bell pepper, cut into 1½-inch pieces
3 tablespoons olive oil

1. Preheat oven to 350°F. Coat a large baking dish with nonstick vegetable spray.

2. In a large pot of salted boiling water, cook the rotini until tender but still slightly firm, 10 to 12 minutes. Drain and transfer to a large bowl.

3. Add spaghetti sauce, eggs, fresh herbs, lemon pepper, and ½ teaspoon salt to pasta. Turn into prepared baking dish.

4. Arrange peppers on top of pasta mixture to cover. Drizzle olive oil over top. Sprinkle with the remaining 1 teaspoon salt. Cover loosely with aluminum foil.

5. Bake in preheated oven for 40 minutes. Remove foil and bake until center is set and peppers are beginning to brown, about 20 minutes longer. Serve hot or at room temperature.

FRESH PINEAPPLE-APPLESAUCE KUGEL

With three married daughters and their families, my Aunt Eva's used to cooking for a crowd. I use fresh pineapple for superb flavor but you can substitute a 16-ounce can of undrained crushed pineapple.

8 TO 10 SERVINGS

½ pound medium egg noodles
5 eggs, beaten
¼ cup vegetable oil
2 cups chopped fresh pineapple
1 (16-ounce) jar chunky applesauce
¾ cup sugar
1½ teaspoons cinnamon
½ teaspoon salt
⅓ cup crushed cornflakes

1. Preheat oven to 375°F. Coat a 9-by-12-inch baking dish with non-stick vegetable spray. In a large pot of lightly salted boiling water, cook noodles until tender but still slightly firm, 5 to 7 minutes.

2. In a large bowl, blend eggs, oil, pineapple, applesauce, sugar, 1 teaspoon cinnamon, and salt. Add noodles and stir gently to mix.

3. Transfer to prepared baking dish. Mix cornflakes with ½ teaspoon cinnamon; sprinkle evenly over kugel.

4. Bake in preheated oven about 50 minutes, until browned and firm in center when touched lightly with fingers. This kugel is equally delicious hot, cold, or at room temperature.

VEGETABLE AND MUSHROOM KUGEL

8 TO 10 SERVINGS

¼ cup Italian salad dressing
1 medium Vidalia onion, chopped
2 cups sliced mushrooms
1 large yellow bell pepper, cut into ½-inch dice
1 large red bell pepper, cut into ½-inch dice
½ pound asparagus, thinly sliced (2 cups)
1 (10-ounce) package thawed frozen French-style green beans
½ cup chopped fresh parsley
1 (10-ounce) package thawed frozen pureed butternut squash
3 eggs, beaten
⅓ cup matzoh meal
2 teaspoons dried oregano
1½ teaspoons salt
1 teaspoon pepper
2 tablespoons margarine

1. Preheat oven to 350°F. Coat a large baking dish with nonstick vegetable spray.

2. In a medium skillet, heat salad dressing. Add onion and mushrooms and cook over medium-high heat until onion is translucent, stirring often, about 10 minutes.

3. Transfer to a large mixing bowl. Add yellow and red bell peppers, asparagus, green beans, parsley, squash, eggs, matzoh meal, oregano, salt, and pepper. Pour into prepared baking dish. Dot with margarine.

4. Bake in preheated oven 45 minutes, or until nicely browned and firm in center. Cut into squares and serve hot.

BEEF-NOODLE KUGEL

*F*or a simple, everyday supper, here's a tasty main dish that freezes well. All it needs is a green vegetable or tossed salad on the side. To lighten the dish, ground turkey can be substituted for all or half of the beef.

4 SERVINGS

½ pound bow-tie pasta (farfalle)
2 tablespoons oil
1 pound lean ground beef
2 medium onions, chopped
1 (14½-ounce) can stewed tomatoes
1 cup sliced fresh mushrooms
1 cup thawed frozen peas
1 teaspoon dried tarragon
½ teaspoon dried basil
1 teaspoon salt
¼ teaspoon pepper
3 eggs, beaten

1. Preheat oven to 350°F. Coat a 9-inch square baking dish with nonstick vegetable spray. In a large saucepan of salted boiling water, cook the pasta until tender but still slightly firm, about 12 minutes; drain.

2. Meanwhile, in a large skillet, heat oil over medium-high heat. Add beef and cook, stirring, until no pink remains, about 5 minutes. Remove from heat.

3. Add onions, stewed tomatoes, mushrooms, peas, cooked bow ties, tarragon, basil, salt, and pepper to beef. Stir lightly to mix. Let cool 5 minutes, then stir in eggs. Transfer to prepared baking dish.

4. Bake in preheated oven 1 hour, or until kugel is until nicely browned on top and firm in center. Serve hot.

M E A T

FEINEKUCHEN

Sometimes it's nice to have a dish just for one. Think of this big pancake whenever there are some leftover noodles in your fridge. I like it either for breakfast or for a light supper.

1 SERVING

2 eggs
2 tablespoons milk
½ teaspoon salt
¼ teaspoon pepper
½ cup cooked noodles
1 tablespoon butter
1 tablespoon cinnamon-sugar or fruit preserves

1. In a small bowl, whisk eggs, milk, salt, and pepper. Stir in cooked noodles.

2. In a small skillet, melt butter over medium-high heat. Pour in noodle mixture. Reduce heat to medium and cook 3 to 4 minutes, until pancake is browned and firm enough to flip. Turn over and cook 3 to 4 minutes longer, until both sides are nicely browned and crisp.

3. Sprinkle with cinnamon-sugar or spread with preserves. Fold over and eat out of hand like a sandwich or conventionally with knife and fork.

DAIRY

BUTTER-CRUMB MACARONI

*T*his is a favorite childhood recipe of my friend and colleague, Myra Chanin. It proves that the best dishes are often the simplest. Here there is no substitute for butter.

4 SERVINGS

3 tablespoons butter
1¼ cups coarse fresh white bread crumbs
2 cups cottage cheese
2 scallions, chopped
4 cups hot cooked macaroni
1 teaspoon salt
1 teaspoon pepper

1. In a small skillet, melt butter over medium heat. Add bread crumbs. Cook, stirring often, until crumbs take on a deep golden color, about 10 minutes.

2. Stir cottage cheese and scallions into macaroni.

3. Fold in browned buttered crumbs. Season with salt and pepper to taste. Eat while warm.

DAIRY

TRIPLE-CHEESE MACARONI CASSEROLE

I serve this easy dish on Shavuot, as it fits right in with the concept of dairy dishes for this holiday. Serve with Israeli Salad (page 191) or crisp greens.

4 TO 6 SERVINGS

12 ounces elbow macaroni
¼ cup Dijon mustard
⅛ teaspoon grated nutmeg
2 cups shredded sharp Cheddar cheese
2 cups low-fat cottage cheese
⅓ cup grated Parmesan cheese
¼ cup milk
1 large tomato, cut into 12 thin wedges

1. Preheat oven to 375°F. Coat a 2½-quart baking dish with nonstick vegetable spray. In a large saucepan of salted boiling water, cook the macaroni until tender but still firm, about 7 to 9 minutes. Drain into a colander.

2. In a large bowl, mix macaroni, mustard, nutmeg, Cheddar cheese, cottage cheese, ¼ cup Parmesan cheese, and milk. Spoon into prepared baking dish.

3. Overlap tomato wedges in an attractive design on top of macaroni mixture. Sprinkle remaining Parmesan on top.

4. Bake in preheated oven until heated through and browned, about 20 minutes. Serve hot.

DAIRY

OMA'S NOODLES AND BLUEBERRIES

My husband, Walter, remembers his grandmother handing him a tin pail and sending him out to a nearby farm to pick blueberries for this hot compote. Use margarine in place of butter to turn this into a parve dish.

4 TO 6 SERVINGS

8 ounces medium egg noodles
⅓ cup sugar
2 tablespoons fresh lemon juice
4 cups blueberries
2 tablespoons butter
2 tablespoons cinnamon-sugar

1. In a large saucepan of boiling water, cook noodles until tender but still firm, 5 to 7 minutes. Drain into a colander.

2. Meanwhile, in a nonreactive medium saucepan, mix sugar, lemon juice, blueberries, and 3 tablespoons water. Bring to a boil over medium-high heat, stirring to dissolve sugar, about 5 minutes. Immediately remove from heat.

3. In a large bowl, toss hot noodles with butter and cinnamon-sugar. Divide among bowls. Pour blueberry sauce over noodles. Serve hot.

DAIRY

CREAMY DESSERT KUGEL WITH CAPPUCCINO TOPPING

A dairy-rich, irresistible kugel, which absolutely melts in the mouth. Serve at Shavuot or a large gathering, such as a brit. Ingredients may be halved and baked in a 9-inch square baking dish.

12 TO 15 SERVINGS

1 (8-ounce) package fine egg noodles
2 sticks (8 ounces) unsalted butter, at room temperature
1 (8-ounce) package cream cheese, at room temperature
1 cup sugar
6 eggs
1 pint sour cream
2 teaspoons vanilla extract
¼ cup crushed cornflakes
2 teaspoons instant cappuccino coffee mix

1. Preheat oven to 350°F. Coat a large baking dish with nonstick vegetable spray. In a large pot of lightly salted boiling water, cook noodles until just tender, about 5 minutes; drain. Spread cooked noodles over bottom of baking dish.

2. In a large bowl, cream butter, cream cheese, and sugar until light and fluffy, 2 minutes. Beat in eggs, sour cream, and vanilla until well blended. Pour over noodles.

3. In a small bowl, mix cornflakes and instant cappuccino coffee mix. Sprinkle evenly over kugel.

4. Bake in preheated oven for 1 hour, or until firm to touch in center and nicely browned. Serve warm or at room temperature.

DAIRY

PECAN-CRUSTED FIG KUGEL

Sephardic flavors combine with traditional Ashkenazic ingredients here to make a delicious kugel pie.

6 TO 8 SERVINGS

1 (8-ounce) package fine egg noodles
½ cup vanilla yogurt
½ cup cottage cheese
½ cup chopped dried figs
2 eggs
¼ cup packed brown sugar
½ teaspoon ground cardamom
½ teaspoon salt
¼ cup coarsely chopped pecans

1. Preheat oven to 350°F. Coat a 10-inch pie dish with nonstick vegetable spray. In a large pot of lightly salted boiling water, cook noodles until just tender, 5 to 7 minutes; drain.

2. In a medium bowl, blend yogurt, cottage cheese, figs, eggs, 2 tablespoons brown sugar, cardamom, and salt. Add noodles and stir gently to mix. Pour into prepared dish.

3. In a small bowl, mix chopped pecans with remaining 2 tablespoons brown sugar. Sprinkle over noodles.

4. Bake in preheated oven 35 minutes, or until browned on top and firm in center. Cut into wedges and serve hot or at room temperature.

DAIRY

PINEAPPLE BABKA PUDDING

Any leftover, day-old babka or other plain yeast coffee cake will do nicely for this kugel. Serve the old-fashioned way with a pitcher of milk to pour over it.

8 SERVINGS

6 tablespoons butter, at room temperature
¾ cup sugar
3 eggs
2 tablespoons fresh lemon juice
1 teaspoon grated lemon zest
½ teaspoon almond extract
1 (20-ounce) can crushed pineapple, undrained
⅓ cup dried cherries
6 slices of babka, torn into bite-size chunks (about 4 cups)

1. Preheat oven to 350°F. Coat a 2-quart casserole with nonstick vegetable spray. In a large bowl, beat butter and sugar until pale and fluffy. Beat in eggs, lemon juice, lemon zest, almond extract, pineapple, and dried cherries. Fold in babka chunks.

2. Transfer to prepared casserole. Let stand 10 minutes at room temperature for babka to soak up some of the liquid.

3. Bake in preheated oven 45 minutes, or until puffy and browned. Serve warm.

NOTE: To make parve, use a parve babka and substitute margarine for butter.

DAIRY

UPSIDE-DOWN PINEAPPLE KUGEL

*T*hanks to Pearl Gendason for sharing her kugel for a crowd. This was a prizewinning recipe in the *Baltimore Jewish Times*.

12 TO 15 SERVINGS

1 pound no-yolk noodles, cooked and drained
1 stick (4 ounces) low-calorie margarine, melted
¼ cup packed light brown sugar
2 teaspoons cinnamon
1 (16-ounce) can pineapple slices, drained
16 to 20 dried apricots
1 cup low-fat sour cream
3 ounces light cream cheese, at room temperature
1 pound fat-free cottage cheese
2½ tablespoons granulated sugar
1 cup egg substitute, such as Egg Beaters
1 (8-ounce) can crushed pineapple, drained
⅓ cup raisins
½ teaspoon salt

1. Preheat oven to 350°F. In a large pot of lightly salted boiling water, cook noodles until tender but still slightly firm, 5 to 7 minutes. Pour 4 tablespoons margarine into a large baking dish and tilt to spread. Stir in brown sugar and cinnamon. Arrange pineapple slices and apricots attractively in brown sugar mixture.

2. Blend sour cream and cream cheese. Add remaining margarine, cottage cheese, granulated sugar, egg substitute, crushed pineapple, raisins, and salt. Mix well. Add noodles and stir lightly to mix. Pour over fruit in baking dish.

3. Cover loosely with aluminum foil. Bake 1 hour in preheated oven. Remove foil and bake until browned and firm in center, about 30 minutes longer. Let cool 10 minutes.

4. Loosen edges with a knife. Turn out onto a serving dish large enough to hold kugel. Cut into squares. Serve hot or at room temperature.

DAIRY

STICKY BUN KUGEL

My friend Jewel treasures old-fashioned recipes collected over the years. This loaf-pan kugel, crowned with brown sugar and nuts, is certain to become a family favorite. To make it parve, substitute margarine for butter.

8 SERVINGS

½ pound wide egg noodles
1 stick (4 ounces) butter, at room temperature, softened
⅓ cup brown sugar
½ cup pecan halves
2 eggs
2 tablespoons granulated sugar
1½ teaspoons cinnamon
2 tablespoons fresh lemon juice

1. Preheat oven to 350°F. Coat a 9-by-5-by-3-inch loaf pan with nonstick vegetable spray. In a large saucepan of lightly salted boiling water, cook egg noodles until tender but still slightly firm, about 7 minutes; drain.

2. Meanwhile, in a small bowl, mix 6 tablespoons butter with brown sugar until well blended. Spread over bottom of loaf pan. Press pecan halves, flat sides up, into brown sugar.

3. Beat remaining butter, eggs, granulated sugar, cinnamon, and lemon juice. Fold in cooked noodles. Transfer to prepared loaf pan.

4. Bake in preheated oven 45 minutes, or until kugel is firm and browned on top. Let cool 5 minutes. Loosen edges of kugel with a knife and turn out onto serving platter. Serve hot.

DAIRY

CHAPTER NINE

Blintzes, Knishes, and Latkes

*P*ractically every country in the world has some kind of thin dough wrapper or pancake that it uses to enclose any variety of fillings. In France, for example, it's the crepe; in China, the wonton skin or Mandarin pancake. In Jewish cooking, it's the blintz leaf, of course, which Jewish cooks wrap around all sorts of sweet and savory fillings. Cook up a batch of blintz leaves, using a nonstick skillet, then freeze to fill when you have time. Or fill a batch and freeze to pull out as needed. Here I've included a recipe for blintz leaves plus at least half a dozen assorted fillings. There are also a number of recipes that take prepared blintzes—your own leftovers or purchased—and turn them into something even more delicious than they were to begin with. Most of these recipes are simple and quick, so you don't have to save them just for weekends.

Knishes, pastry wrapped around meat, potato, and even grain fillings and then baked, are akin to Polish pirogi. Savory and hot, they can be baked and then frozen, ready whenever you need them as a warming snack, hot appetizer, or filling accompaniment to a bowl of soup. While they can take some time to assemble, I've given foolproof food processor directions for the dough. And one recipe for Quick Knishes with Bulgur, Potatoes, and Browned Onions is made with prepared puff pastry and formed in long rolls, which are sliced after baking, so labor is kept to a minimum.

After chicken soup and matzoh balls, latkes are probably one of the most treasured Jewish foods. Now they come in all sorts of sizes and flavors. Along with Classic Potato Latkes, traditional during Chanukah to commemorate the miracle of the oil that miraculously lasted the Maccabeans eight days, I've included such recipes as Glick's Colossal Butternut Latkes, Fresh Salmon Latkes, and Maple-Drenched Almond Latkes, perfect for a Chanukah dessert.

Besides the big three of the title, I've used this chapter as a catch-all for other Jewish savories, including a vegetarian version of kishke, wrapped in aluminum foil rather than casings, and Kreplach, beef dumplings not unlike Italian ravioli. Contemporary ingredients and appliances make preparation of all these Jewish pastries simpler and easier than ever before.

CLASSIC POTATO LATKES

Here is my food processor method for traditional potato latkes, the most popular latkes in America. These originated in Eastern Europe, where potatoes were cheap and plentiful.

MAKES 24

2 eggs
¼ small onion, cut into 3 pieces
4 medium potatoes, peeled and cut into 1-inch pieces
¼ teaspoon baking powder
3 tablespoons flour
1 teaspoon salt
¼ teaspoon pepper
Vegetable oil for frying
Applesauce or sour cream

1. Break eggs into a food processor. Add onion and potatoes. Process until potatoes are coarsely chopped. Add baking powder, flour, salt, and pepper. Pulse 3 or 4 times to mix.

2. Heat ⅛ inch of oil in a large skillet over medium heat. Drop rounded tablespoonfuls of potato mixture into skillet; press lightly with back of a spoon to flatten slightly. Cook on both sides until brown, about 3 minutes per side. Continue frying, adding more oil as needed, until all of batter is used up.

3. Drain on paper towels. Serve hot with applesauce for a meat meal or sour cream for a dairy meal.

GLICK'S COLOSSAL BUTTERNUT LATKES

*A*t Glick's kosher bakery-delicatessen in Melbourne, Australia, these oversize classic latkes are popular take-away food at Chanukah. To reduce cooking time, use two skillets.

4 SERVINGS

1 pound butternut squash, peeled and shredded
2 medium baking potatoes (about ¾ pound), coarsely grated
¼ cup chopped fresh cilantro
2 eggs, beaten
½ cup matzoh meal
2 teaspoons lemon pepper seasoning
1 teaspoon ground ginger
1 teaspoon salt
3 to 4 tablespoons peanut oil

1. In a large bowl, combine squash, potatoes, and cilantro. Add beaten eggs, matzoh meal, lemon pepper, ginger, and salt. Mix well.

2. Heat 1 tablespoon oil in a 7-inch nonstick skillet over medium heat. Pour in 1½ cups mixture. Cook until underside is browned and latke firm enough to be flipped over, 5 to 7 minutes.

3. Reduce heat to medium-low and cook 5 to 7 minutes longer, until underside is browned. Keep warm. Repeat with remaining mixture, stirring well before transferring to skillet and adding more oil as needed. Serve hot.

QUICK KNISHES WITH BULGUR, POTATOES, AND BROWNED ONIONS

*U*sing packaged puff pastry instead of homemade dough saves time here. So does making two long rolls and cutting them into individual slices, rather than forming individual knishes.

MAKES 16

2 medium baking potatoes, peeled and cut into 1-inch chunks
2 tablespoons bulgur
2 tablespoons garlic-flavored oil
2 large onions, halved and thinly sliced
¼ cup chopped fresh parsley
1 teaspoon salt
½ teaspoon lemon pepper seasoning
½ teaspoon dried tarragon
1 (17¼-ounce) package frozen puff pastry (2 sheets), thawed

1. Preheat oven to 400°F. In a medium saucepan of salted boiling water, cook potatoes until tender, 10 to 15 minutes; drain. Meanwhile, in a small bowl, pour enough hot water over bulgur to cover. Soak 10 minutes; drain.

2. In a medium skillet, heat oil over medium heat. Add onions. Cook, stirring often, until soft and golden brown, about 15 minutes.

3. Place onions in a food processor with bulgur, potatoes, parsley, salt, lemon pepper, and tarragon. Process to chop coarsely.

4. Spread half of mixture lengthwise down center of 1 pastry sheet. Brush pastry edges with water. Fold over to cover filling, shaping into a roll. Press to seal.

5. Place roll, seam side down, on an ungreased baking sheet. Repeat

with remaining ingredients. Score each roll crosswise into 8 slices, cutting only halfway through.

6. Bake in preheated oven 20 minutes, or until golden. Use a serrated knife to cut rolls where scored into individual knishes. Serve hot.

MAPLE-DRENCHED ALMOND LATKES

I like to serve these as dessert with fresh sliced strawberries or, in winter, with thawed and sweetened frozen raspberries.

MAKES 10 TO 12

1½ cups cold unseasoned mashed potatoes
½ cup almond paste, softened
¼ cup finely chopped blanched almonds
3 tablespoons matzoh meal
2 tablespoons sugar
1 egg white, lightly beaten
¼ to ⅓ cup vegetable oil
Warmed maple syrup

1. In a medium bowl, combine mashed potatoes, almond paste, almonds, matzoh meal, sugar, and egg white. Beat until well blended.

2. Heat 2 tablespoons oil in a large, heavy skillet, preferably nonstick, over medium-high heat. Drop mixture by rounded tablespoonfuls into heated skillet. Flatten slightly with a wide spatula. Cook until golden, about 3 minutes on each side. Transfer to a serving dish.

3. Repeat with remaining batter, adding more oil as needed to prevent sticking. While latkes are hot, drizzle warm maple syrup over them and serve.

SOUR PLUM CHUTNEY

Walnuts and sour plums are common in Georgian cuisine. Since we don't have sour plums here, I use Italian prune plums and lemon. I tasted this tongue-tingler spooned over an oversize cheese blintz at a north Tel Aviv café run by Georgian-Russian immigrants. I offer it as a tart sauce with blintzes or kugels or as a relish with meats and poultry.

MAKES 1⅓ CUPS

½ pound Italian prune plums
½ lemon, seeded and cut into 4 pieces
2 tablespoons sugar
1 teaspoon ground cardamom
Pinch of hot red pepper flakes
⅓ cup chopped walnuts

1. Halve plums and remove pits. In a food processor, coarsely chop plums and lemon, peel and all.

2. Transfer to a small nonreactive saucepan. Stir in sugar, cardamom, and hot pepper flakes. Cook over medium-low heat, stirring often, until sugar is melted and fruit is beginning to soften, 10 to 15 minutes.

3. Add walnuts. Reduce heat to low and cook 5 minutes longer. Serve at room temperature.

VEGETABLE KISHKE

*I*f you love kishke but think this traditional Jewish dish is heavy and complicated, try my version. Using ready-to-eat prepared baby carrots cuts preparation time in half. This dish is especially good with braised brisket.

4 TO 6 SERVINGS

12 baby carrots
1 medium onion, quartered
1 small red bell pepper, cut into 1-inch chunks
½ medium zucchini, cut into 1-inch chunks
¼ cup chopped fresh parsley
¼ cup vegetable oil
1 tablespoon schmaltz
1 teaspoon paprika
1 teaspoon salt
¼ teaspoon pepper
1¼ cups matzoh meal

1. Preheat oven to 350°F. Coat a sheet of foil, 12 by 10 inches, with nonstick vegetable spray.

2. In a food processor, place carrots, onion, bell pepper, zucchini, parsley, oil, and schmaltz. Pulse several times, then process 30 seconds to chop finely.

3. Add paprika, salt, pepper, and matzoh meal and process briefly to mix. Shape into a roll 10 inches long and 1 inch thick. Place on prepared foil. Fold foil over to cover tightly.

4. Place roll on a baking sheet and bake in preheated oven 1¼ hours. Unwrap and discard foil. Kishke will be nicely crusted outside and moist inside when sliced. Serve hot.

GOLDEN ONION KNISHES

MAKES 12; 4 TO 6 SERVINGS

2 cups flour
2 teaspoons baking powder
1 teaspoon dried dill
2 teaspoons salt
4 tablespoons margarine, cut into 4 pieces
About ½ cup cold water
¼ cup olive oil
2 large onions, chopped
½ cup mashed potatoes
½ teaspoon pepper
1 egg, beaten

1. In a food processor, combine flour, baking powder, dill, and 1 teaspoon salt. Add margarine and process until dough is consistency of coarse bread crumbs. Add ½ cup water and process until dough forms a ball. Gradually add more water, 1 tablespoon at a time, if needed. Refrigerate 30 minutes while making filling.

2. Preheat oven to 375°F. Coat a large baking sheet with nonstick vegetable spray.

3. In a medium skillet, heat olive oil. Add onions and cook over medium heat until soft and just beginning to brown, about 10 minutes. Remove from heat. Add mashed potatoes, pepper, and remaining 1 teaspoon salt. Mix well.

4. Divide dough in half. On a floured board, roll out dough to a ¼-inch thickness. Cut into 3-inch rounds with a cookie cutter. Place 1 rounded teaspoonful of onion mixture in center of each dough round. Dampen edges and fold over into half-moon shapes to cover filling. Press edges to seal. As they are formed, place knishes on prepared baking sheet. Brush with beaten egg.

5. Bake in preheated oven 15 minutes, or until knishes are browned. Serve hot.

KREPLACH

*T*raditionally eaten on the eve of the Yom Kippur fast, these small, meat-filled dumplings, sometimes dubbed "Jewish ravioli," are boiled and served in soup or fried and presented as a side dish.

MAKES 18

1 cup minced cooked beef
1 small onion, minced
2 tablespoons steak sauce
1 tablespoon minced fresh parsley
½ teaspoon garlic powder
Pinch of pepper
2 cups flour
2 eggs, beaten
½ teaspoon salt
1 tablespoon vegetable oil

1. In a small bowl, mix beef, onion, steak sauce, parsley, garlic powder, and pepper. Set filling aside.

2. In a food processor, mix flour, eggs, salt, oil, and 1 tablespoon water. Mixture should form a ball. Add a little more water, 1 teaspoonful at a time, if needed.

3. Divide dough in half. On a floured board, roll out dough as thinly as possible, almost paper thin. Cut out 3-inch circles with a cookie cutter. Repeat until all dough is used up.

4. Place 1 teaspoonful of meat filling in center of each circle. Dampen edges. Bring edges towards middle and pinch to seal.

5. Gently drop kreplach into a pan of boiling salted water. Cook over medium heat until kreplach float to top, about 20 minutes. Drain and serve.

TO FRY: Heat 2 tablespoons oil in a large nonstick skillet. Fry kreplach over medium heat, turning once, until golden brown on both sides, 4 minutes.

EASY APPLE BLINTZES

4 TO 6 SERVINGS

1 cup apple pie filling
1 apple, cored and chopped
2 tablespoons currants
12 prepared Blintz Leaves (recipe follows)
2 to 3 tablespoons butter or oil
Sour cream or vanilla yogurt

1. In a small bowl, mix together apple pie filling, chopped apple, and currants.

2. Place 1 heaping tablespoonful in center of each blintz leaf. Fold 2 opposite sides of leaf over filling to almost cover. Then fold up ends to overlap, completely covering filling and forming a rectangle 3½ by 2 inches. Repeat with remaining leaves and filling.

3. Heat 2 tablespoons butter or oil in a large nonstick skillet over medium-high heat. Add blintzes, seam side down, in 2 batches if necessary, and fry 2 minutes on each side, or until nicely browned. Serve hot, topped with a dollop of sour cream or vanilla yogurt.

TO BAKE RATHER THAN FRY BLINTZES: Preheat oven to 425°F. Coat bottom of shallow baking dish with nonstick vegetable spray. Place blintzes in dish, seam side down. Brush tops with oil or melted butter. Bake in preheated oven for 15 minutes, or until golden brown.

DAIRY

BLINTZ LEAVES

A blintz is really a Jewish crepe, or leaf, *blet lach* in Yiddish. In my mother's kitchen, blintzes were never looked on as fancy food, just delicious wrappers for the fruit jams that lined our winter pantry. I have reduced the number of eggs traditionally used and increased the liquid. A nonstick skillet makes blintz cooking a breeze. Following are an assortment of sweet and savory fillings you can roll up in the leaves.

MAKES 12

1 cup flour
¼ teaspoon salt
2 eggs
1½ cups milk
1 tablespoon oil
Vegetable oil for frying

1. Measure flour and salt into a medium bowl. Make a well in center and beat in eggs, milk, and oil; batter will be thin. Pour into a pitcher and set aside for 10 minutes.

2. Heat a 7-inch nonstick skillet over medium heat. Dip a crumpled paper towel into vegetable oil and rub over surface of skillet to grease lightly. Raise heat to medium-high.

3. Pour just enough batter into skillet to cover bottom. Tilt to spread thinly and pour excess back into pitcher. Cook 30 seconds, or until center is dry.

4. Flip onto a warm platter. Cover with a clean kitchen towel or wax paper. Repeat with remaining batter, greasing pan between each blintz leaf.

PARVE BLINTZ LEAVES: Substitute nondairy creamer for the milk.

DAIRY

BLINTZ FILLINGS: SAVORY AND SWEET

APRICOT-CHERRY (parve): In a small bowl, mix ½ cup prepared apricot pie filling with 2 tablespoons dried cherries. Enough for 6 to 8 blintzes.

SPICED MIXED FRUIT (parve): In a small bowl, mix ½ cup diced mixed fruit with ¼ cup parve cake crumbs, 1 tablespoon orange juice, and ¼ teaspoon cinnamon. Enough for 6 to 8 blintzes.

CHOPPED CHICKEN (meat; use with parve blintz leaves): In a small bowl, mix together 1½ cups shredded cooked chicken, 1 tablespoon chopped fresh parsley, 1 beaten egg, 2 tablespoons matzoh meal, and salt and pepper to taste. Enough for 8 blintzes.

CHOPPED CHILI BEEF (meat; use with parve blintz leaves): In a small bowl, combine 1 cup cooked ground beef, 2 tablespoons steak sauce, and ⅛ teaspoon chili powder. Enough for 6 to 8 blintzes.

CHEESE AND CILANTRO (dairy): In a small bowl, mix together 1 cup farmer cheese, 1 egg white, 2 tablespoons chopped fresh cilantro, ½ teaspoon salt, and a pinch of pepper. Enough for 6 to 8 blintzes.

SWEET CINNAMON-CHEESE (dairy): In a small bowl, mix together 8 ounces farmer cheese, 1 tablespoon cream cheese, 2 tablespoons beaten egg, and 1 tablespoon cinnamon-sugar. Enough for 8 to 10 blintzes.

BLUEBERRY BLINTZ BAKE

This is an adaptation of a recipe that regularly makes the rounds during the holidays. The sauce surrounding the blintzes puffs up when baked. In summer, I use fresh berries, ripe plums, or peaches. In winter, try sliced bananas, diced pineapple, and dried cherries.

10 TO 12 SERVINGS

10 to 12 frozen cheese blintzes
¼ cup ginger preserves
1 cup blueberries
1 cup blackberries
6 eggs
2 cups sour cream
6 tablespoons unsalted butter, melted
3 tablespoons sugar

1. Coat a large shallow baking dish with nonstick vegetable spray. Fit blintzes into dish in a single layer.

2. In a small saucepan, melt ginger preserves over medium heat. Add blueberries and blackberries and cook 1 minute, stirring to mix and glaze the fruit. Spoon over blintzes.

3. In a medium bowl, whisk eggs, sour cream, melted butter, and sugar. Pour over blintzes and berries. At this point, the dish can be covered and refrigerated overnight. Remove from refrigerator 1 hour before cooking.

4. Preheat oven to 350°F. Bake for 1 hour, until nicely browned and center is set. Serve warm or at room temperature.

NOTE: To lighten this recipe, margarine can be substituted for the butter, 1 cup low-fat vanilla yogurt and 1 cup low-fat sour cream for the sour cream, and 3 eggs plus 6 egg whites for the eggs.

DAIRY

SWEET BUCKWHEAT BLINTZES

Buckwheat, which grew easily in poor, rocky soil, was a staple Russian grain. While the upper classes enjoyed buckwheat crepes as blini with caviar, the peasants turned them into cheese-filled blintzes. The gluten-free, distinctively flavored flour can be stored in a plastic bag and frozen to be used as needed. Serve them with Sour Plum Chutney (page 254).

MAKES 12

½ cup buckwheat flour
½ cup all-purpose flour
½ teaspoon salt
1 egg
1¾ cups milk
2 to 3 tablespoons vegetable oil
1 cup farmer cheese
¼ cup cottage cheese
2 tablespoons sugar
1 teaspoon grated lemon zest
¼ teaspoon cinnamon
2 tablespoons butter or oil

1. Sift buckwheat flour, all-purpose flour, and salt into a medium bowl. Make a well in center. Add egg, milk, and 1 tablespoon oil and beat until smooth. Pour batter into a pitcher and let stand 5 minutes.

2. Dip a crumpled paper towel in vegetable oil and rub over surface of 7-inch nonstick skillet to grease lightly. Heat over medium-high heat.

3. Pour about 3 tablespoons batter into skillet. Tip to cover entire bottom of pan thinly, pouring any excess back into pitcher. Cook, shaking pan once or twice, for 1 minute, or until center looks dry. Flip crepe onto a warmed platter and cover with a clean kitchen towel or wax paper. Repeat with remaining batter, greasing skillet lightly between each crepe.

DAIRY

4. In a small bowl, combine farmer cheese, cottage cheese, sugar, lemon zest, and cinnamon. Mix to blend well. Place 1 rounded tablespoon of cheese filling in center of each crepe. Fold 2 opposite sides over filling to almost meet, then fold over edges to overlap, enclosing filling and forming a rectangle about 3½ by 2 inches. (Blintzes can be refrigerated or frozen at this point.)

5. Shortly before serving, heat 2 tablespoons butter or oil in a large nonstick skillet over medium heat. Add blintzes, seam side down. Cook 2 minutes on each side over medium-high heat, until golden brown. Serve hot.

SKILLET BLINTZ BREAKFAST

Here's a great way to dress up leftover blintzes. I especially like these for a lazy Sunday brunch for two.

2 SERVINGS

¼ cup apricot preserves
1 tablespoon fresh lemon juice
1 cup blueberries
Pinch of grated nutmeg
4 cheese blintzes
Ricotta cheese or vanilla yogurt

1. In a medium skillet, melt preserves with lemon juice over medium heat. Add blueberries and nutmeg and bring to a boil.

2. Reduce heat to medium-low. Place blintzes in berry sauce. Cover pan and simmer until heated through, 3 to 5 minutes.

3. Serve blintzes and berry sauce hot, topped with ricotta cheese or vanilla yogurt.

DAIRY

POTATO LATKES FROM NORMANDY

*I*n Normandy, where the best French dairy products are produced, everything is cooked in butter. These latkes contain only potatoes and cook into a thin, crisp pancake. If you are doubling the recipe, use two skillets for faster preparation.

2 SERVINGS

1 large baking potato
2 tablespoons butter
Salt and pepper

1. Scrub potato. No need to peel. Shred on large holes of a box grater.

2. In a 7-inch skillet, melt 1 tablespoon butter over medium heat.

3. Spoon half of shredded potatoes into hot butter in skillet. With a spatula, spread and press evenly over bottom of pan. Season lightly with salt and pepper.

4. Raise heat to high and cook 1 minute. Reduce heat to medium-high and cook until crisp on bottom, about 3 minutes longer. Flip over and cook until underside is browned and crisp, about 2 minutes.

5. Drain on paper towels and keep warm. Repeat with remaining ingredients. Serve hot.

DAIRY

CAULIFLOWER-POTATO LATKES

*T*hese buttery, crusty latkes are eaten out of hand in the streets of the Marais, the old Jewish neighborhood in Paris. Use thawed frozen cauliflower florets if you like, to speed up preparation. If served with meat, oil should be used for frying, and the mashed potatoes should not contain any dairy products.

MAKES 12

1 cup cauliflower florets
1½ cups mashed potatoes
3 tablespoons matzoh meal
2 teaspoons minced garlic
1 teaspoon salt
¼ teaspoon white pepper
1 egg, beaten
2 tablespoons kasha
4 to 6 tablespoons butter

1. In a large pot of salted boiling water, cook cauliflower until it is very soft, 10 to 15 minutes. Drain and pat dry.

2. In a mixing bowl, mash cauliflower to small bits with a fork. Add mashed potatoes, matzoh meal, garlic, salt, pepper, and egg. Blend thoroughly.

3. Shape into 12 patties 3 inches in diameter and about ½ inch thick. Sprinkle with kasha, pressing into both sides.

4. Melt 3 tablespoons butter in a large skillet over medium-high heat. Fry latkes in batches, adding more butter as necessary, until they are browned and crust is crisp, about 3 minutes per side. Drain on paper towels. Serve hot.

DAIRY

PARMESAN POTATO LATKES

Parmesan cheese adds a distinct bite to the classic latke. These make a tempting platter, which I sometimes garnish with pesto sauce.

MAKES 24; 6 TO 8 SERVINGS

2 eggs
¼ small onion, cut into 3 pieces
4 medium potatoes, peeled and cut into 1-inch chunks
¼ cup matzoh meal
¼ cup grated Parmesan cheese
2 tablespoons chopped fresh parsley
1 tablespoon Dijon mustard
⅓ to ½ cup olive or vegetable oil

1. In a food processor, combine eggs, onion, and potatoes. Process until onion and potatoes are finely chopped.

2. Transfer to a mixing bowl and blend in matzoh meal, cheese, parsley, and mustard.

3. Heat ¼ cup oil in a large nonstick skillet over medium heat. Slide rounded tablespoonfuls of potato batter into the hot oil, pressing each with a wide spatula to flatten slightly. Cook until golden brown and crisp on both sides, about 3 minutes per side. Drain on paper towels. Serve hot.

DAIRY

FRESH SALMON LATKES

*I*f you're in Paris, don't miss a visit to Jo Goldenberg's deli on Rue de Rosiers in the Marais; he's a character. This is one of his sell-out signature dishes, especially popular at Chanukah.

MAKES 12; 6 SERVINGS

¾ pound salmon fillet, cut into 6 pieces
½ lemon, thinly sliced
1 egg
½ cup milk
¾ cup all-purpose flour
½ teaspoon baking powder
1 teaspoon salt
¼ teaspoon pepper
6 tablespoons butter or vegetable oil
Lemon wedges

1. Place the salmon pieces in a deep, medium-size skillet or shallow saucepan. Pour in enough boiling water to almost cover fish. Add lemon slices. Bring to a boil over high heat. Reduce heat to low, cover, and simmer 10 minutes, or until salmon is opaque in center when flaked. Remove salmon with a slotted spatula. Remove skin and bones and flake fish into a medium bowl.

2. In a separate bowl, whisk together egg and milk. Add flour, baking powder, salt, and pepper. Whisk just until blended. Pour batter over cooked salmon. Stir gently to mix.

3. Melt 3 tablespoons butter in a large skillet over medium heat. Pour batter, ¼ cup for each latke, into the hot butter. Raise heat to medium-high and cook latkes until nicely browned and crisp on bottom, about 4 minutes. Turn over and cook until second side is crisp and browned, about 2 minutes longer. Repeat in 1 or 2 more batches to use remaining batter, adding more butter as needed.

4. Drain on paper towels. Serve warm, with lemon wedges.

DAIRY

SPINACH BOUREKAS

*P*repared puff pastry makes short work of these savory pastry pies, which were introduced to Israel by Greek and Turkish Jews.

MAKES 8; 4 SERVINGS

1 (10-ounce) package frozen chopped spinach, thawed and
  squeezed dry
1 egg
½ cup shredded Cheddar cheese
¼ cup low-fat cottage cheese
2 teaspoons Dijon mustard
⅛ teaspoon grated nutmeg
½ teaspoon salt
1 (17¼-ounce) package frozen puff pastry, thawed (2
  sheets)
Sesame seeds

1. Preheat oven to 400°F. In a mixing bowl, combine spinach, egg, Cheddar cheese, cottage cheese, mustard, nutmeg, and salt. Mix well.

2. Unfold 1 pastry sheet. With fingers, press out any lines or perforations. Cut into quarters.

3. Place 2 tablespoons spinach mixture on 1 half of each quarter. Moisten edges with water and fold over to cover filling as in a turnover. Press to seal. Brush with water; sprinkle with sesame seeds. With scissors, snip pastry to make a small V for steam to escape. Place on baking sheet. Repeat with remaining pastry and filling.

4. Bake in preheated oven 15 minutes. Lower heat to 375°F. and bake until pastries are puffed and browned, 15 minutes longer. Cover loosely with foil if browning too quickly. Serve hot or at room temperature.

DAIRY

MACCABEAN RAREBIT

Here's a perfect combination of my Scottish and Jewish backgrounds. If you can find it, use Israeli Maccabee beer, perfect for this holiday, which commemorates the victory of the Maccabees in their fight for religious freedom.

4 SERVINGS

3 cups shredded sharp Cheddar cheese
¾ cup beer
2 tablespoons butter
2 tablespoons Dijon mustard
Pinch of grated nutmeg
2 English muffins, split and toasted
1 medium tomato, thinly sliced

1. In a medium saucepan, stir cheese and beer together over low heat until cheese is melted and smooth, 10 to 15 minutes.

2. Add butter, mustard, and nutmeg. Cook, stirring, until butter melts.

3. Spoon rarebit onto English muffin halves. Top each portion with 1 or 2 slices of tomato. Eat with a knife and fork.

DAIRY

Cakes, Cookies, and Pastries

Sweets have a rich tradition in the Jewish home. We eat honey cake and *teiglach* on Rosh Hashanah to symbolize the happiness of the coming year. That same association between sweetness and happiness carries over into the three-cornered *hamantaschen* pastries that celebrate victory on Purim and even the coffee cake or rugelach kept on hand every day. Sponge cakes, strudels, and kuchens of every variety arise from a long tradition of Central and Eastern European baking, as do *mandelbrot*—the Jewish biscotti—cheese cakes, and *kichel.*

You'll find Jewish pastries from all over the world here, from the Gesundheit Kuchen of German Jews to the Fried Lemon-Honey Puffs, or *bimuelos,* of Greek and Turkish Jews to Sufganiot, the popular jelly doughnuts of Israel. To fit in with today's hectic schedules, I've included plenty of simple one-bowl cakes and cookies—Easy Carrot Cake and Chocolate-Ginger Mandelbrot, for example.

More elaborate pastries, such as Almond Konafa from the Middle East and Hasty Hamantaschen, are simplified by using prepared filo pastry and biscuit dough to save time. Even the more complicated rich pastry, such as buttery *meurbe teig* for Aunt Hanni's Apple Tart, can be made ahead and refrigerated for up to 24 hours until needed. (Just be sure to let it return to room temperature before using so that it can be handled easily.)

This generous assortment of parve and dairy desserts will serve well for everyday eating and for Shabbat, for special holidays, or anytime you have a *simchah*, or celebration, that calls for coffee and something sweet.

ONE-BOWL HONEY CAKE

Honey cake, which symbolizes a sweet year, is traditional for Rosh Hashanah. Leftovers—if you have any—can be wrapped and frozen to serve when the fast is broken after Yom Kippur.

MAKES 36 SQUARES; 12 TO 16 SERVINGS

3 cups flour
¾ cup sugar
1 teaspoon baking soda
¼ teaspoon baking powder
½ teaspoon grated nutmeg
3 eggs
½ cup vegetable oil
½ cup honey
¾ cup strongly brewed black coffee
¼ cup thawed frozen orange juice concentrate
1 ounce unsweetened parve chocolate, melted
36 walnut halves

1. Preheat oven to 350°F. Coat an 11-by-14-inch baking dish with nonstick vegetable spray.

2. In a large bowl, mix flour, sugar, baking soda, baking powder, and nutmeg. Make a well in center and beat in eggs, oil, honey, coffee, orange juice, and chocolate.

3. Pour batter into prepared baking dish. Arrange walnuts on top. Bake in preheated oven for 1 hour, or until a toothpick inserted in center comes out clean. Let cool, then cut into squares.

VARIATION: Cashew Honey Cake—Substitute 36 cashews for walnuts. Brush baked cake with ¼ cup warm honey mixed with ¼ teaspoon powdered ginger.

MARLENE'S SPONGE CAKE

*I*n every Jewish home in Glasgow, sponge cake, like this one from Marlene Morrison, is always on hand to dunk in Russian tea or, as my father liked it, in sweet red wine. This cake, which is so easy to make, is still sold in the Morrison deli.

10 TO 12 SERVINGS

4 eggs
1 cup sugar
1 teaspoon vanilla extract
¾ cup flour
2 teaspoons baking powder

1. Preheat oven to 350°F. Coat an 8½-by-4½-by-2½-inch loaf pan with nonstick vegetable spray.

2. In a mixing bowl, whisk together eggs, sugar, and vanilla until thick and pale, 3 to 4 minutes.

3. Sift flour and baking powder. With a large metal spoon or rubber spatula, fold dry ingredients into egg mixture. Pour into prepared loaf pan.

4. Bake in preheated oven until top is firm when pressed gently in center and cake has shrunk slightly from sides of pan, 30 to 35 minutes.

5. Let cake cool slightly in pan, about 5 minutes. Loosen edges with a round-bladed knife. Turn out onto a wire rack. Let cool completely before slicing with a serrated knife. To store, wrap tightly in plastic wrap and refrigerate.

EASY CARROT CAKE

Carrots are symbolic of a sweet, fulfilling year, which is why they are popular on Rosh Hashanah. Here I use them in an unlikely processed form—baby food—to produce a rich-tasting, moist cake with none of the work of peeling and grating that is usually involved.

20 TO 24 SERVINGS

3 cups flour
2 cups granulated sugar
2 teaspoons baking powder
1 teaspoon baking soda
2 teaspoons cinnamon
½ teaspoon salt
1½ cups vegetable oil
2 (6-ounce) jars junior baby food carrots
4 eggs, beaten
2 teaspoons vanilla extract
½ cup crystallized ginger, chopped
3 tablespoons powdered sugar

1. Preheat oven to 350°F. Coat a 13-by-9-by-2-inch baking pan with nonstick vegetable spray.

2. In a large bowl, mix flour, granulated sugar, baking powder, baking soda, cinnamon, and salt. Make a well in center and add oil, carrots, eggs, and vanilla. Beat with a wooden spoon to mix well. Fold in chopped ginger.

3. Pour into prepared pan. Bake in preheated oven for 1 hour, or until a toothpick inserted in center comes out clean.

4. Let cool completely, then cut into squares. Before serving, dust with powdered sugar.

BLUEBERRY KUCHEN

*K*uchen is a German coffee cake. This one is easy and only mildly sweet. I like it at breakfast with a cup of coffee or tea.

8 TO 10 SERVINGS

4 tablespoons margarine
⅓ cup plus 1 tablespoon sugar
1 egg
¾ cup flour
½ teaspoon baking powder
2 cups blueberries
1 teaspoon cornstarch

1. Preheat oven to 375°F. Coat a 9-inch baking pan with nonstick vegetable spray.

2. In a mixing bowl, cream margarine and ⅓ cup sugar until pale, 3 to 4 minutes. Add egg with ¼ cup flour and beat until incorporated, 1 to 2 minutes longer. Add baking powder and remaining flour gradually. Press into prepared pan.

3. In a small saucepan, cook blueberries with remaining 1 tablespoon sugar and 2 tablespoons water over high heat for 1 minute, stirring constantly. With a slotted spoon, place berries on top of pastry in baking dish.

4. Blend cornstarch with 1 tablespoon cold water and stir into blueberry liquid in saucepan. Bring to boil, stirring constantly, until liquid is thickened and smooth, 1 to 2 minutes. Remove from heat and let cool for a few minutes, then drizzle over blueberries.

5. Bake in preheated oven for 40 minutes, or until pastry is golden. Serve warm or at room temperature.

CHOCOLATE-GINGER MANDELBROT

Mandelbrot is a kind of Jewish biscotti—a hard, delicious finger cookie to be dunked in tea or coffee. They keep for weeks in an airtight container in a cool, dry place or for months in the freezer. These are relatively low in fat.

MAKES 36

2 cups flour
1 cup sugar
1 teaspoon baking powder
1 teaspoon powdered ginger
¼ cup chopped crystallized ginger
¼ cup chopped parve semisweet chocolate chips
3 eggs
2 teaspoons vanilla extract

1. Preheat oven to 325°F. Coat a large cookie sheet with nonstick cooking spray.

2. In a large bowl, mix flour, sugar, baking powder, powdered ginger, crystallized ginger, and chocolate.

3. Make a well in center of dry ingredients. Add eggs and vanilla and mix until completely blended.

4. Divide dough in half. Shape into 2 logs about 12 inches long and ¾ inch thick. Place on cookie sheet at least 2 inches apart.

5. Bake in preheated oven for 45 minutes, until golden brown. Remove from oven and turn oven off.

6. Let cool 5 minutes. With a large serrated knife, cut dough logs crosswise on a diagonal into slices ½ inch thick. Lay slices flat on cookie sheet. Return to warm oven for 1 hour to dry out. (Be sure not to peek; oven door should remain closed.) Let cool on a wire rack.

MARBLEIZED MANDELBROT

After dunking a piece of traditional rock-hard mandelbrot in her coffee at my house, Sheila Epstein sent me this recipe, which she described as "a cookie you won't break your teeth on." Its cake-like texture is achieved by using crumbly walnuts rather than crisp almonds and allowing only a brief second baking.

MAKES 30 TO 36

3 eggs
¾ cup vegetable oil
1 cup plus 2 tablespoons sugar
1½ teaspoons vanilla extract
1 teaspoon almond extract
1½ teaspoons baking powder
3½ cups flour
1 cup chopped walnuts
1 ounce parve unsweetened chocolate, melted

1. Preheat oven to 375°F. Spray a large cookie sheet with nonstick vegetable spray.

2. In a mixing bowl, beat eggs, oil, 1 cup sugar, vanilla, and almond extract.

3. Blend baking powder with ½ cup flour and stir into egg mixture. Add remaining flour, 1 cup at a time, beating well after each addition.

4. Stir in walnuts. Drizzle melted chocolate over batter and cut in with a knife to marbleize.

5. With lightly floured hands, shape dough into 3 rolls, each about 10 inches long and ¾ inch thick. Place on prepared cookie sheet. Sprinkle remaining 2 tablespoons sugar over the rolls.

6. Bake in preheated oven for 18 minutes. Remove from oven briefly and cut each roll crosswise on a slight angle into slices ½ inch wide. Return to oven and bake 5 minutes longer.

APPLE-RAISIN STRUDEL

Making strudel used to involve lengthy preparations. Filo dough is cheap, easily available, and good quality. Remove as many sheets as you need, then immediately rewrap the remainder tightly and freeze or refrigerate.

8 SERVINGS

6 filo leaves
2 tablespoons margarine, melted
3 tablespoons dry bread crumbs
2 tablespoons apricot or other preserves, warmed
½ cup raisins
1 medium apple, peeled and coarsely grated
1 tablespoon grated lemon zest
⅛ teaspoon cinnamon
Powdered sugar

1. Preheat oven to 375°F. Coat a baking sheet with nonstick vegetable spray.

2. Lay 1 sheet of filo on a flat, dry surface. Brush with melted margarine. Sprinkle 1 teaspoon bread crumbs over pastry. Repeat with 4 more filo sheets, using same amount of melted butter and bread crumbs.

3. Top with last sheet of filo and spread with preserves to within ½ inch of edges. Sprinkle on raisins, grated apple, lemon zest, and cinnamon. Roll up lengthwise like a jelly roll.

4. Place on prepared baking sheet, seam side down. Brush with melted butter and sprinkle remaining bread crumbs on top. Bake in preheated oven for 20 minutes, or until top is golden and crisp.

5. Let cool on a wire rack. Before serving, sprinkle with powdered sugar and cut crosswise on a slight angle into 1-inch-thick slices.

NOTE: Strudel freezes well. To crisp after thawing, bake uncovered in a 350°F. oven for 10 minutes.

MINI APPLE STRUDEL TARTS

Miniature filo pastry shells certified kosher are now available in the freezer sections of supermarkets right next to the filo dough. Fill them with fruits, cream, preserves, or this old-fashioned apple and raisin mixture.

MAKES 15

1 (2.1-ounce) package miniature filo pastry shells
1 medium apple, peeled, cored, and chopped
2 teaspoons grated lemon zest
¼ teaspoon cinnamon
⅓ cup apricot preserves
⅓ cup raisins
1 tablespoon margarine, melted

1. Preheat oven to 375°F. Remove shells from package and place on a large baking sheet. Toss chopped apple with lemon zest and cinnamon.

2. Place 1 teaspoon apricot preserves on bottom of each shell. Top with 1 rounded teaspoon chopped apple and 1 teaspoon raisins. Brush edges of shells with melted margarine.

3. Bake tarts 10 minutes, or until filling is bubbly and pastry is pale golden brown. Cover loosely with aluminum foil if browning too fast. Transfer to a wire rack and let cool before serving.

JEWISH SCOTTISH STRUDEL

*T*he women in the small, tight-knit Glasgow Jewish community are famous as good bakers. Their Chanukah strudel pastry is actually a spongy cake dough instead of traditional filo leaves. It freezes well.

MAKES 36; 12 TO 18 SERVINGS

4 eggs
1 cup sugar
1 cup vegetable oil
3¾ cups self-rising flour*
6 tablespoons apricot preserves, melted
1 cup golden raisins
¾ cup currants
6 tablespoons chopped walnuts
Cinnamon

1. Preheat oven to 350°F. Coat a large baking sheet with nonstick vegetable spray.

2. In a large bowl, whisk eggs and sugar until thick and pale, about 3 minutes. Stir in oil. Fold in flour. Refrigerate for 1 hour.

3. Divide dough into 3 pieces. On a floured board, press 1 piece of dough into a rectangle about 6 by 10 inches. Spread 2 tablespoons preserves over the dough. Sprinkle on ⅓ cup raisins, ¼ cup currants, and 2 tablespoons nuts. Dust lightly with cinnamon. Roll up as for a jelly roll. Place on prepared baking sheet. Repeat with remaining ingredients.

4. Bake in preheated oven 35 minutes. Let cool. Cut into slices ½ inch thick.

*In place of self-rising flour, you can substitute 3¾ cups all-purpose flour mixed with 4 teaspoons baking powder.

LEMON-SCENTED KICHEL

*T*hese light, spongy cookies go with wine for a kiddush, prayers of sanctification on Shabbat or other holiday.

MAKES 20 TO 24

3 eggs
5 tablespoons sugar
¼ cup vegetable oil
½ teaspoon lemon oil
1¼ cups flour

1. Preheat oven to 325°F. Coat 2 large cookie sheets with nonstick vegetable spray.

2. In a mixing bowl, beat eggs and 3 tablespoons sugar until thick and pale, 3 to 4 minutes. Beat in vegetable oil and lemon oil. Gradually add flour, ¼ cup at a time, beating after each addition, until flour is incorporated.

3. Drop tablespoonfuls of dough about 2 inches apart onto prepared baking sheets. Sprinkle remaining 2 tablespoons sugar over cookies.

4. Bake in preheated oven for 25 minutes, or until edges are nicely browned. Transfer to a wire rack and let cool. Store in a tight-lidded container at room temperature.

CHOCOLATE-WALNUT PUFF PASTRIES

MAKES 24

1 (17¼-ounce) package frozen puff pastry, thawed (2 sheets)
2 cups chopped walnuts
½ cup parve miniature semisweet chocolate chips
¼ cup sugar
1 teaspoon cinnamon
½ cup honey
3 tablespoons fresh lemon juice
1 teaspoon vanilla extract

1. Preheat oven to 375°F. Place 1 sheet of pastry in bottom of a 9-inch square baking pan. Trim to fit the bottom. With a fork, prick all over and bake in preheated oven for 12 minutes. Remove pastry from oven; leave oven on.

2. In a small bowl, mix walnuts, chocolate chips, sugar, and cinnamon. Sprinkle over baked pastry.

3. Top with remaining pastry sheet; trim to fit. Prick all over with a fork. Score into 24 pieces, cutting through top pastry layer.

4. Return to oven and bake 25 to 30 minutes, or until top layer of pastry is puffed and golden.

5. Meanwhile, in a small saucepan, combine honey, lemon juice, vanilla, and 2 tablespoons water. Cook over medium-low heat, stirring occasionally, until tiny bubbles begin to appear at side of pan.

6. As soon as pastry comes out of oven, pour honey syrup over pastry, letting it drip through into filling. Let cool. Serve at room temperature.

CHOCOLATE MERINGUES

*C*ontrary to what you might hear, meringues are incredibly simple to make. No need for copper bowls or cream of tartar. Just be sure all the utensils are scrupulously clean and not a speck of yolk gets into the whites; even a trace of fat or grease will prevent the whites from expanding to their full volume. Separate each egg over a cup before adding the white to the bowl. That way, if you break a yolk, it won't spoil the rest of the whites.

MAKES 26 TO 30

4 egg whites
1 cup sugar
¼ cup chopped parve sweet, bittersweet, or semisweet chocolate

1. Preheat oven to 225°F. Line 2 cookie sheets with parchment or aluminum foil. Coat lightly with nonstick vegetable spray.

2. In a large bowl, beat egg whites until they peak softly. Add sugar gradually, 2 tablespoons at a time, and continue beating until stiff, glossy peaks form. Fold in chopped chocolate.

3. Drop tablespoonfuls of meringue onto prepared cookie sheets or press through a pastry bag with a large star nozzle.

4. Bake in preheated oven for 1 hour. Turn oven off and leave meringues inside without opening door for 3 to 4 hours, or overnight, to dry completely. Store in an airtight container in a cool, dry place. Do not refrigerate.

P A R V E

TEIGLACH—MY WAY

Instead of rolling out the mixture, these "dough balls" are simply cooked in honey and served rather like miniature sticky buns. If you have a *bubbe* or *zayde* at your Rosh Hashanah table, teiglach will stir both conversation and memories.

MAKES 3 DOZEN

2 eggs
¼ cup vegetable oil
½ teaspoon baking powder
1¾ to 2 cups flour
1 cup honey
½ cup sugar
1 teaspoon powdered ginger
36 pecan halves

1. Preheat oven to 375°F. Coat a large cookie sheet with nonstick vegetable spray.

2. In a medium bowl, beat eggs and oil until well blended. Add baking powder and enough flour to make a soft dough.

3. Break off 1-inch pieces of dough, roll each into a ball, and place on cookie sheet. Bake in preheated oven 10 minutes, until pale brown.

4. In a large, heavy saucepan, combine honey, sugar, and ginger. Bring to a boil, reduce heat to low, and simmer 2 to 3 minutes. Add dough balls and pecans.

5. Cook, stirring gently, until dough balls are golden brown, about 10 minutes. Remove from heat immediately. Let cool 5 minutes.

6. With 2 spoons, carefully lift dough balls from hot syrup and place on an oiled cookie sheet. Top each with a pecan half. Let cool. Set in individual miniature paper cups. Store in an airtight container in a cool, dry place.

PRUNE FILLING

MAKES 1½ CUPS; ENOUGH FOR 25 TO 30
HAMANTASCHEN

1 (12-ounce) package pitted prunes
1 cup orange juice
½ cup sugar
½ teaspoon allspice
½ teaspoon cinnamon

1. Place prunes in a medium saucepan. Add orange juice and enough water to barely cover. Bring to a boil over medium-high heat. Reduce heat to medium and cook until only ¼ cup liquid remains, 10 to 15 minutes.

2. Remove from heat and stir in sugar, allspice, and cinnamon. Transfer to a food processor and pulse to a coarse paste. Cool completely before using.

HASTY HAMANTASCHEN

*T*hese small, triangular pastries, symbolic of the wicked Haman's three-cornered hat, are traditional treats for Purim celebrations.

MAKES 10

½ cup prepared poppy seed filling or Prune Filling
(recipe precedes)
1 tablespoon grated lemon zest
½ teaspoon cinnamon
1 (12-ounce) package refrigerated biscuits (10)
2 tablespoons warm honey or powdered sugar

1. Preheat oven to 400°F. In a small bowl, combine poppy seed filling with lemon zest and cinnamon. Mix well.

2. Separate refrigerated biscuits. On a lightly floured board, flatten each biscuit into a round about 2½ inches in diameter.

3. Place 1 rounded teaspoonful of filling in center of each biscuit. Dampen edges with water. Fold dough edges up over filling to form a flat 3-sided pyramid. Leave some of filling in center uncovered. As they are formed, place *hamantaschen* on a large ungreased cookie sheet.

4. Bake in preheated oven for 10 to 12 minutes, or until golden at edges. Brush with warm honey or dust with powdered sugar.

DAIRY

APPLE SPONGE CAKE

Known as *apfel auflauf* in the old country, this mildly sweet dessert is a special favorite with German Jews.

4 TO 6 SERVINGS

3 tablespoons butter, melted
3 tablespoons cinnamon-sugar
¼ teaspoon pure lemon oil or 1 tablespoon grated lemon zest
6 medium apples, peeled, cored, and thinly sliced
2 eggs, separated
½ cup sugar
½ cup flour
½ teaspoon baking powder
2 tablespoons milk
½ teaspoon vanilla extract

1. Preheat oven to 350°F. In a 1½-quart baking dish, mix butter, cinnamon-sugar, and lemon oil.

2. Add apples, stirring to coat with butter mixture. Cover loosely with foil and bake in preheated oven for 10 minutes.

3. Meanwhile, in a medium bowl, whisk egg whites or beat with an electric hand mixer until stiff peaks form.

4. In a separate bowl, beat egg yolks and sugar until pale, 2 to 3 minutes. Stir in flour, baking powder, milk, and vanilla. Fold in stiffly beaten egg whites.

5. Spoon batter over apples. Return to oven and bake for 30 minutes, or until a toothpick comes out clean when inserted in center. Serve warm.

DAIRY

AUNT HANNI'S APPLE TART

My husband Walter's Aunt Hanni, who owned a New York bakery, is a fabulous home baker. She makes applesauce from scratch for this rich, buttery tart, but I save time with a good store-bought chunky brand.

8 TO 10 SERVINGS

1 stick (4 ounces) unsalted butter, at room temperature
½ cup plus 1 tablespoon sugar
1 egg
1½ cups flour
½ teaspoon baking powder
1½ cups chunky applesauce
1½ teaspoons unsweetened cocoa powder

1. Preheat oven to 350°F. Coat a 10-inch springform pan with non-stick vegetable spray.

2. In a food processor or with an electric mixer, blend butter, ½ cup sugar, egg, and ¼ cup flour. Add baking powder and remaining 1¼ cups flour gradually to make a stiff dough. Set aside 1 rounded tablespoon of this mixture.

3. Press remaining dough into prepared springform to reach 1 inch up sides of pan. Bake in preheated oven for 15 minutes.

4. Spoon applesauce over cake. Mix reserved dough with cocoa and 1 tablespoon sugar until crumbly. Sprinkle over top.

5. Return to oven and bake 30 minutes longer. Let cool before cutting. Serve at room temperature.

DAIRY

APRICOT-HONEY LOAVES

*L*ightly sweetened with honey to ensure a sweet year, this symbolic cake is often served on Rosh Hashanah or after the fast is broken on Yom Kippur. I like to make the cake in small loaves; they are the perfect size for snacking or for giving as a little hostess gift.

MAKES 2 MINI-LOAVES

3 eggs, separated
¼ cup sugar
2 tablespoons honey
⅓ cup chopped dried apricots
¼ cup slivered almonds
1 tablespoon grated lime zest
2 tablespoons butter, melted
1 teaspoon vanilla extract
1 cup flour
1 teaspoon baking powder

1. Preheat oven to 350°F. Coat 2 miniature loaf pans, 6 by 3 by 2 inches, with nonstick vegetable spray.

2. In a medium bowl, beat egg whites until stiff. In a separate bowl, beat egg yolks, sugar, and honey until pale and thickened. Stir in apricots, almonds, lime zest, melted butter, and vanilla. Add flour and baking powder and mix well. Lastly, fold in beaten egg whites. Divide batter between prepared pans.

3. Bake in preheated oven for 25 minutes, or until a toothpick inserted in center comes out clean. Let cool on a wire rack before slicing.

DAIRY

GESUNDHEIT KUCHEN

Gesundheit, or "blessing," cake is a favorite recipe brought over by German Jews in the early part of the century. It is often served at a bris, engagement party, or other happy occasion.

10 TO 12 SERVINGS

1 stick (4 ounces) butter, at room temperature
9 ounces cream cheese, at room temperature
1½ cups granulated sugar
4 eggs
2 cups cake flour
2 teaspoons vanilla extract
2 teaspoons baking powder
Powdered sugar

1. Preheat oven to 350°F. Coat a 10-inch bundt pan with nonstick vegetable spray.

2. In a mixing bowl, beat butter, cream cheese, and sugar until light and fluffy. Add eggs, 1 at a time, with 1 tablespoon of the flour to prevent curdling, beating after each addition.

3. Add vanilla, baking powder, and remaining flour, ½ cup at a time, beating well after each addition. Spoon batter into bundt pan.

4. Bake in preheated oven for 55 to 60 minutes, or until cake is golden and a toothpick inserted in center comes out clean. Let cool 5 minutes in pan before turning out onto a wire rack to cool. Dust with powdered sugar just before serving.

JOSIE'S PLUM TORTE

When I first arrived in the United States, a Viennese colleague, Josie Pollack, gave me this recipe. It quickly became a family favorite. *Meurbe teig* is a rich buttery cake that forms the base of many European fruit tarts.

8 TO 10 SERVINGS

1 stick (4 ounces) butter, at room temperature
½ cup sugar
1 egg
1½ cups flour
½ teaspoon baking powder
¼ cup sugar
3 cups pitted and quartered Italian prune plums (about
    1½ pounds)
1 teaspoon cornstarch
2 tablespoons cinnamon-sugar
Frozen vanilla yogurt or lightly sweetened whipped cream

1. Preheat oven to 375°F. Coat a 9-inch square baking pan with nonstick vegetable spray. In a mixing bowl, cream butter, sugar, and egg until pale and creamy. Gradually add flour and baking powder. Blend well. Press into bottom of prepared baking pan.

2. In a small saucepan, combine sugar with 3 tablespoons water. Stir over high heat until sugar is dissolved. Reduce heat to medium-low. Add plums and cook until skin color begins to change, 5 to 10 minutes. Remove from heat.

3. With a slotted spoon, transfer plums to pastry base, arranging them in overlapping pattern. Blend cornstarch with 1 tablespoon cold water. Stir into plum cooking juices and bring to a boil over medium-high heat, stirring constantly. Drizzle cooking syrup over plums. Sprinkle cinnamon-sugar on top.

4. Bake in preheated oven for 45 minutes, or until pastry is golden at edges. Let cool at least 15 minutes before cutting into squares. Serve warm, topped with frozen yogurt or lightly sweetened whipped cream.

DAIRY

PLUM KUCHEN

*I*n this unusual recipe from my friend Ruth Bloom, the butter is melted and blended with the flour rather than cut in. The vinegar, which is undetectable, tenderizes the dough. It's a fabulous dessert, but seasonal, since it must be made with small, blue Italian prune plums, which are normally seen only in the fall.

8 TO 10 SERVINGS

1 stick (4 ounces) butter, melted
1 tablespoon distilled white vinegar
⅔ cup plus 2 tablespoons sugar
1¼ cups plus 2 tablespoons flour
1 tablespoon cinnamon
1 pound Italian prune plums, pitted and quartered

1. Preheat oven to 350°F. In a medium bowl, mix butter and vinegar. Blend in 2 tablespoons sugar and 1¼ cups flour to make a smooth dough. Press into bottom and sides of a 10-inch pie plate. Prick with a fork. Bake in preheated oven for 10 minutes.

2. In a medium bowl, mix remaining 2 tablespoons flour, ⅔ cup sugar, and cinnamon. Add plums and toss to coat.

3. Arrange plums, cut side up, in concentric circles on top of dough to cover bottom. Sprinkle any remaining flour mixture over the plums. Sprinkle 3 tablespoons water over kuchen.

4. Bake in preheated oven for 40 minutes, or until pastry is golden at edges. Cover loosely with foil if pastry appears to be browning too quickly. Let cool before cutting into wedges.

DAIRY

SOUR CREAM COFFEE CAKE

*E*nriched with sour cream, this loaf cake turns out light and spongy. Because it's so moist, it freezes well. The batter can also be baked in muffin tins to make mini cakes.

12 TO 15 SERVINGS

1½ sticks (6 ounces) butter, at room temperature
1¼ cups sugar
2 eggs
2 cups flour
1 cup sour cream
1 teaspoon vanilla extract
1½ teaspoons baking powder
3 tablespoons cinnamon-sugar
1 teaspoon instant coffee powder
¼ cup chopped pecans

1. Preheat oven to 350°F. Coat a 9-by-5-by-3-inch loaf pan or a tray of 12 muffin pans with nonstick vegetable spray.

2. In a mixing bowl, cream butter, sugar, eggs, and ¼ cup flour until pale and blended. Stir in sour cream and vanilla extract. Add baking powder and remaining flour, ½ cup at a time. Mix well.

3. Pour half of batter into prepared pan or muffin pans. Combine cinnamon-sugar, coffee powder, and pecans; sprinkle half over batter. Repeat with remaining batter and cinnamon-sugar mixture.

4. Bake in preheated oven for 1 hour for loaf, 35 minutes for muffins, or until a toothpick inserted in center comes out clean. Let cool on a wire rack. To serve, cut into slices ½ inch thick.

DAIRY

WHITE NIGHT COCONUT MACAROONS

White chocolate is my contemporary twist on an old favorite. These are perfect for the *shalach manos* baskets of goodies sent to friends and neighbors at Purim.

MAKES 24

3 egg whites
¾ cup sugar
2½ cups flaked coconut
⅓ cup white chocolate chips

1. Preheat oven to 225°F. Coat 2 cookie sheets with nonstick vegetable spray.

2. Beat egg whites to soft peaks. Gradually beat in sugar, ¼ cup at a time, beating well after each addition.

3. Fold in coconut, then white chocolate chips. Drop by tablespoonfuls onto prepared cookie sheets.

4. Bake in preheated oven for 2 hours. Turn off oven and leave in oven without opening door overnight.

5. Transfer to a wire rack and let stand 1 hour. Store in an airtight container in a cool, dry place.

DAIRY

CREAMY SHERRY-VANILLA CHEESECAKE

This is a rich, unpretentious, but surprisingly easy recipe, jazzed up with a dash of sherry. Don't worry if the cake cracks—the topping forms a good camouflage. Serve at a *simchah* ("celebration"), or at Shavuot, when dairy dishes are customary.

10 TO 12 SERVINGS

1 cup graham cracker crumbs
½ cup gingersnap crumbs
¾ cup plus 2 tablespoons sugar
5 tablespoons butter, melted
1½ pounds cream cheese, cut up, at room temperature
3 eggs
1 tablespoon cornstarch
2 tablespoons sherry
1 teaspoon vanilla extract
1 cup sour cream
2 tablespoons cinnamon-sugar

1. Preheat oven to 350°F. Coat an 8-inch springform pan with non-stick vegetable spray.

2. In a medium bowl, mix graham cracker crumbs, gingersnap crumbs, and 2 tablespoons sugar. Stir in melted butter and press into springform, covering bottom and about 1 inch of sides. Refrigerate while making filling.

3. Place cream cheese in a large mixing bowl and beat with an electric mixer on high speed for about 2 minutes, until smooth and fluffy. Add remaining ¾ cup sugar and beat 2 minutes longer. Add eggs, 1 at a time, beating on low speed until mixed into batter. With the last egg, add cornstarch, sherry, and ½ teaspoon vanilla.

4. Carefully pour into crust. Bake in preheated oven for 45 minutes. Cake should be set in center when touched lightly with fingers. Let cool 10 minutes on a wire rack; leave oven on.

DAIRY

5. Mix sour cream with remaining ½ teaspoon vanilla. Spread evenly over top of cheesecake. Return to oven and bake for 10 minutes. Before serving, sprinkle cinnamon-sugar over top. Serve at room temperature.

ALMOND KONAFA

Konafa, a Middle Eastern shredded pastry, is available in the frozen food case of supermarkets and Middle Eastern food stores. Made by the producers of filo dough, it comes in the same long package.

MAKES 16

½ pound almonds, chopped
¾ cup plus 2 teaspoons sugar
½ pound frozen konafa, thawed
6 tablespoons butter, melted
1 tablespoon fresh lemon juice

1. Preheat oven to 400°F. Coat a 9-inch square baking pan with nonstick vegetable spray.

2. Place almonds in a small saucepan with water to cover. Bring to a boil. Cook until softened, about 3 minutes. Drain well, transfer to a small bowl, and toss with 2 teaspoons sugar.

3. In a large bowl, pull konafa apart into thin threads. Mix in half of melted butter. Spread half of konafa mixture over bottom of prepared baking dish. Cover with almonds. Spread remaining konafa on top. Drizzle remaining butter over all.

4. Bake in preheated oven for 35 minutes, or until golden.

5. While konafa is baking, prepare syrup. Bring 1 cup water, remaining ¾ cup sugar, and lemon juice to a boil, stirring to dissolve sugar. Boil over high heat without stirring, until syrupy, about 8 minutes.

6. Spoon syrup over hot konafa. Let cool, then cut into squares with a serrated knife.

CREAM-FILLED KONAFA

This recipe is an adaptation of one given to me by an Egyptian Jewish cook. Konafa, or *kataifi,* is finely shredded filo dough, widely used in Middle Eastern pastries. You can find it in the freezer section next to the filo dough.

MAKES 24

2 tablespoons cornstarch
1¼ cups milk
2 tablespoons sugar
2 tablespoons grated orange zest
1 cup sour cream
¼ teaspoon ground cardamom
½ pound konafa
1 stick (4 ounces) margarine or butter, melted
½ cup honey, warmed
2 tablespoons orange juice

1. Preheat oven to 400°F. Coat a 9-inch square baking dish with nonstick vegetable spray.

2. In a heavy, medium saucepan, mix cornstarch with ¼ cup milk. Add remaining milk and bring to a boil over medium-high heat, stirring constantly with a wooden spoon to make sure milk doesn't burn and stick to bottom of pan. Boil, stirring, for 1 minute, until thickened and smooth. Remove from heat.

3. Stir in sugar, orange zest, sour cream, and cardamom. Set cream filling aside.

4. In a large bowl, mix konafa and half of melted margarine. Pull into thin threads with your hands, tossing to coat all strands with margarine.

5. Spread half of konafa mixture over bottom of prepared baking dish. Spoon cream filling over konafa, spreading to edge of dish. Cover with remaining konafa. Drizzle remaining margarine over top.

DAIRY

6. Bake in preheated oven until golden brown, 35 minutes. Mix honey with orange juice. Spoon over hot konafa. Let cool before cutting into squares with a serrated knife. Serve at room temperature.

BERLINKRANZ

*T*his unusual cookie was brought to the United States at the turn of the century by German Jews.

MAKES 15 TO 18

1 hard-cooked egg yolk
½ cup powdered sugar
1 raw whole egg
1 teaspoon vanilla extract
1 stick (4 ounces) butter, cut into 8 pieces, softened
1½ cups flour
2 tablespoons milk
2 tablespoons granulated sugar

1. In a food processor, chop cooked egg yolk with powdered sugar. Add raw egg, vanilla, and butter. Process until well blended.

2. Add flour, ½ cup at a time, processing to mix thoroughly after each addition. Transfer dough to a bowl, cover, and refrigerate at least 1 hour, or overnight.

3. Preheat oven to 375°F. Coat a large cookie sheet with nonstick vegetable spray.

4. Roll dough into a thin rope about 3 inches long and ½ inch thick, like a short pencil. Tie each strip into a loose loop. Place on prepared cookie sheet. Brush with milk and sprinkle with granulated sugar.

5. Bake cookies in preheated oven for 8 to 10 minutes, until golden brown. Transfer to a wire rack and let cool before serving.

DAIRY

BUTTER KICHEL

A soft, not-too-sweet butter cookie equally good with a glass of wine or a cup of coffee. Cinnamon-sugar, which I suggest below, is the traditional topping, but I like to sprinkle half the cookies with sugar mixed with powdered ginger.

MAKES 36

1½ sticks (6 ounces) unsalted butter, softened
1 cup sugar
2 eggs
1½ teaspoons vanilla extract
2½ cups all-purpose flour
1 teaspoon baking powder
3 tablespoons cinnamon-sugar

1. Cream butter and sugar until light and fluffy, 3 to 4 minutes. Add eggs, vanilla, and ¼ cup of the flour. Mix well.

2. Add baking powder and remaining flour, about ½ cup at a time, mixing well between each addition. Refrigerate dough 1 hour or overnight.

3. Preheat oven to 325°F. Coat 2 baking sheets with nonstick vegetable spray.

4. Divide dough into thirds. Press one-third into a rectangle 12 inches long and about 3 inches wide. Sprinkle with 1 tablespoon cinnamon-sugar and cut into 12 bars 1 inch wide. Place on prepared baking sheets. Repeat with remaining dough.

5. Bake in preheated oven until nicely browned, about 25 minutes. Let cool on a wire rack before serving.

DAIRY

FRIED LEMON-HONEY PUFFS

*T*hese light, yeasty pastry puffs, called *bimuelos,* are the customary Chanukah dessert for Greek and Turkish Jews. I make the dough in one step using rapid-rise yeast, which needs no "proofing."

MAKES 30

2 cups flour
1 (¼-ounce) package rapid-rise yeast
1 teaspoon sugar
1 cup warm water (105° to 115°F.)
¼ cup warm milk (105° to 115°F.)
1 cup honey
3 tablespoons fresh lemon juice
Vegetable oil for frying

1. In a medium bowl, mix flour, yeast, and sugar. Add warm water and milk and mix well. Cover and let rise in a warm place until volume has doubled, about 30 minutes.

2. Meanwhile, in a medium skillet, heat honey and ¼ cup water, stirring to dissolve honey, until hot. Stir in lemon juice. Reduce heat to low and keep honey syrup warm.

3. Pour 1 inch of oil into a large, heavy saucepan and heat over medium-high heat to 375°F. on a deep-frying thermometer.

4. Dip a tablespoon in the hot oil, then use it to scoop up a rounded spoonful of batter. Slide batter gently into hot oil. Fry, turning often, until *bimuelos* puff up to more than twice their original size and are browned all over, 4 to 5 minutes. Dip spoon in oil before each addition of batter so that batter slides off easily.

5. With tongs, dip hot pastries into honey syrup, letting excess run back into skillet. Arrange on a platter. Eat while hot.

DAIRY

APRICOT RUGELACH

*A*t my house, the most popular filling for these irresistible little crescent cookies is a mixture of apricot preserves and dried apricots or dried cherries. These freeze well.

MAKES 24

1 stick (4 ounces) butter, softened
3 ounces cream cheese, at room temperature
1 tablespoon sugar
1 egg, separated
2 cups flour
¼ cup apricot preserves, warmed
¼ cup plus 2 tablespoons chopped dried apricots or
   dried cherries
2 tablespoons cinnamon-sugar

1. In a food processor, blend butter, cream cheese, sugar, and egg yolk. Add flour, ½ cup at a time, blending well after each addition, until dough forms a soft ball. Wrap and refrigerate 30 minutes or freeze 5 minutes to firm up slightly.

2. Preheat oven to 350°F. Coat a large cookie sheet with nonstick vegetable spray. Divide dough into 3 equal portions. On a floured surface, roll out 1 portion into an 8-inch round.

3. Spread about 1 tablespoon apricot preserves over dough to edges. Sprinkle with 2 tablespoons dried apricots. Cut into 8 wedges. Roll up each wedge, beginning from the wide end, like a jelly roll. Bend in ends to form a crescent. Repeat with remaining pastry and filling.

4. As they are formed, place rugelach on prepared cookie sheet. Brush with beaten egg white and sprinkle with cinnamon-sugar.

5. Bake rugelach in preheated oven for 20 minutes, or until golden brown. Transfer to a wire rack and let cool before serving.

DAIRY

RAPID RUGELACH

*I*nstead of the customary sour cream pastry, prepared pie crust dough is used here to speed up preparation. I make sour cream part of the filling. Include some of these with *hamantaschen* in *shalach manos* baskets to deliver to friends at Purim.

MAKES 16

¼ cup sour cream
½ cup ground almonds
2 (9-inch) pastry shells, chilled
⅓ cup mini semisweet chocolate chips
¼ cup currants or raisins
3 tablespoons cinnamon-sugar

1. Preheat oven to 375°F. Coat a baking sheet with nonstick vegetable spray.

2. In a small bowl, blend sour cream and ground almonds. Remove a pastry shell from its aluminum pie pan; press pastry out flat. Spread half of almond mixture over pastry to within ½ inch of edges.

3. Sprinkle with half of chocolate bits and half of currants. Cut into 8 pie-shaped wedges. Roll each piece, like a jelly roll, from wide end to narrow end in center and curve slightly to make a crescent. Place on prepared baking sheet. Repeat with remaining ingredients. Brush with water and sprinkle with cinnamon-sugar.

4. Bake in preheated oven for 10 to 15 minutes, or until golden. Let cool before serving. Store in a tightly covered container in a cool place.

DAIRY

SUFGANIOT

These jelly donuts without the hole are the foremost Chanukah delicacy in Israel—way ahead of potato latkes. This quick version is made with baking powder rather than yeast.

MAKES 20 TO 24

2 cups flour
2 tablespoons granulated sugar
3 tablespoons butter
1 tablespoon baking powder
1 cup buttermilk or sour milk*
3 tablespoons strawberry preserves or your favorite flavor
Vegetable oil for frying
Powdered sugar

1. In a medium bowl, mix flour and granulated sugar. Rub in butter to resemble coarse bread crumbs. Stir in baking powder.

2. Make a well in center of dry ingredients. Mix in enough buttermilk to make a soft, slightly sticky dough.

3. With floured hands, roll 1 rounded tablespoon of dough into a ball about 1½ inches in diameter. With your finger or the handle end of a wooden spoon dipped in flour, make an indentation large enough to hold ½ teaspoon preserves. Work dough around preserves to seal completely. Repeat with rest of dough and preserves.

4. In a large saucepan or deep-fryer, heat 2 inches of oil to 375°F. on a deep-frying thermometer. Gently slide dough balls into hot oil in batches without crowding. Cook over medium heat, turning often, until crisp and brown, 3½ to 4 minutes. Drain on paper towels and toss in powdered sugar. Serve hot.

*To sour milk, mix 1 cup milk with 2 teaspoons distilled white vinegar. Let stand for 10 minutes without stirring.

DAIRY

CHAPTER ELEVEN

Fruit Desserts and Puddings

Desserts you can eat with a spoon hold a major place on the Jewish table, from the old-fashioned dried fruit compotes of Grandmother's house to more contemporary recipes designed with an eye to the citrus, fresh dates, and melons that are the bounty of modern Israel. There are a number of creamy dairy puddings, which are traditionally served on Shavuot.

Many of the fruit desserts in this chapter are fat-free. These range from Eastern European Raspberry-Peach Kissel and Dried Fruit Compote with Tokay Wine to Middle Eastern-inspired Fresh Figs in Lime Syrup and my own Pears in Ginger Syrup. Some of my childhood favorites also appear here: Rhubarb-Strawberry Compote and Rosy Stewed Apples.

With the use of nondairy creamer and whipped topping, I've managed to include a wide selection of both dairy and parve desserts from all over the world. Coconut Tapioca Pudding comes from the Black Jews of Cochin, India, and Papaya with Lemon Cream and Coconut from Jews living in the Caribbean. I've even included a recipe for a glamorous-looking Australian Pavlova, which was given to me by a Jewish family living in Melbourne. And, of course, there's my mother's comforting Baked Custards, which were her nourishing backup to chicken soup.

QUICK-BAKED APPLES

With a microwave, you can enjoy the old-fashioned taste of baked apples prepared with contemporary speed. These can be eaten warm, at room temperature, or chilled.

4 SERVINGS

4 medium baking apples, cored
¼ cup currants or raisins
2 teaspoons brown sugar
1½ teaspoons grated orange zest
¼ teaspoon vanilla extract

1. Peel a ¼-inch band of skin around each apple about 1 inch from the top to allow steam to escape and to prevent bursting.

2. In a cup or small bowl, mix currants, brown sugar, and orange zest. Fill apple centers with currant mixture.

3. Place apples in a 9-inch glass pie plate. Mix vanilla with 3 tablespoons water and pour into plate around apples. Cover loosely with dampened microwave-safe paper towel.

4. Microwave on High for 6 minutes, or until apples are tender to the touch. Check after 5 minutes. Remove from microwave and let stand at room temperature for 4 minutes before serving.

ROSY STEWED APPLES

Grape juice adds a subtle hue to these stewed dried apples. Dried fruit compote is an all-purpose Jewish dessert that can be served with any meal, meat or dairy.

4 TO 6 SERVINGS

½ cup apple juice
½ cup grape juice
3 thin slices of lemon
3 or 4 cloves
2½ cups dried unsweetened apples (6 ounces)

1. In a medium saucepan, mix apple juice, grape juice, lemon slices, cloves, and 3 cups water.

2. Add dried apples. Liquid should come about ½ inch above apples. If it doesn't, add more water.

3. Bring to a boil over medium-high heat. Reduce heat to medium-low. Cover and cook until apples are plump, 25 minutes, stirring occasionally. Serve at room temperature.

HOMEMADE DRIED APPLES

Drying was a popular method of preserving fresh fruits before the days of refrigerators and freezers. It's surprisingly easy to dry fruit in the oven.

MAKES 2 CUPS

3 tablespoons sugar
6 apples

1. Preheat oven to 225°F. Line 2 large baking sheets with aluminum foil. Sprinkle each sheet with 1½ tablespoons sugar.

2. Peel and core apples. Slice into rings ¼ inch thick. Arrange in a single layer on prepared baking sheets.

3. Bake in preheated oven for 4 hours. Turn oven off. Leave apples in closed oven 8 hours longer, or overnight. When done, they should be wrinkled, golden, and chewy.

4. Let cool at room temperature for 4 to 6 hours before storing in a tightly lidded container.

PINK APPLESAUCE

*T*his applesauce is completely natural, with very little sugar and the skins left on. Many Jews serve this as a condiment with almost any meal, but I like it as a parve dessert.

6 TO 8 SERVINGS

3 pounds McIntosh apples, cored (skins left on)
2 tablespoons fresh lemon juice
1 cinnamon stick
2 to 4 tablespoons sugar

1. Cut each apple into 8 wedges and place in a large nonreactive saucepan. Toss with lemon juice. Add cinnamon stick and ½ cup water.

2. Cover and cook over low heat, stirring often, until apples begin to soften, about 20 minutes. Remove from heat and let stand, covered, 30 minutes longer. (Apples will soften completely from retained heat.) Remove cinnamon stick and discard.

3. Chop coarsely in food processor. Stir in sugar. Serve chilled or at room temperature.

APRICOT PRESERVES

*H*omemade preserves are so easy to make and such a treat. This tangy, golden spread is excellent on scones, toast, or matzohs. If the dried apricots are soft and plump, less soaking time will be needed.

MAKES 2 CUPS

½ pound dried apricots, chopped
1 orange, skin and all, cut into 1-inch pieces
¾ cup sugar
¼ cup fresh lemon juice

1. Cover apricots with cold water to come ½ inch above fruit. Soak 4 hours or overnight. Drain, reserving ¾ cup soaking liquid.

2. Pour reserved liquid and orange into blender or food processor. Process until orange is coarsely chopped.

3. Pour mixture into a heavy, medium saucepan. Add apricots and sugar. Cook over medium-high heat, stirring often, until boiling.

4. Reduce heat to low. Add lemon juice. Cook, stirring occasionally, until thickened, 30 to 35 minutes.

5. Pour preserves into 2 half-pint sterilized jars. Cover loosely with the lids and let cool. Tighten bands and store in refrigerator. Preserves will keep in refrigerator for at least 6 months.

CHOCOLATE-DIPPED APRICOTS AND ALMONDS

*T*hese make an attractive addition to a cookie tray. In summer, use fresh strawberries with the stems attached.

MAKES ABOUT 1 POUND

1 (6-ounce) package dried apricots
6 ounces parve semisweet chocolate chips, melted
1 cup whole almonds

1. Line a baking sheet with wax paper. With tongs, dip apricots into melted chocolate to cover half of each apricot. Place on prepared baking sheet.

2. Repeat with almonds, dipping to cover half of each almond.

3. Refrigerate fruit and nuts 30 minutes to harden chocolate. Store between layers of wax paper in a tightly covered container in a cool, dry place.

CRANBERRY KISSEL

Kissel, a jelled fruit dessert favored by German Jews, may be prepared with almost any fresh fruit. At a dairy meal, top with a dab of sour cream; at a meat meal, with nondairy frozen dessert whip.

4 SERVINGS

3 cups fresh cranberries
¾ cup sugar
1 tablespoon plus 1 teaspoon cornstarch
2 tablespoons cherry brandy

1. In a large nonreactive saucepan, mix cranberries, sugar, and 1½ cups water. Bring to a boil over high heat.

2. Reduce heat to low and cook until cranberries pop, about 10 minutes. Strain through a sieve and return to rinsed saucepan.

3. Mix cornstarch and ½ cup water until smooth. Stir into cranberry puree. Bring to a boil over medium heat, stirring constantly, until thickened and smooth. Cook, stirring, for 1 minute.

4. Stir in cherry brandy. Remove from heat and let cool slightly, then spoon into small glasses or demitasse cups. Cover and refrigerate until cold. Serve chilled.

CRIMSON COMPOTE

Since according to the Jewish laws of kashruth any dessert that accompanies a meat meal must be nondairy, fruit compotes have become an essential part of the cuisine. Here I use frozen berries, which are especially convenient.

4 SERVINGS

¼ cup sweet red wine, such as Malaga, or fortified wine, such as Madeira
¼ cup orange marmalade
1 teaspoon dried mint
2 cups frozen blueberries
2 cups frozen strawberries
1 cup frozen raspberries

1. In a medium nonreactive saucepan, combine wine and marmalade. Warm over medium heat, stirring, until marmalade is melted.

2. Stir in mint, blueberries, strawberries, and raspberries. Reduce heat to medium-low and cook until berries thaw, 7 to 10 minutes.

3. Remove from heat and let cool. Serve at room temperature or chilled.

FRESH FIGS IN LIME SYRUP

Fresh figs, limes, and sesame seeds are popular ingredients in Sephardic cooking. Figs taste very much alike whether they have green skins or dark purple skins. They are ripe when they yield to gentle pressure.

4 SERVINGS

⅔ cup white grape juice
⅓ cup lime marmalade
¼ teaspoon powdered ginger
12 fresh green or black figs
1 tablespoon toasted sesame seeds (optional)

1. In a medium nonreactive saucepan, stir grape juice, lime marmalade, and ginger over medium heat until marmalade is melted.

2. Add figs. Cover and reduce heat to medium-low. Cook until figs feel soft when pressed gently with a spoon, about 10 minutes.

3. Remove from heat. Let stand, covered, 15 minutes longer. Green figs will change to a yellowish green.

4. Spoon into 4 small serving dishes. Pour juices over figs. Sprinkle sesame seeds on top. Serve at room temperature.

DRIED FRUIT COMPOTE WITH TOKAY WINE

*T*oday's prunes and raisins are plump and moist. With sweet amber Tokay wine, this fragrant compote is made in minutes. Spoon into crystal glasses or, for less formal occasions, serve in dessert bowls.

4 TO 6 SERVINGS

1 (12-ounce) package pitted prunes
¼ cup raisins
2 tablespoons dried cherries
1 cup Tokay wine
1 tablespoon honey
¼ teaspoon ground allspice
1 bay leaf

1. In a medium saucepan, place prunes, raisins, cherries, wine, honey, allspice, bay leaf, and ⅓ cup water. Cover and bring to a boil over medium heat.

2. Reduce heat to low and cook for 15 minutes. Remove from heat. Discard bay leaf. Let cool. Serve chilled or at room temperature.

TIPSY GOLDEN FRUITS

Brandied fruits keep almost indefinitely in the refrigerator. They can be eaten in small portions by themselves or spooned over ice cream or cake.

MAKES 1 QUART

1½ cups diced (½-inch) dried pears
1 small orange, unpeeled and sliced ¼ inch thick
1 cup diced (½-inch) dried peaches
½ cup dried cherries
2 tablespoons sliced crystallized ginger
1 to 1½ cups cherry brandy

1. Place ¾ cup pears in a quart jar. Top with half of orange, ½ cup dried peaches, ¼ cup dried cherries, and 1 tablespoon crystallized ginger. Repeat with remaining ingredients. Pour in enough brandy to come ¼ inch above fruits.

2. Cover tightly. Let stand at room temperature 1 week before using as compote or dessert topping. Add more brandy to keep fruits covered as needed. Keeps indefinitely in refrigerator.

ROASTED FRUITS IN CIDER

*P*an-roasted winter fruits and glazed dried fruits give a new twist to the traditional "Jewish" compote. Make at Chanukah when glazed dried fruits and nuts are easily available.

4 SERVINGS

2 tablespoons walnut oil
¼ cup maple syrup
2 teaspoons balsamic vinegar
2 pears, cored and sliced ¼ inch thick
2 apples, cored and sliced ¼ inch thick
⅓ cup chopped glazed mixed dried fruits
½ cup apple cider
2 tablespoons chopped glazed pecans

1. Heat oil in a large skillet over medium heat. Stir in maple syrup and balsamic vinegar.

2. Add pears and apples. Partially cover and cook over medium-high heat until barely tender, 8 to 10 minutes.

3. Remove from heat. Stir in dried fruits and apple cider.

4. Transfer to a serving bowl. Sprinkle pecans over top. Serve at room temperature.

PARVE

CHOCOLATE KUMQUAT COMPOTE

*K*umquats are tiny, zesty, oval oranges available in the winter months. They are too tart to eat raw. Cook in a simple syrup and serve small portions as the Israelis do.

4 TO 6 SERVINGS (2½ TO 3 CUPS)

½ pound fresh kumquats
¾ cup sugar
¼ teaspoon pepper
2 tablespoons shelled pistachio nuts, halved
¼ cup grated parve semisweet chocolate

1. Rinse kumquats in cold water. Pierce each kumquat once with a sharp-pointed knife.

2. In a medium saucepan, dissolve sugar in 1¼ cups water. Bring to a boil over high heat.

3. Add kumquats and pepper. Reduce heat to medium-low. Cook until kumquats are easily pierced with a knife and have lost their raw look, 20 to 25 minutes. Stir in pistachios.

4. Let compote cool, then transfer to a serving bowl. Cover and refrigerate. Serve chilled, with grated chocolate sprinkled on top.

PEARS IN GINGER SYRUP

4 SERVINGS

1 cup ginger ale
2 tablespoons brown sugar
1 teaspoon grated fresh ginger
½ teaspoon vanilla extract
4 pears, cored, peeled, and sliced ¼ inch thick

1. In a large skillet, combine ginger ale, brown sugar, ginger, and vanilla. Bring to a simmer over medium-high heat, stirring to dissolve brown sugar.

2. Add pears and baste with liquids from skillet. Cover and cook over medium-low heat until pears are tender when pierced with a knife, 10 to 15 minutes.

3. Let cool. Serve at room temperature, with the syrup drizzled over the top.

BAKED PINEAPPLE STREUSEL

*S*ave time and buy pineapple already peeled and cored. Two 16-ounce cans of drained pineapple chunks may also be used.

6 TO 8 SERVINGS

2 tablespoons margarine
½ cup oatmeal (not instant)
2 tablespoons brown sugar
½ cup chopped walnuts
1 pineapple, peeled and cored
¼ teaspoon cinnamon
2 tablespoons honey

1. Cut margarine into oatmeal. Add brown sugar and walnuts. Set oatmeal streusel aside.

2. Preheat oven to 375°F. Cut pineapple into 1-inch chunks. Place in a shallow 9-inch square baking dish.

3. Sprinkle cinnamon over pineapple. Drizzle with honey. Top with oatmeal streusel.

4. Bake in preheated oven until topping is nicely browned, 15 to 20 minutes. Serve warm.

PURPLE PLUMS IN PORT

My dad never drank port, but he loved this compote. The blue-black, slightly tart Italian prune plums are best here, but any purple or black variety will work.

4 SERVINGS

1 pound Italian prune plums
½ cup port wine
3 tablespoons sugar
3 drops pure lemon oil or 1 tablespoon fresh lemon juice

1. Cut plums in half. Remove pits and then halve each piece again.

2. In a large nonreactive saucepan, combine port and sugar. Stir over medium heat until sugar dissolves, 3 to 4 minutes.

3. Add plums, stirring to baste with port syrup. Cook over low heat until plums are tender but still hold their shape, about 15 minutes. Stir in lemon oil. Serve at room temperature.

STEWED PRUNES

A bowl of stewed prunes used to be standard in every Jewish refrigerator. Here's my version.

4 TO 6 SERVINGS

1 (12-ounce) package pitted prunes
2 tablespoons fresh lemon juice plus 4 to 6 thin slices
  of lemon
2 clementines or seedless tangerines or oranges, peeled
  and sectioned
2 tablespoons sugar
Slivers of lemon peel, for garnish

1. Place prunes in a nonreactive medium saucepan. Add enough cold water to come about ½ inch above prunes.

2. Add lemon juice, clementine sections, and sugar. Bring to a simmer over medium heat, stirring to dissolve sugar.

3. Reduce heat to low. Cover and cook for 15 minutes. Uncover and continue cooking for 10 minutes more. Remove from heat and let cool. Serve at room temperature or chilled. Garnish with a lemon twist.

RASPBERRY-PEACH KISSEL

*S*un-kissed summer fruits make a silky pudding, popular with Eastern European Jews. Any berries or fruits in season may be substituted.

4 SERVINGS

4 ripe peaches, thinly sliced
1 cup raspberries
⅓ cup sugar
3 tablespoons fresh lemon juice
3 tablespoons cornstarch

1. In a medium saucepan, combine peaches, raspberries, sugar, lemon juice, and 2 cups water. Bring to a boil over medium-high heat. Reduce heat to medium-low. Cover and cook until fruit is soft, about 10 minutes.

2. Blend cornstarch and ½ cup water to a smooth paste. Stir into fruit. Bring to a boil over medium heat, stirring constantly, until thickened and clear, 3 to 4 minutes.

3. Transfer to a blender or food processor and puree until smooth. Strain to remove any seeds.

4. Pour pudding into small glass dessert dishes. Cover and refrigerate until cold. Serve chilled.

GINGERED RHUBARB COMPOTE

*T*o dress up this simple compote, spoon it into the center of a dish of creamy vanilla pudding or tapioca.

4 TO 6 SERVINGS

6 cups sliced rhubarb, cut ½ inch thick
1½ to 2 cups sugar
2 tablespoons chopped crystallized ginger

1. In a large nonreactive saucepan, place rhubarb, 1½ cups sugar, and 3 tablespoons water. Cook over medium-low heat, stirring often, until sugar dissolves, 5 to 7 minutes.

2. Raise heat to medium and cook, stirring often, until rhubarb is soft and beginning to break down, about 5 to 7 minutes longer.

3. Taste and add more sugar if it's needed. Stir in crystallized ginger and remove from heat. Serve at room temperature or chilled.

RHUBARB-BANANA PUDDING

Rhubarb grows wild all over Europe. Even cultivated, it comes up year after year, needing little attention. Since tartness varies considerably, I have given a range for the sugar here.

4 TO 6 SERVINGS

2 cups fresh or frozen rhubarb, sliced ¼ inch thick
⅔ to ¾ cup sugar
⅔ cup orange juice
⅛ teaspoon powdered ginger
¼ cup parve vanilla pudding mix (not instant)
2 cups sliced bananas

1. In a nonreactive medium saucepan, mix rhubarb, ⅔ cup sugar, orange juice, and ginger. Bring to a simmer over medium heat.

2. Reduce heat to medium-low. Cover and continue cooking until rhubarb is soft, 10 to 15 minutes.

3. In a small bowl, blend vanilla pudding mix with 6 tablespoons water. Stir into rhubarb mixture. Add bananas.

4. Raise heat to high and bring to a boil, stirring constantly. Cook 1 minute. Remove from heat.

5. Taste and add more sugar if desired. Let cool. Serve at room temperature in dessert glasses.

RHUBARB-STRAWBERRY COMPOTE

R hubarb grew wild, sprawling all over our backyard in the Shetland Isles. My mother didn't have time for complicated cooking, so she created easy desserts like this one.

4 TO 6 SERVINGS

½ pound rhubarb, trimmed and cut into ½-inch slices
   (4 cups)
½ cup sugar
2 tablespoons orange juice
½ teaspoon vanilla extract
2 cups sliced strawberries

1. In a nonreactive medium saucepan, stir together rhubarb, sugar, and orange juice. Cover and cook over medium-low heat for 10 minutes, stirring occasionally, until rhubarb breaks down.

2. Stir in vanilla and strawberries. Raise heat to medium-high and cook 1 to 2 minutes longer. Remove from heat and let cool, then cover and refrigerate until cold. Serve chilled.

FOAMY WINE SAUCE

*C*ardamom adds a distinct Middle Eastern flavor to this rich egg sauce, similar to a French sabayon or Italian zabaglione. Pass the sauce in a pitcher to spoon over fruit and cake.

MAKES 1 ¼ CUPS

4 egg yolks
¼ cup sugar
2 tablespoons fresh lime juice
Pinch of ground cardamom
½ cup dry white wine, such as Chardonnay

1. In top of double boiler over medium heat, whisk yolks and sugar until pale and fluffy, about 2 minutes.

2. Add lime juice, cardamom, and wine in a slow, steady stream, stirring constantly. Cook, stirring constantly, until mixture is thickened and foamy, 6 to 8 minutes.

3. Remove from heat and whisk for 1 minute to cool slightly and aerate. Serve warm or at room temperature.

WINTER FRUIT COMPOTE

*T*his easy mix of fresh, prepared, and dried fruit will keep well in the refrigerator for up to five days.

6 TO 8 SERVINGS

8 ounces dried apricots
⅓ cup dried cherries
1 (16-ounce) can pear halves, juices reserved
1 (16-ounce) jar citrus fruit sections, juices reserved
⅛ teaspoon whole cloves
2 cinnamon sticks
2 kiwifruit
3 tablespoons amaretto liqueur

1. Place dried apricots and cherries in a medium saucepan. Pour reserved juices drained from pears and citrus sections over dried fruit. Add cloves and cinnamon sticks. If needed, add enough water to barely cover fruit. Cook over low heat for 20 minutes. Remove from heat and let cool slightly.

2. Cut canned pears into ½-inch dice and place in a serving bowl. Add citrus sections, cloves, and cinnamon sticks. Pour plumped dried fruits with their liquid into bowl.

3. Peel kiwi and cut them into 8 wedges each. Add amaretto and kiwifruit to compote. Stir gently to mix. Serve warm, at room temperature, or chilled.

SHABBAT WINE MOLD

*S*weet Concord grape wine, customarily used to say the blessing to welcome the Sabbath, is used as part of the liquid for this gelatin mold.

4 TO 6 SERVINGS

1 (3-ounce) package black cherry gelatin
1 cup boiling water
1 cup sweet red kosher wine
1 cup pitted fresh or canned sweet cherries
½ cup chopped celery
½ cup chopped walnuts

1. In a medium bowl, dissolve gelatin in boiling water. Stir in wine. Let cool slightly, then refrigerate until mixture is beginning to set, about 2 hours.

2. Fold in cherries, celery, and walnuts. Transfer to a 6-cup ring mold. Refrigerate until firm and completely set, at least 3 to 4 hours.

SABRA SAUTEED BANANAS

*T*his chunky, glazed compote is perfumed with Israeli orange liqueur. Spoon the hot compote over coffee ice cream or frozen yogurt.

4 SERVINGS

2 tablespoons butter
2 tablespoons brown sugar
2 tablespoons Sabra or other orange liqueur
1 teaspoon fresh lemon juice
3 medium bananas, peeled and sliced lengthwise ½ inch thick

1. Melt butter in a medium nonstick skillet. Add brown sugar and stir over medium heat until bubbly, 2 minutes.

2. Remove from heat and stir in Sabra liqueur and lemon juice.

3. Add sliced bananas. Return to medium heat and turn bananas to coat with butter-sugar mixture. Cover partially and cook until bananas are barely softened, 2 to 3 minutes, stirring several times. Serve warm or at room temperature.

DAIRY

SPICED CANTALOUPE WITH DATES

*M*ade ahead and chilled, this honeyed fruit dessert is especially fitting for a Yom Kippur break-the-fast dairy meal.

6 SERVINGS

1 medium cantaloupe
½ cup sour cream
⅛ teaspoon cinnamon
Pinch of grated nutmeg
2 tablespoons honey, warmed
8 pitted dates
2 tablespoons chopped pistachios

1. Quarter the cantaloupe. Scoop out the seeds and cut off the rind. Cut the cantaloupe into ¾-inch dice.

2. In a large bowl, mix sour cream, cinnamon, and nutmeg. Add cantaloupe and stir to coat. Transfer to a serving dish.

3. Drizzle honey over melon. Arrange dates around edge of dish. Garnish with pistachios and serve chilled.

DAIRY

PAPAYA WITH LEMON CREAM AND COCONUT

Enclaves of Jews can be found all over the world, even in the Caribbean. Wherever they dwell, they incorporate local ingredients into their traditional cuisine. In St. Thomas, I found tropical fruits transformed into enticing parve desserts. Use store-bought lemon curd or make your own Lemon-Lime Curd (see recipe on page 339) for the filling.

4 SERVINGS

2 papayas, halved and seeded
¼ cup whipped cream
½ cup lemon curd
2 tablespoons toasted coconut

1. Cut a thin slice of skin off bottom of each papaya half so that it stands firm.

2. In a small bowl, fold whipped cream into lemon curd. Spoon into cavities of papaya halves. Refrigerate until ready to serve.

3. Just before serving, sprinkle toasted coconut on top.

DAIRY

AUSTRALIAN PAVLOVA

*T*his is a popular Australian dessert that I first enjoyed at the Melbourne home of a Jewish family. For a stunning Passover dessert, adapt the recipe by substituting potato starch for the cornstarch and Passover macaroons for the toasted cake crumbs.

8 TO 10 SERVINGS

3 egg whites
½ cup sugar
1 teaspoon cornstarch
1 teaspoon distilled white vinegar
¾ cup heavy cream
2 kiwifruits, peeled and thinly sliced
2 cups strawberries, halved
2 tablespoons toasted white or yellow cake crumbs

1. Preheat oven to 325°F. Coat a 10-inch pie dish with nonstick vegetable spray.

2. Beat egg whites until they form soft peaks. Gradually beat in sugar, ¼ cup at a time. Continue to beat until meringue is stiff and glossy. Fold in cornstarch and vinegar.

3. Spoon meringue into prepared pie dish. Smooth bottom with a spatula and work meringue evenly up sides of dish.

4. Bake in center of preheated oven for 20 minutes, or until pale golden. Let cool.

5. Beat cream until it forms soft peaks. Spread whipped cream over meringue to cover. Arrange kiwi and strawberries attractively on top. Sprinkle with toasted cake crumbs. Serve at room temperature.

DAIRY

CREAMY APRICOT AND RAISIN RICE PUDDING

4 TO 6 SERVINGS

2 egg whites
3 ounces low-fat cream cheese, at room temperature
¼ cup powdered sugar
½ cup low-fat sour cream
1 whole egg, lightly beaten
3 cups cooked rice
1 teaspoon cinnamon
1 cup dried apricots, chopped
½ cup golden raisins

1. Preheat oven to 350°F. Coat a 1½-quart baking dish with nonstick vegetable spray.

2. Beat egg whites until stiff. In a separate bowl, whip cream cheese and sugar until light, 2 minutes. Add sour cream and egg and beat until smooth, 1 minute longer.

3. Stir in rice, cinnamon, apricots, and raisins. Fold in stiffly beaten egg whites.

4. Transfer to prepared baking dish. Bake in preheated oven for 30 minutes, until golden and puffy. Serve warm.

NOTE: 1 cup long-grain white rice cooked with 1¾ cups water and ½ teaspoon salt yields 3 cups cooked rice.

DAIRY

COCONUT TAPIOCA PUDDING

Coconuts are abundant in Southern India, the home of the Black Jews of Cochin, so many of their dishes use coconut as a main ingredient as in this creamy tropical dessert. Coconut milk is parve and available canned in supermarkets or use fresh.

4 SERVINGS

2 teaspoons Asian sesame oil
¼ cup flaked coconut
¼ cup slivered almonds
3 tablespoons instant tapioca
2 tablespoons sugar
1 cup unsweetened coconut milk
1 cup milk

1. In a medium saucepan, heat sesame oil over medium heat. Add coconut and almonds. Cook, stirring often, until pale golden brown, about 2 minutes. Transfer to a bowl.

2. In same pan (no need to wash), mix tapioca, sugar, coconut milk, and milk. Let stand 5 minutes. Bring to a boil over medium-high heat, stirring constantly. Mixture will be thin but will thicken as it cools.

3. Pour tapioca into dessert dishes. Let cool 10 minutes. Cover and refrigerate until chilled, at least 2 hours. Just before serving, sprinkle toasted coconut and almonds on top.

DAIRY

FRUIT AND RICE TZIMMES

*T*his is really a substantial rice pudding laced with dried fruit, which I like to serve after a light meal.

6 TO 8 SERVINGS

1 (11-ounce) package mixed dried fruit
1 lemon
4 tablespoons butter, cut into 4 pieces
1 cup long-grain white rice
¼ cup packed brown sugar
1½ teaspoons cinnamon
½ teaspoon salt

1. In a large saucepan, mix dried fruit with 3½ cups cold water. Bring to a boil over high heat. Reduce to low heat. Cover and cook for 10 minutes.

2. Slice lemon thinly, then cut slices in quarters. Add to fruits in saucepan along with butter, rice, brown sugar, cinnamon, and salt.

3. Cover and cook over low heat, stirring often, until rice is tender, 30 to 35 minutes. Serve warm or at room temperature. (If refrigerated, mixture will thicken. Reheat over low heat, with a little apple or orange juice.)

NOTE: To turn this into a parve dessert, substitute margarine for the butter.

DAIRY

SHAVUOT RICE PUDDING

Dairy products are traditionally served at Shavuot. One explanation for this is that "the honey and milk" in the Song of Songs refers to the sweetness and purity of the Torah, the first five books of the Bible. Some Sephardic Jews flavor Shavuot sweets and puddings with rose water, which is available in specialty stores and some markets.

4 TO 6 SERVINGS

½ cup long-grain white rice
3 cups milk
2 tablespoons sugar
2 tablespoons honey
1 teaspoon rose water or vanilla extract
½ cup chopped mixed dried fruits

1. In a double boiler, mix rice, milk, sugar, and honey. Cover and cook over medium heat for 30 minutes, stirring occasionally.

2. Stir in rose water or vanilla and chopped dried fruits. Cover, reduce the heat to medium-low, and cook until thick and creamy, about 30 minutes longer. Serve warm or at room temperature.

DAIRY

BAKED CUSTARDS

Besides chicken soup, these creamy custards were my mother's nourishing cure for colds and sore throats. Buy the freshest eggs possible. I use organic or those bought at farmers' markets.

4 SERVINGS

4 eggs
¼ cup milk
¼ cup sour cream
1 teaspoon salt
⅛ teaspoon white pepper

1. Preheat oven to 325°F. Coat 4 custard cups with nonstick vegetable spray.

2. In a small bowl, whisk eggs, milk, sour cream, salt, and pepper. Divide into prepared cups.

3. Place in a shallow baking dish with enough cool water to come about halfway up the sides of custard cups.

4. Bake 30 minutes, or until center is just set. Serve at room temperature.

DAIRY

LEMON-LIME CURD

Dairy products are linked to Chanukah because, so the story goes, Judith, the beautiful Jewess, fed the enemy general, Holofernes, salty cheese and plenty of wine. As he slept, she beheaded him, thus assuring a Jewish victory. Lemon-Lime Curd is a creamy, tart spread. Mix with whipped cream as a filling for cakes and tarts or to spread on breakfast toast.

MAKES TWO 1-PINT JARS (SCANT 2 CUPS)

2 large lemons
2 limes
5 eggs
1¼ cups sugar
1 stick (4 ounces) butter, melted

1. Grate zest (colored part of rind) from lemons and limes into a blender or food processor. Cut fruits in half and squeeze juice into blender. Add eggs and sugar. Cover and blend on high speed for 10 seconds.

2. With machine on low speed, gradually pour in melted butter in a thin, steady stream. Transfer to a heavy saucepan and cook over medium heat, whisking constantly, until thickened, 4 to 5 minutes. Do not let boil or mixture may curdle.

3. Remove from heat and whisk constantly for 1 minute. Pour into jelly jars. Store in refrigerator for up to 3 weeks.

DAIRY

Passover

*T*he eight-day Passover observance commemorates the Exodus of the Jews from Egypt more than 3,500 years ago. Jews all over the world gather around the table for a Seder, the ceremonial meal, to read and relive the story of the Jews' freedom from Egyptian slavery. The reading is from the Haggadah, a text which has been used throughout the ages, and the symbolic foods, arranged on a special plate, are tasted by everyone. Today the symbolism in many homes has extended to a wish for freedom for people everywhere.

Because Passover calls not just for special plates, but for special foods, it is the most challenging of all the Jewish holidays to cook for. In observant homes, dishes and appliances used only at Passover are taken from storage, washed, and readied for use. The kitchen is thoroughly cleaned and the house rid of all flour and bread, since *chometz*, leavened foods, are forbidden at this time. Besides flour and breads, other foods that include grain or cereal products, as well as any foods made from them, such as grain alcohol, grain vinegar, and corn oil, are forbidden.

All ingredients used during Passover must be certified "kosher for Passover." Even with the extraordinary variety of Passover convenience foods now available, creating tasty appropriate foods three times a day throughout the long week is not easy. Specific dietary rules prevail, and the laws of kashruth are different from keeping a kosher kitchen throughout the rest of the year. "Kosher for Passover" matzohs are made from flour whose production has been scrupulously supervised. Mixing and baking must be completed in 18 minutes or less to avoid any possibility of fermentation or leavening of the dough. Legumes, such as peas and beans, corn, and rice are also forbidden, although some Sephardic Jews do permit rice after it has been carefully picked over to check that no *chometz,* or other grains, are present.

Although there are many symbolic and traditional dishes to be prepared for Passover, the recipes here are easy, and many can be made ahead. Apricot-Cherry Charoseth, for example, will keep, refrigerated, for up to one week, and updated classics, like the eggless, fruit- and vegetable-packed Springtime Kugel, freeze well. Matzoh and eggs may be mixed the night before, ready to pour into the skillet for a breakfast Matzoh Brie. This chapter is a *tzimmes* (wonderful mix) of international Passover dishes from Jewish kitchens all over the world.

APPLE CHAROSETH

*C*haroseth is essential on the Seder plate and this is the most popular version. Its brick red color is symbolic of the mortar made by the Jews, who while in Egyptian slavery, were forced to build the cities of Pithom and Ramses.

MAKES 1½ CUPS

2 tart-sweet apples, such as Stayman or Empire
½ cup walnuts
2 teaspoons cinnamon
2 tablespoons honey
3 tablespoons sweet red wine

1. Peel and core apples and cut into chunks. Place in a food processor. Add walnuts and chop coarsely.

2. Add cinnamon, honey, and 2 tablespoons wine. Pulse 3 or 4 times to mix. *Charoseth* should be moist but stiff. Add a little more wine if needed. Serve at room temperature.

APRICOT-CHERRY CHAROSETH

I am indebted to the Nissimov family, who escaped from Chechnya to Israel in 1995, for this delightful recipe. The summer fruits grown in their garden were dried for year-round cooking, as in this *charoseth* for the Passover Seder.

MAKES 1½ CUPS

1 cup dried apricots
¼ cup dried cherries
3 large dried peaches (about 4 ounces), cut into ½-inch chunks
¼ cup slivered almonds
1 tablespoon packed fresh mint leaves
2 tablespoons sweet wine
1 tablespoon honey

1. In a medium nonreactive saucepan, place dried apricots, cherries, and peaches. Add enough cold water to cover. Bring to a boil over high heat. Reduce heat to low. Simmer 15 minutes; drain.

2. Place drained fruits in a food processor and pulse to chop coarsely. Add almonds, mint, and wine. Pulse again to mix and chop finely.

3. Transfer to a small bowl. Sweeten with honey to taste. Serve at room temperature.

COCONUT CHAROSETH

*C*haroseth is a fruit/nut paste, symbolic of the mortar used by Jewish slaves during their captivity in Egypt and served at the Passover Seder. My friend and colleague Judy Stern toasts the nuts for her *charoseth* for richer flavor.

MAKES 3 CUPS

½ cup walnut pieces
½ cup slivered almonds
2 medium apples, peeled, cored, and cut into chunks
½ cup shredded coconut
1 teaspoon pumpkin pie spice
2 tablespoons honey
¼ cup blackberry wine

1. Preheat oven to 350°F. Spread out nuts on a small baking sheet. Toast in oven, stirring several times, until lightly browned and fragrant, 5 to 7 minutes. Remove to a plate and let cool.

2. In a food processor, coarsely chop apples, walnuts, and almonds.

3. Transfer to a medium bowl. Add coconut, pumpkin pie spice, honey, and enough wine to make a stiff paste. Serve at room temperature.

NOTE: If using fresh coconut, grate finely, spread on a baking sheet, and dry in a 200°F. oven for 3 hours, stirring occasionally.

PESACH "ORANGES"

These are fun to make with children while retelling the Passover story. Serve as one of several *charoseths* at the Seder.

MAKES 20 TO 24

14 pitted dates
1 cup dried apricots
¼ cup walnuts
¼ seedless orange, skin on, cut into 1-inch pieces
2 tablespoons orange juice
1 to 2 tablespoons honey
20 to 24 pistachio halves

1. In a food processor, finely chop dates, apricots, walnuts, and orange.

2. Transfer to a small bowl and stir in orange juice and enough honey to hold fruits together. Cover and refrigerate 15 minutes.

3. Roll into small balls about 1 inch in diameter. Insert a pistachio half in each to resemble an orange stem. Set in miniature paper cups, if desired. Serve at room temperature or slightly chilled.

SEPHARDIC SEDER EGGS

*T*raditionally served at the Sephardic Passover Seder, I found that these slow-cooked brown eggs, called *huevos haminados*, cook very well, without any fuss, in an electric slow cooker. Eggs are pasteurized by cooking at 140°F. for 30 minutes, so start off on High.

MAKES 12

Brown skins of 3 or 4 medium onions
12 eggs in shell
1 teaspoon instant coffee

1. Spread onion skins over bottom of slow cooker. Gently place raw eggs in their shells on top.

2. Sprinkle coffee over eggs. Pour in enough warm water to cover eggs by about 2 inches.

3. Cover and turn to High. After 2 hours, reduce heat to low and cook overnight. Eggshells will be brown.

4. To serve, shell eggs; yolks will be hard-cooked, and whites a creamy beige color. Arrange on drained onion skins, which resemble golden brown wafers. Serve at room temperature.

FOOLPROOF TINY KNAIDLACH

*T*hese mini matzoh balls are so easy, I make them to serve in chicken soup year-round, not just at Passover. Parsley or another herb can be substituted for the dill, or the herb can be omitted altogether.

MAKES 30 TO 36

3 tablespoons margarine, softened
3 eggs
1 tablespoon minced dill
1½ teaspoons salt
¼ teaspoon pepper
Pinch of grated nutmeg
About 1 cup matzoh meal

1. In a small bowl, beat margarine into eggs; the mixture will be slightly lumpy. Add dill, salt, pepper, nutmeg, and enough matzoh meal to make a dough that is slightly sticky. Cover and refrigerate 30 minutes.

2. With wet hands, roll matzoh dough into small balls about ¾ inch in diameter.

3. Drop knaidlach gently into a pan of simmering salted water. Cook 15 minutes.

MATZOH BRIE WITH BROCCOLI AND TOMATO

*T*his is a recipe I created for my diet-conscious husband, Walter. With only one egg, half a sheet of matzoh, and vegetables galore, this makes a filling, low-calorie breakfast.

1 SERVING

½ sheet matzoh
1 egg
1 teaspoon vegetable oil
1 cup broccoli florets
1 medium onion, cut into ½-inch dice
1 medium tomato, chopped
½ teaspoon lemon pepper seasoning

1. Crumble matzoh into a small bowl. Add warm water to cover. Let soak 5 minutes to soften. Drain off water and squeeze matzoh dry. Return to bowl and beat in egg.

2. Heat oil in a 7-inch nonstick skillet. Add broccoli and cook over medium heat for 3 minutes. Add onion, tomato, and lemon pepper seasoning. Cook until onion is softened and translucent and broccoli is crisp-tender, about 3 minutes longer.

3. Pour egg and matzoh mixture over vegetables. Cook over medium heat, stirring, to desired doneness, 3 to 4 minutes. Serve at once.

REDUCED-FAT MATZOH BRIE

Here's a sweet, fluffy Passover pancake that contains less fat than usual, but is satisfying enough to serve for brunch or lunch. You can double or even triple the quantities if you wish. Just be sure to use a larger nonstick skillet when you do.

1 SERVING

1 matzoh, crumbled
1 whole egg, separated
1 egg white
1 tablespoon brown sugar
½ teaspoon grated lemon zest
Pinch of grated nutmeg
1 teaspoon peanut oil
Honey or preserves

1. Place matzoh in a bowl and cover with hot water. Soak to soften, 3 to 5 minutes. Drain and squeeze dry.

2. In a small bowl, beat egg yolk, brown sugar, lemon zest, and nutmeg. Add softened matzoh and stir to mix.

3. In a medium bowl, beat egg whites until stiff. Fold into matzoh mixture.

4. Heat oil in 7-inch nonstick skillet. Pour matzoh mixture into skillet. Cook over medium heat 3 minutes on each side, until nicely browned.

5. Serve immediately with honey or preserves.

MATZOH VEGETABLE BAKE

*F*or a dairy supper, sprinkle shredded Cheddar cheese over the vegetables between the matzoh layers. Serve with a crisp green salad.

8 SERVINGS

1 large onion, thinly sliced
3 matzohs
4 medium tomatoes, sliced ½ inch thick
2 yellow bell peppers, cut into ¼-inch-wide strips
2 celery ribs, chopped
1 teaspoon sugar
½ teaspoon salt
¼ teaspoon pepper
1 cup marinara sauce

1. Preheat oven to 350°F. Coat a 9-inch square baking dish with nonstick vegetable spray.

2. Spread half of onion over bottom of baking dish. Cover with 1 matzoh. Place half of tomatoes, peppers, and celery on top. Sprinkle with ½ teaspoon sugar, ¼ teaspoon salt, and ⅛ teaspoon pepper. Drizzle ¼ cup marinara sauce over vegetables.

3. Cover with second matzoh and repeat with remaining vegetables, seasonings, and ¼ cup sauce.

4. Top with third matzoh and drizzle remaining ½ cup sauce over entire dish. Cover with aluminum foil and bake in preheated oven for 20 minutes. Remove foil and bake 10 minutes longer. Serve hot as a side dish.

ROASTED PEPPER AND PARSLEY STUFFING

*T*his is enough stuffing for a six-pound capon. Or it can be baked separately as directed below.

6 TO 8 SERVINGS

4 cups farfel
1 large red bell pepper, cut into ½-inch dice
1 medium green bell pepper, cut into ½-inch dice
¼ cup bottled vinaigrette salad dressing
1 tablespoon coarse kosher salt
1 cup coarsely chopped fresh parsley
4 tablespoons margarine, melted
½ teaspoon pepper

1. Preheat oven to 350°F. Preheat broiler. Coat a baking sheet with nonstick vegetable spray.

2. In a large bowl, cover farfel with cold water. Let stand 5 minutes. Drain well.

3. Spread diced peppers on prepared baking sheet. Brush with salad dressing and sprinkle with salt. Broil about 4 inches from heat until peppers are just beginning to brown, 4 to 5 minutes.

4. Transfer to a medium bowl. Add drained farfel, parsley, margarine, and pepper. Mix well.

5. Spoon into an oiled 9-inch square baking dish or 2-quart baking dish. Bake in preheated oven until crisp and browned on top, about 35 minutes.

PARSLEY "BREAD" STICKS

By the middle of the Passover week, everyone's looking for something different to munch. These crisp, garlicky sticks make a welcome change from matzoh.

MAKES 12

½ cup vegetable oil
1 teaspoon salt
⅛ teaspoon pepper
2 tablespoons chopped fresh parsley
2 cups matzoh meal
4 eggs

1. Preheat oven to 400°F. Coat a baking sheet with nonstick vegetable spray. In a medium saucepan, bring oil, salt, pepper, and 1 cup water to a boil over high heat. Remove pan from heat and stir in parsley.

2. Add matzoh meal all at once and beat with a wooden spoon until mixture leaves sides of pan, about 2 minutes.

3. Transfer to a food processor. Add eggs, 1 at a time, and process to mix thoroughly after each addition.

4. With wet hands, shape dough into 12 sticks, each about 4 inches long and ¾ inch wide. Place on prepared baking sheet.

5. Bake in preheated oven until puffed and golden, 25 minutes. Cool on a wire rack before serving.

SALT STICKS: Before baking, sprinkle each stick with kosher salt.

POTATO AND ZUCCHINI KUGEL

As with many kugels, this one freezes well. To use, defrost in the refrigerator overnight, cover tightly with foil, and bake in a 350°F. oven until heated through, about 30 minutes.

8 TO 10 SERVINGS

1½ pounds baking potatoes, peeled
1 medium carrot, peeled
1 medium onion, peeled
1⅓ cups matzoh meal
3 eggs
2 garlic cloves, minced
1½ teaspoons salt
½ teaspoon pepper
2 medium zucchini
¼ cup chopped fresh dill

1. Preheat oven to 375°F. Coat a 9-inch square baking dish with nonstick vegetable spray.

2. Cut potatoes, carrot, and onion into 1-inch chunks. Chop coarsely in a food processor.

3. Transfer to a mixing bowl. Add ⅔ cup of matzoh meal, 2 eggs, garlic, 1 teaspoon of salt, and ¼ teaspoon of pepper. Spread half of mixture over bottom of prepared baking dish.

4. In a food processor with grater blade, shred zucchini. Transfer to a bowl. Add remaining egg, dill, and remaining ⅔ cup matzoh meal, ½ teaspoon salt, and ¼ teaspoon pepper. Spread over potato mixture in baking dish. Cover with remaining potato mixture to make 3 layers.

5. Bake in preheated oven until nicely browned and firm in center, 1 to 1¼ hours. Cut into squares and serve hot.

ZUCCHINI-CARROT KUGEL

6 TO 8 SERVINGS

3 medium green zucchini (about ¾ pound)
3 medium yellow zucchini or summer squash (about ¾ pound)
1 large carrot, peeled
3 scallions, chopped
¼ cup chopped fresh parsley
4 eggs, beaten
¼ cup matzoh meal
2 teaspoons salt
¾ teaspoon pepper
2 tablespoons peanut oil

1. Preheat oven to 375°F. Coat a 9-inch square baking dish with nonstick vegetable spray.

2. Coarsely grate green and yellow zucchini and carrot on grating blade of a food processor or on large holes of a hand grater.

3. Transfer to a large bowl. Add scallions, parsley, eggs, matzoh meal, salt, and pepper. Mix well.

4. Pour into prepared baking dish. Drizzle oil over top. Bake in preheated oven until browned on top and set in center, 45 to 50 minutes. Let cool about 10 minutes, then cut into squares and serve.

SPRINGTIME KUGEL

*C*hop apples and vegetables in a food processor before beginning this refreshing, lemony kugel. It freezes well and so can be made ahead and reheated. I serve it as a side dish, particularly with chicken, or as a nibble with coffee.

8 TO 10 SERVINGS

½ cup matzoh meal
½ cup sugar
½ teaspoon nutmeg
1 teaspoon cinnamon
2 large apples, coarsely chopped
2 medium sweet potatoes, peeled and coarsely chopped
1 large baking potato, peeled and coarsely chopped
1 large carrot, peeled and coarsely chopped
½ cup golden raisins
2 tablespoons frozen orange juice concentrate, thawed
Grated zest and juice of 1 lemon
1 stick (4 ounces) margarine, melted

1. Preheat oven to 350°F. Coat a 9-inch square baking dish with nonstick vegetable spray.

2. In a large bowl, combine matzoh meal, sugar, nutmeg, and cinnamon. Add apples, sweet potatoes, baking potato, carrot, raisins, orange juice, lemon zest, lemon juice, and melted margarine. Stir to mix well. Transfer to prepared baking dish.

3. Bake kugel in preheated oven until firm and nicely browned on top, 1¼ hours. If browning too quickly, cover loosely with foil. Let cool slightly, then cut into squares. Serve hot or warm.

ALMOND KUGEL WITH GLAZED PEARS

10 TO 12 SERVINGS

1 (12-ounce) package Passover noodles
4 eggs, lightly beaten
¼ cup thawed frozen orange juice concentrate
½ cup finely ground almonds
½ cup chopped almonds
1 teaspoon cinnamon
½ teaspoon salt
⅓ cup plus 2 tablespoons sugar
7 tablespoons margarine, melted
½ teaspoon vanilla extract
3 medium pears, cored and cut into ¼-inch-thick wedges

1. Preheat oven to 350°F. Grease a 9-by-12-inch baking dish. Cook noodles as directed on package; drain.

2. In a large bowl, mix cooked noodles with eggs, orange juice, ground almonds, chopped almonds, cinnamon, salt, ⅓ cup of sugar, and 6 tablespoons of melted margarine. Spoon into prepared baking dish. Bake in preheated oven for 45 minutes.

3. In a large skillet, combine remaining 1 tablespoon margarine, 2 tablespoons sugar, and vanilla extract. Add pears and cook over medium-high heat, stirring gently, just until sugar melts and pears are glazed, about 5 minutes.

4. Arrange glazed pears attractively on top of kugel. Drizzle any juices in skillet over top.

5. Return to oven. Bake until pears are golden and kugel is nicely browned, about 20 minutes. Let cool 10 minutes before cutting into squares. Serve warm or at room temperature.

CHOCOLATE RASPBERRY ROLL

*T*his can also be baked in a 9-by-12-inch baking dish, topped with nondairy topping, berries, and chocolate, and then cut into squares.

10 SERVINGS

4 eggs, separated
¾ cup plus 1 tablespoon sugar
1 tablespoon fresh lemon juice
⅓ cup potato starch
1 tablespoon matzoh cake meal
1 cup nondairy topping
¼ cup chopped parve semisweet chocolate plus 3 table-
    spoons semisweet chocolate, melted
½ pint raspberries

1. Preheat oven to 350°F. Line a 15½-by-10-inch jelly-roll pan with wax paper. Coat with nonstick vegetable spray.

2. Whisk egg whites until stiff and set aside. Whisk yolks with ¾ cup sugar until pale. Beat in lemon juice.

3. Sift potato starch and matzoh cake meal. Gradually fold into egg yolk mixture. Fold in beaten egg whites.

4. Spread batter in prepared pan. Bake in preheated oven until cake springs back when touched, 18 to 20 minutes.

5. Turn out onto wax paper sprinkled with 1 tablespoon sugar. Immediately peel paper from cake, then roll up as for jelly roll. Let cool. Unroll and remove wax paper.

6. Mix nondairy topping with chopped chocolate. Spread over cake to within ¼ inch of edges. Sprinkle with raspberries and roll up again. Drizzle melted chocolate over cake. Slice with a serrated knife.

TOASTED HAZELNUT CAKE

*I*f you don't have a box of superfine sugar, grind granulated sugar in a food processor for 20 seconds. Roasting gives hazelnuts a much deeper, richer flavor. I like to heap fresh sliced sugared strawberries or raspberries on top of slices of this moist cake. Whipped cream or nondairy topping is optional.

10 TO 12 SERVINGS

1 cup finely ground toasted hazelnuts
1 cup superfine sugar
2 tablespoons matzoh cake meal
½ teaspoon cinnamon
Pinch of salt
9 eggs, separated

1. Preheat oven to 350°F. Spread out hazelnuts on a lightly greased baking sheet. Toast in preheated oven, shaking pan once or twice, until skins are cracked and nuts are pale golden brown. Roll warm nuts in a kitchen towel to remove most of the dark brown outer skins. Let cool, then grind nuts as fine as possible, preferably in a nut grinder. (If you use a food processor, add 2 tablespoons of the sugar to help keep the nuts from turning to a paste.)

2. Coat a 10-inch tube pan with nonstick vegetable spray. In a medium bowl, combine ground hazelnuts with cake meal, cinnamon, and salt.

3. In a large bowl, beat egg yolks lightly. Gradually beat in sugar and continue to beat until thick and pale, about 3 minutes. In another large bowl, beat egg whites until they form stiff peaks.

4. Fold dry hazelnut mixture into egg yolks. Add one-fourth of egg whites and fold to lighten. Add remaining egg whites and fold in gently just until no streaks of white remain. Turn batter into prepared tube pan.

5. Bake in preheated oven for 45 minutes, or until a toothpick inserted in center comes out clean. Let cake cool on a wire rack. Run knife around edges to loosen before turning out onto serving platter.

CITRUS-SCENTED SPONGE CAKE

I've baked this delicate sponge cake for more than twenty years. Whether served plain, soaked with wine, made into a trifle, or topped with fruit compote, it's a Hofman family tradition.

12 TO 15 SERVINGS

½ cup matzoh cake meal
¾ cup potato starch
8 eggs, separated
1¼ cups sugar
1 tablespoon grated orange zest
2 tablespoons orange juice
2 tablespoons fresh lemon juice

1. Preheat oven to 350°F. Sift together cake meal and potato starch.

2. In a large bowl, beat egg whites until they form soft peaks. Gradually add ¾ cup sugar and continue beating until stiff peaks form.

3. In another large bowl, whisk egg yolks and remaining ½ cup sugar until thick and pale, 3 to 4 minutes. Mix in orange zest, orange juice, and lemon juice.

4. Fold egg whites into egg yolk mixture, then fold in dry ingredients. Turn into an ungreased 10-inch tube pan.

5. Bake in preheated oven for 1 hour, or until a toothpick inserted in center comes out clean and cake springs back when touched.

6. Invert pan until cake is cool. With a round-bladed knife, cut around edges to loosen before turning out onto a cake plate.

PRUNE PUDDING WITH ALMOND DUMPLINGS

*P*runes, which are dried plums, are a very popular fruit with Jews all over the world. Whether you call this pudding, or as my grandmother would say, *flaumen kugel with almond knaidlach*, it's a fine Passover dessert, best after a light lunch or supper.

4 TO 6 SERVINGS

2 eggs, separated
2 tablespoons sugar
¾ cup matzoh meal
2 tablespoons margarine, melted
12 to 15 slivered almonds
3 cups Stewed Prunes (page 322)
Orange or apple juice (optional)

1. Preheat oven to 350°F. In a mixing bowl, beat egg whites until they form stiff peaks.

2. In another bowl, beat egg yolks and sugar until pale and thick, about 2 minutes. Stir in matzoh meal and melted margarine. Fold in beaten egg whites. Let stand 10 to 15 minutes to firm up.

3. Roll matzoh mixture into 1½-inch balls. Press a slivered almond into each. Arrange over bottom of 2-quart baking dish. Pour stewed prunes over dumplings. There should be enough liquid to cover prunes in dish. If not, add a little orange or apple juice.

4. Bake in preheated oven for 35 minutes, until bubbly. Serve warm or at room temperature. For a dairy meal, pass a pitcher of light cream to pour over pudding.

KUMQUAT SORBET

*I*ntensely flavored and refreshing, this sweet ice creates a perfect ending to a heavy meal. A Passover kumquat wine is produced by the Hills of Galilee Wine Company. Serve with a chocolate Passover sweet.

4 SERVINGS

1 cup sugar
2 cups water
2 cups kumquat wine
2 tablespoons fresh lime juice
⅓ cup chopped preserved kumquats

1. In a small saucepan, stir sugar with 2 cups water over medium heat until sugar dissolves. Bring to a boil and cook 5 minutes. Remove from heat. Let cool to room temperature.

2. Stir wine, lime juice, and chopped kumquats into cooled syrup. Pour into a shallow dish. Freeze 3 hours, or until slushy and beginning to harden at edges.

3. Whisk 2 minutes to break up ice crystals. Return to freezer and freeze until fairly firm, 6 to 8 hours; this is a soft sorbet. Serve spooned into small dessert dishes or stemmed glasses.

CHOCOLATE WHIP

*T*his creamy German-Jewish dessert is really parve, with not a trace of dairy. It is very rich, so I recommend presenting it in demitasse cups or wineglasses. A dab of nondairy topping and a candied violet turn a simple sweet into an upscale dessert.

6 SERVINGS

6 ounces parve bittersweet chocolate, coarsely chopped
3 tablespoons sweet red Concord grape wine
4 eggs, separated
2 tablespoons nondairy topping
Candied violets or mint leaves (optional)

1. Melt chocolate in a double boiler over simmering water or in a microwave on High for 1½ to 2 minutes, stirring after 1 minute, then after 30 seconds.

2. Whisk in wine, then egg yolks, 1 at a time, until mixture is smooth. Remove from heat.

3. Beat egg whites until stiff peaks form. Fold into chocolate mixture.

4. Spoon into 6 demitasse cups or wineglasses. Top with a dab of nondairy topping and a candied violet.

NOTE: This recipe contains uncooked egg whites. If you are uncomfortable eating raw eggs, choose another dessert.

ALMOND AND RAISIN COOKIES

*K*ids love to make these quick no-fuss cookies. They can be mixed and baked inside half an hour. Farfel is matzohs broken into rough one-fourth-inch pieces. You can buy it, or make your own by pulsing cut-up matzohs in a food processor until they are coarsely chopped.

MAKES 24

1 cup matzoh meal
1 cup farfel
½ cup plus 2 tablespoons sugar
1 cup raisins
½ cup slivered almonds
1 teaspoon cinnamon
⅓ cup peanut oil
2 eggs, lightly beaten
1 teaspoon almond extract

1. Preheat oven to 350°F. Coat 2 baking sheets with nonstick vegetable spray.

2. In a large bowl, combine matzoh meal, farfel, sugar, raisins, almonds, and cinnamon. Stir to mix. Make a well in center. Pour in oil, eggs, and almond extract. Mix until moistened. Drop by tablespoonfuls onto prepared baking sheets.

3. Bake in a preheated oven for 20 minutes, or until browned at edges. Immediately remove to wire rack to cool. Store in a tight-lidded container in freezer or refrigerator or at room temperature for up to 1 week.

FRUIT AND NUT CHREMSLACH

A matzoh fritter heavy with nuts and raisins. Serve as dessert with Honey Raisin Sauce.

MAKES 12 TO 15

¼ cup slivered almonds
3 matzohs
2 eggs, separated
⅛ teaspoon salt
⅓ cup raisins or currants
1 tablespoon cinnamon-sugar
Vegetable oil for frying
Honey Raisin Sauce (recipe follows)

1. Spread out almonds on a plate and microwave on High for 1 minute. Stir and microwave 20 to 30 seconds longer, until golden. Or toast in a toaster oven, 1 to 2 minutes, watching carefully to avoid scorching.

2. Soak matzohs in water until soft, 5 to 10 minutes. Squeeze out as much water as possible.

3. Place in a medium bowl and mash together with egg yolks, salt, raisins, almonds, and cinnamon-sugar. Mix well.

4. In another medium bowl, beat egg whites until they form stiff peaks. Fold into matzoh mixture.

5. In a large skillet, heat ¼ inch of oil over medium-high heat. Carefully slide mixture by heaping tablespoonfuls into hot oil. Cook in batches without crowding for 3 to 4 minutes, turning, until crisp and golden all over. Drain on paper towels. Serve with a pitcher of warm Honey Raisin Sauce.

HONEY RAISIN SAUCE

MAKES 1 CUP

1 cup raisins
½ cup sweet red wine
2 tablespoons honey
¼ teaspoon ground ginger

In a small nonreactive saucepan, combine raisins, wine, and ¾ cup water. Cook over medium-low heat until raisins are plump and liquid is reduced by about half, 10 to 15 minutes. Stir in honey and ginger. Serve warm.

MINTED STRAWBERRY APPLESAUCE

*A*pplesauce is almost a condiment in many Jewish homes. Here's a refreshing springtime variation, which you can offer as a dessert or as a side dish.

4 SERVINGS

¼ cup apple juice
2 tablespoons strawberry preserves
1 pint fresh strawberries, halved
1 (16-ounce) jar applesauce
1 tablespoon chopped fresh mint or 1 teaspoon dried

1. In a small saucepan, mix apple juice and strawberry preserves. Cook over medium heat, stirring, until preserves are melted, 3 to 4 minutes.

2. Add strawberries and cook, stirring to coat them with glaze, 2 minutes. Remove from heat. Stir in applesauce and mint. Serve at room temperature or chilled.

CHICKEN SOUP WITH MATZOH BALLS

A must in many homes as one course of the Seder, *knaid-lach,* or matzoh balls, served in chicken soup are a year-round Jewish favorite.

10 TO 12 SERVINGS

1 small onion, chopped
3 tablespoons schmaltz
3 eggs
¾ cup matzoh meal
½ cup plus 1½ tablespoons chopped fresh parsley
¾ teaspoon salt
¼ teaspoon pepper
Old-Fashioned Chicken Soup (page 46)
2 medium carrots, peeled and thinly sliced

M E A T

1. In a small skillet, cook onion in schmaltz over medium heat until onion is golden and beginning to brown, about 10 minutes. Remove from the heat and let cool slightly.

2. In a mixing bowl, beat the eggs lightly. Beat in matzoh meal, 1½ tablespoons parsley, salt, and pepper. Scrape the onion and schmaltz from the skillet into the bowl. Add ⅓ cup of the cold chicken soup and blend well. Cover and refrigerate at least 1 hour.

3. Form the matzoh meal dough into 10 to 12 balls. Bring a large pot of salted water to a boil over high heat. Add the matzoh balls, reduce the heat to medium, cover, and cook for 30 minutes.

4. Bring the remaining chicken soup to a boil. Add the carrot slices and boil 10 minutes, or until tender. Add the matzoh balls just to heat through.

5. To serve, place a matzoh ball in each soup plate. Ladle the hot soup over the matzoh balls, making sure everyone gets at least a few carrot slices. Garnish each serving generously with chopped parsley.

POT ROAST PIE WITH
MASHED POTATO TOPPING

4 TO 6 SERVINGS

2 tablespoons peanut oil
2 pounds beef chuck, cut into 1-inch chunks
12 small white boiling onions (½ pound), peeled
1 medium carrot, peeled and sliced
1½ cups beef broth
1 tablespoon Dijon mustard
1½ teaspoons salt
1 bay leaf
4 cups mashed potatoes
1 egg
2 tablespoons margarine, melted
1 tablespoon chopped fresh parsley

1. In a large heavy pot, heat oil over medium-high heat. Add chuck and cook, turning, to brown all sides, about 8 minutes.

2. Add onions, carrot, broth, mustard, salt, and bay leaf. Bring to a boil over high heat. Reduce heat to low, cover, and simmer for 2 hours, or until meat is very tender. Remove and discard bay leaf.

3. Preheat oven to 400°F. In a medium bowl, mix mashed potatoes with egg, melted margarine, and parsley.

4. Transfer beef stew to 2½-quart casserole. Spoon potato mixture on top, spreading to the edges with a fork.

5. Bake in preheated oven for 20 minutes, or until nicely browned. Serve hot.

PESACH-STUFFED TURKEY BREAST

*I*f you have family members who don't eat red meat, this is a fine choice for a gala main course. Vegetable oil can be substituted for the chicken fat to keep the cholesterol down.

8 SERVINGS

½ cup crumbled matzoh
2 tablespoons schmaltz or vegetable oil
1 medium onion, chopped
1 Granny Smith apple, chopped
1 large green bell pepper, cut into ¼-inch dice
2 tablespoons chopped fresh cilantro or parsley
1 teaspoon salt
¼ teaspoon pepper
2½-pound boneless turkey breast
2 tablespoons peanut oil
Paprika

1. Preheat oven to 375°F. Cover matzoh with warm water and soak for 5 minutes to soften. Drain and set aside.

2. Heat schmaltz in a large skillet. Add onion and apple. Cook over medium heat until onion is softened and translucent, about 5 minutes. Remove from heat.

3. Stir matzoh, bell pepper, cilantro, salt, and pepper into onion and apples. Spoon stuffing into center of turkey breast. Bring ends together and fasten with metal poultry picks.

4. Brush turkey breast with oil and dust with paprika. Place in a roasting pan and cover with foil.

5. Roast in preheated oven for 1 hour, basting often with pan juices. Turkey is done when juices run clear when pierced at thickest part with a fork. Let stand 5 minutes. Slice and serve hot.

CHICKEN AND MATZOH PIE

Mina de Pesach is a traditional Sephardic main course for a Passover meal. Leftover chicken from chicken soup can be used for this dish.

6 TO 8 SERVINGS

¼ cup peanut or olive oil
1 medium onion, chopped
1 celery rib, thinly sliced
1 garlic clove, minced
4 cups sliced mushrooms
3 cups cooked diced (¾-inch) chicken
2 tablespoons chopped fresh parsley
2 tablespoons chopped sun-dried tomatoes
1 teaspoon salt
¼ teaspoon pepper
4 eggs, beaten
1 cup chicken stock
3 whole wheat matzohs

MEAT

1. Preheat oven to 375°F. Coat a 9-inch square baking dish with nonstick vegetable spray.

2. In a large skillet, heat 3 tablespoons oil over medium heat. Add onion, celery, and garlic. Cook, stirring occasionally, until softened, about 5 minutes. Add mushrooms and cook 5 minutes longer.

3. Remove from heat and add chicken, parsley, sun-dried tomatoes, salt, and pepper. Let cool 10 minutes, then quickly stir in eggs. Set aside.

4. Pour chicken stock into a shallow dish. Lay matzohs in stock, 1 at a time, to moisten both sides well. Cover bottom of prepared baking dish with 1½ matzohs, breaking to fit.

5. Spoon the chicken-mushroom mixture over matzohs, spreading to edge of dish. Dip remaining matzohs and place on top to cover completely.

6. Brush with 1 tablespoon oil. Bake in preheated oven until top is browned and filling is firm, about 30 minutes. Cover loosely with foil if casserole browns too quickly. Let cool 10 minutes before serving. Cut into squares. Serve warm.

FARFEL STUFFING WITH SPRING HERBS

*T*his may be baked in a baking dish or lightly stuffed into the cavity of a five- to six-pound capon. Matzohs crumbled into one-fourth-inch pieces may be substituted for farfel.

4 TO 6 SERVINGS

3 cups farfel
3 tablespoons schmaltz or vegetable oil
1 large onion, chopped
2 eggs, beaten
1 cup coarsely chopped fresh parsley
2 tablespoons chopped fresh sage or 1½ teaspoons dried
1 teaspoon garlic powder
1½ teaspoons salt
¼ teaspoon pepper

1. Place farfel in a medium bowl and cover with cold water. Let stand 5 minutes. Drain well.

2. In a large skillet, heat schmaltz or oil. Add onion and cook over medium-high heat, stirring occasionally, until browned at edges, 4 to 6 minutes. Remove from heat.

3. Scrape onion into bowl with farfel. Add eggs, parsley, sage, garlic powder, salt, and pepper. Mix well.

4. Stuff loosely into poultry cavity for roasting or bake in an oiled 2-quart baking dish in a 350°F. oven until browned and crusty on top, about 35 minutes.

MEAT

PASSOVER SCOTCH EGGS

Children especially enjoy these crusty meat-covered eggs. I often make them with hard-cooked eggs left over from the Seder. Tuck these into Passover brown bag lunches or serve them at home with tomato relish or a salsa.

4 SERVINGS

6 ounces ground turkey
6 ounces ground beef
1 tablespoon (kosher for Passover) dry salad dressing mix
4 hard-cooked eggs, shelled
¼ cup matzoh meal
1 teaspoon paprika

1. Preheat oven or toaster oven to 375°F. Mix ground turkey and beef with salad dressing mix until thoroughly blended. Divide into 4 equal portions.

2. Carefully mold 1 portion of meat around each egg, smoothing out any cracks and pinching to seal, so that the egg is completely surrounded.

3. Mix matzoh meal and paprika. Roll eggs in matzoh meal to coat all over.

4. Bake in preheated oven for 10 to 15 minutes, or until meat is cooked through and browned and crusty outside. Serve hot or cold.

FEINEKUCHEN

Passover breakfasts are always a challenge. This big pancake is good cut into wedges and served simply, as suggested below, or with sliced bananas and sour cream.

2 SERVINGS

4 eggs
¼ cup milk
¼ teaspoon vanilla extract
¼ teaspoon salt
Pinch of pepper
2 matzohs, crumbled
2 tablespoons butter or vegetable oil
Sugar or warm honey

1. In a medium bowl, whisk together eggs, milk, vanilla, salt, and pepper. Add matzohs and let soak until slightly soft, about 5 minutes.

2. In a medium nonstick skillet, heat butter or oil. Pour in matzoh mixture. Cook over medium heat until browned on bottom and firm enough to flip over without breaking, 5 to 6 minutes.

3. Cook 2 minutes longer. Serve sprinkled with sugar or with warm honey.

DAIRY

MATZOH BRIE

*I*t wouldn't be Passover without fried matzohs. Prepare this family-size mix the night before, then a delicious breakfast is less than 10 minutes away. Serve sweet, sprinkled with cinnamon sugar, or savory, topped with salsa. Mixture may also be scrambled over medium heat to desired doneness.

4 SERVINGS

3 matzohs, crumbled into bite-size pieces
4 eggs
½ teaspoon salt
¼ teaspoon pepper
4 to 6 tablespoons butter

1. Place matzohs in a bowl and pour hot water over to cover. Let soak 5 minutes, until softened; drain.

2. In a wide shallow bowl, beat eggs, salt, and pepper until blended. Add matzohs and stir with a fork to mix.

3. In a large, heavy skillet, melt 4 tablespoons butter over medium heat. In batches, if necessary, drop egg-matzoh mixture by tablespoonfuls into hot butter. Cook about 3 minutes on each side, until golden and cooked through. Serve hot.

DAIRY

SALMON PIE WITH PEANUT CRUST

Even during Passover, there are nights when supper from a can is all a busy cook has time for. All this needs is a green salad or a plate of sliced cucumbers and tomatoes.

6 TO 8 SERVINGS

½ cup finely chopped peanuts
½ cup matzoh meal
1 teaspoon lemon pepper
¼ cup peanut oil
3 ounces cream cheese, softened
3 tablespoons butter, softened
½ cup sour cream
3 eggs
½ teaspoon salt
⅛ teaspoon pepper
3 tablespoons chopped chives
2 (7¾-ounce) cans pink salmon, drained

1. Preheat oven to 375°F. Mix together peanuts, matzoh meal, and lemon pepper. Stir in oil and 2 tablespoons water. Press into bottom and sides of a 10-inch pie dish. Bake crust in preheated oven for 10 minutes. Remove from oven. Reduce heat to 350°F.

2. In a medium bowl, beat cream cheese and butter until blended. Add sour cream, eggs, salt, and pepper and beat until smooth. Stir in chives.

3. Flake salmon and spread over bottom of partially cooked pie shell. Pour cream cheese mixture over salmon.

4. Bake until filling is firm and set, about 40 minutes. Serve hot or at room temperature.

DAIRY

SPINACH-TOMATO MATZOH STRATA

I adapted this recipe from one given to me by Jill Horn, the creative owner/chef at Vorspeise (Yiddish for hors d'oeuvres), at the Reading Terminal Market in Philadelphia. Prepare and refrigerate overnight to bake the next day.

4 SERVINGS

1 (10-ounce) box frozen chopped spinach, thawed
1 cup ricotta cheese
2 eggs
¼ cup chopped fresh dill
½ teaspoon plus ⅛ teaspoon salt
½ teaspoon pepper
3 to 4 matzohs
1 pound fresh mushrooms, thinly sliced
2 tablespoons vegetable oil
1 large beefsteak or 2 medium tomatoes, thinly sliced
½ cup milk
½ cup shredded Cheddar cheese

1. Coat a 1½-quart baking dish with nonstick vegetable spray. Squeeze spinach dry and mix with ricotta, 1 egg, dill, and ¼ teaspoon each salt and pepper. Spread half of spinach mixture over bottom of baking dish. Cover with a layer of matzohs, breaking them to fit, if necessary.

2. In a large skillet, cook mushrooms in oil over high heat, 3 to 4 minutes, or until lightly browned. Season with ¼ teaspoon salt and ⅛ teaspoon pepper. Spread half of cooked mushrooms over matzohs in dish. Cover with a second matzoh layer.

3. Spread remaining spinach mixture and then mushrooms over matzohs. Arrange all of tomatoes over mushrooms. Cover with remaining matzoh.

DAIRY

4. In a small bowl, whisk together milk, remaining 1 egg, and remaining ⅛ teaspoon each salt and pepper until blended. Gently pour over ingredients in baking dish. Top with Cheddar cheese. Cover and refrigerate overnight so matzohs can absorb liquid.

5. Preheat oven to 350°F. Bake strata for 50 to 60 minutes, until puffy, golden, and firm in center. Serve warm or at room temperature.

GESCHMIERTE MATZOHS I

Geschmierte means "smeared" in Yiddish. My South African neighbors nostalgically remember this after-school Passover snack, thickly spread with cream cheese and seasonings.

2 SERVINGS

2 matzohs
¼ cup cream cheese, softened
½ teaspoon garlic powder
1 teaspoon coarse kosher salt
½ teaspoon pepper

1. Preheat broiler. Smear matzohs thickly with cream cheese.

2. Sprinkle with garlic powder, kosher salt, and pepper.

3. Place under preheated broiler 2 to 3 minutes, until cheese is softened. Let cool for 5 minutes before eating.

BANANA YOGURT KUGEL WITH PINEAPPLE AND BLACK WALNUTS

Black walnuts have a very distinctive flavor, which is slightly sharper and more aromatic than the ordinary kind. At holiday time, you'll find them in the supermarket. They are also available in nut shops and specialty stores and by mail order in baking catalogs.

8 TO 10 SERVINGS

6 matzohs
4 eggs
½ cup sugar
1 (8-ounce) container banana yogurt
1 cup sour cream
½ cup crushed pineapple with juice
1 teaspoon cinnamon
¼ cup black walnut pieces
2 teaspoons butter
¼ cup pineapple preserves, warmed

1. Preheat oven to 350°F. Coat a 2½-quart baking dish with nonstick vegetable spray.

2. Crumble matzohs into a bowl and cover with warm water. Soak 5 minutes. Drain and squeeze dry.

3. In a large bowl, beat eggs with sugar, yogurt, sour cream, pineapple, and cinnamon until well blended. Stir in softened matzohs and black walnuts. Transfer to prepared baking dish. Dot with knobs of butter.

4. Bake in preheated oven until top is golden and center is firm, 45 to 55 minutes. Brush with warmed preserves. Serve hot or at room temperature.

NOTE: This kugel freezes well. Move from freezer to refrigerator the day before serving. Cover with foil and bake in a 325°F. oven for 20 to 30 minutes, until heated through.

DAIRY

PEACH MOCHA TORTE

Some desserts, like this flourless cake, are so good, they're not just for Passover. Raspberries or strawberries can be substituted for the peaches, depending upon availability.

10 TO 12 SERVINGS

6 eggs, separated
1 cup sugar
1 stick (4 ounces) margarine
1¼ cups semisweet chocolate chips
1 tablespoon orange juice concentrate, thawed
2 teaspoons instant coffee
½ cup white chocolate chips, melted
2 ripe peaches, cut into thin wedges
Fresh lemon juice

1. Preheat oven to 325°F. In a mixer bowl, beat egg whites until foamy. Gradually add ½ cup sugar and beat until stiff peaks form.

2. In a small, heavy saucepan, melt margarine and 1 cup semisweet chocolate over low heat. Pour into a large bowl. Whisk in remaining ½ cup sugar, orange juice, and coffee until well blended. Beat in egg yolks, 1 at a time. Fold stiffly beaten egg whites into chocolate mixture.

3. Pour batter into an ungreased 10-inch springform pan. Pour melted white chocolate over batter and cut through with a knife to marbleize.

4. Bake in preheated oven for 35 minutes. Remove springform to a wire rack and let cool. Torte will fall in middle.

5. To unmold, run a knife around edge of cake and remove sides of pan. Arrange fresh peach wedges on top. Brush with lemon juice.

6. In a small bowl in microwave, melt remaining ¼ cup semisweet chocolate chips on High for 45 seconds, stirring after 30 seconds. Drizzle over peaches. Refrigerate before serving.

DAIRY

CHOCOLATE CHERRY SQUARES

*T*hese sweet little morsels should be cut small and set in miniature paper cups. Make ahead and freeze, or store in a tight-lidded container in a cool, dry place.

MAKES 30 TO 36

2 eggs, separated
½ cup vegetable oil
1 cup sugar
½ cup matzoh cake meal
½ cup potato starch
½ cup cherry preserves
Grated zest and juice of ½ lemon
¾ cup chopped walnuts
¼ cup finely chopped chocolate

1. Preheat oven to 350°F. Coat a 9-inch square baking dish with nonstick vegetable spray.

2. Whisk egg yolks, oil, and ½ cup sugar until thick and pale, about 3 minutes. Stir in cake meal and potato starch. Press into prepared baking pan.

3. Mix preserves with lemon zest and juice. Spread over cake layer. Sprinkle walnuts over top. Bake in preheated oven for 15 minutes.

4. Whisk egg whites until foamy. Gradually beat in remaining ½ cup sugar and beat until stiff. Fold in chopped chocolate. Spread over partially baked pastry.

5. Return to oven and bake until meringue is golden, 20 minutes more. Cut into squares while still warm.

DAIRY

CHOCOLATE-COVERED MATZOHS

*T*his Passover treat is expensive to buy, but surprisingly cheap and easy to make. Store these between sheets of wax paper in a tin or other tightly covered container in a cool, dry place.

MAKES 16 PIECES

4 matzohs, broken in quarters
¾ cup apricot preserves, melted and strained
6 ounces dark or semisweet chocolate, chopped

1. Lay matzohs on a baking sheet lined with wax paper. Brush tops with half of preserves. Refrigerate 10 minutes, until chilled and slightly set.

2. Meanwhile, melt chocolate in a double boiler over simmering water or in a microwave oven on High for 1½ minutes, stirring after 1 minute and again at end.

3. Brush half of melted chocolate generously over preserves on same side of matzohs. Return to refrigerator and chill about 15 minutes, until chocolate hardens.

4. Turn matzohs over and repeat, brushing with apricot preserves and chocolate. (If melted chocolate hardens before you brush second side, melt again over low heat or in microwave for about 15 seconds.) Refrigerate at least 1 hour before serving.

DAIRY

TOASTED MARMALADE MATZOHS

*T*raditionally a Passover snack, these could also be offered as cocktail bites or as an accompaniment for a cup of coffee or tea.

MAKES 12

⅓ cup orange juice
3 matzohs
⅓ cup whipped cream cheese
2 tablespoons orange marmalade
¼ cup dried currants

1. Preheat broiler. Pour orange juice into a large shallow dish. Dip matzohs in orange juice. Set matzohs on an oiled baking sheet. Reserve 1 tablespoon orange juice.

2. In a small bowl, blend cream cheese, reserved orange juice, marmalade, and currants. Spread thickly over matzohs.

3. Broil under preheated broiler until cheese is softened, about 2 minutes. Watch carefully to avoid scorching. Let cool slightly before breaking each matzoh into quarters.

DAIRY

Index